ANOTHER
PLACE
&
TIME

VOICES FROM THE CARRISA PLAINS

ANOTHER PLACE

&

TIME

CRAIG DEUTSCHE

ACKNOWLEDGMENTS

This book should properly be credited to the people of the Carrisa Plains with whom I have spoken. They have been incredibly open in talking about their families, their livelihoods, their community, and their forefathers. They have shared meals, photos, and memories, and in some cases they have included me as family. The list of persons with whom I have spoken is in an appendix, and without their help, there would be nothing to tell. It is for these people that the book has been written.

I have also been assisted in compiling the details of this book. Jackie Czapla has been my colleague in the oral history project; my sister Lynn Gray must be thanked for her encouragement in writing; Robin Quinn has been essential in the editing process; and Jason Hashmi designed the cover and interior layout. My wife, Mary, deserves an international award for tolerance. There have been missed meals, astonishing credit card statements, an automobile eternally covered in dirt, and an incoherent husband mumbling something about farm dogs and computer meltdown. I am grateful to you all for help and patience.

CONTENTS

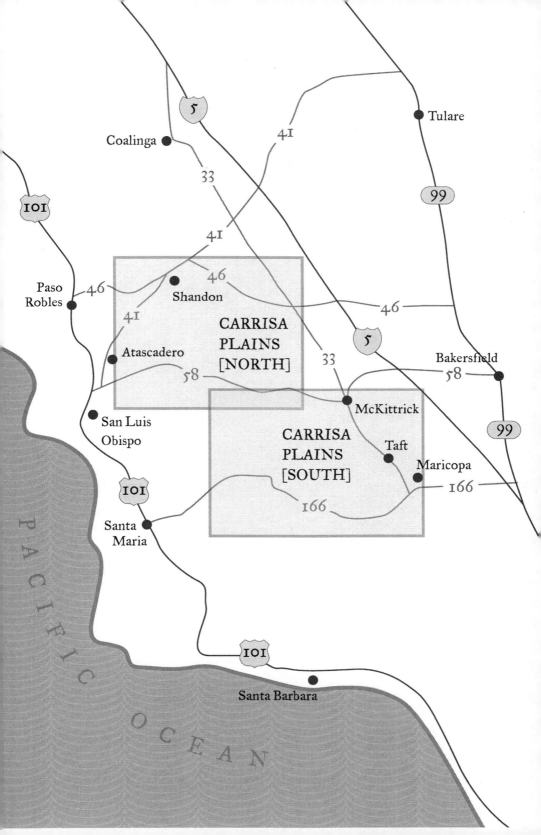

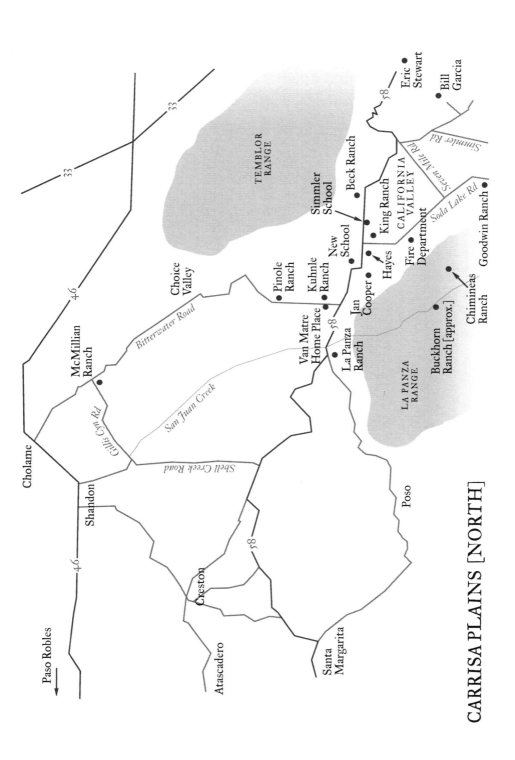

CARRISA PLAINS [NORTH]

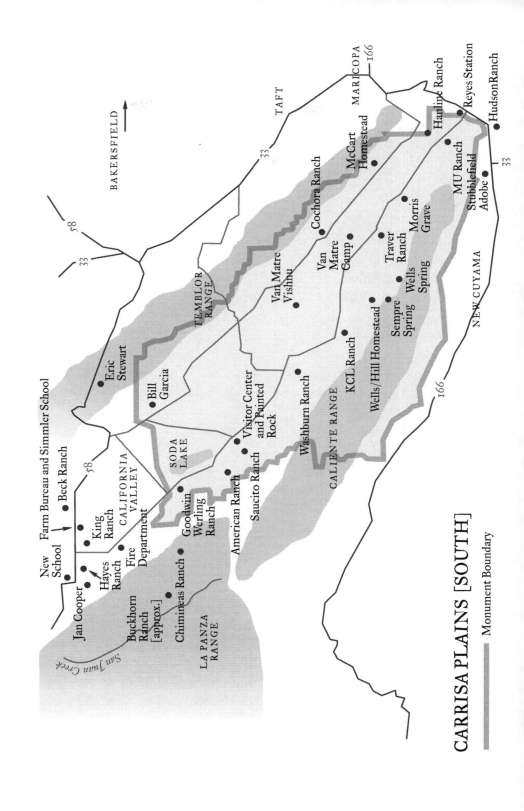

CARRISA PLAINS [SOUTH]

▬▬▬ Monument Boundary

BAKERSFIELD

New School
Farm Bureau and Simmler School
Beck Ranch
King Ranch
CALIFORNIA VALLEY
Fire Department
Hayes Ranch
Jan Cooper
Buckhorn Ranch [approx.]
Chimineas Ranch
LA PANZA RANGE
San Juan Creek
Goodwin Werling Ranch
American Ranch
Saucito Ranch
SODA LAKE
Visitor Center and Painted Rock
Washburn Ranch
Bill Garcia
Eric Stewart
TEMBLOR RANGE
Van Matre Vishnu
KCL Ranch
CALIENTE RANGE
Wells/Hill Homestead
Sempre Spring
Wells Spring
Traver Ranch
Morris Grave
Van Matre Camp
Cochora Ranch
McCart Homestead
MARICOPA
TAFT
166
33
58
Hanline Ranch
Reyes Station
Hudson Ranch
MU Ranch
Stubblefield Adobe
NEW CUYAMA
166
33

PREFACE

Another Place and Time reveals the relatively recent human history of an enigmatic area of Central California tucked between the Temblor Mountains and Caliente Range. The Carrisa Plains is a vast swath of land, sparsely populated, where the sky meets the horizon without interruption from anything manmade. Its personality and countenance changes with the seasons from verdant and colorful to windblown and stark. The first time I encountered the Carrisa Plains, I was struck by a permeating feeling of its vastness, isolation, and beauty. As I drove across Highway 58, questions about who lived here and how they survived kept coming to mind. The author of *Another Place and Time*, Craig Deutsche, answers these questions and recounts an enchanting history of a bygone era.

The book is a time capsule of memories shared by the people and families who lived and worked on the Plains. The Carrisa Plains was not an easy place in which to live or make a living. In order to survive for any length of time, one had to be resourceful, self-reliant, and adaptable. An indefatigable work ethic was a necessity. Isolation was a frequent companion, and conveniences such as indoor plumbing, electricity, and phone service were uncommon. Given the Spartan conditions of life on the Plains, what strikes the reader most is the strong sense of community felt by the residents toward each other and the indelible ties they held to the land. Miles may have separated families and farms, but the people of the Plains were a very tightly knit community that was quick to take people in and lend a helping hand to those in need. Craig relates, "again and again people spoke of help they had either given or received from others." Dances, school activities, and the volunteer fire department brought folks together and forged deep, lasting bonds between families and friends. It is this sense of community that so clearly resonates throughout the history.

I met Craig in 2011, shortly after arriving at Cal Poly as the new head of Special Collections and University Archives. Craig contacted me to inquire if I would be interested in learning more about an oral history project that he and a colleague, Jackie Czapla, were conducting on the Carrisa Plains. We exchanged phone calls and emails for several weeks. With each successive contact, I began to comprehend the extensive and thorough nature of the project. Early in the exchange, Craig sent me an email with the abstracts of fifty-five interviews and with the following explanation:

> The interviews may, or may not, be of a standard form. Jackie and I have no training in this and simply did what seemed to make sense to us. Parts of these interviews are more like conversations. This . . . has the advantage of creating rapport with the subject and encouraging them to tell more and to suggest names for future interviews.

Although Craig purports that he and Jackie had little experience interviewing informants, their work is of a very high caliber and their effort positively herculean. It is evident that the project grew with the mention of unfamiliar names during the interviews, impelling Craig to conduct interviews with former Carrisa Plains residents currently living throughout California and in several western American states. Throughout the interviews both Craig and Jackie have a comfortable rapport with their narrators, as well as a command of and a deep interest in the people and history of the Plains.

As an archivist, I would like to comment on the value of oral history in documenting community. Oral history is one of the more personal and democratic methods of collecting and providing access to history and stories. It serves a valuable role in preserving history that might otherwise not be captured through other primary sources (letters, diaries, census records, photographs, ledgers, etc.). When documenting a community such as the Carrisa Plains, census data will tell researchers how many people lived there, but not what it was like to live there; a diary might provide insight from one person's perspective; and a photograph captures a single moment in time. All of these forms of primary source documentation are vital to the historical record. Oral history, however, expands and complements our understanding of these records; it adds a personal and emotive quality to the history.

Since 2008, Craig and Jackie have devoted themselves to capturing the stories of Carrisa Plains residents, current and former. As of this writing (2012), they have conducted one hundred interviews. Given the sparse population of the area, this remarkable number of interviews provides both a broad and a detailed view of the people, the Plains, and the relationship between the two. The oral histories, housed in the Special Collections and University Archives of the Robert E. Kennedy Library on the campus of Cal Poly, will be a boon to future students, historians, scholars, and anyone interested in the Carrisa Plains. Perhaps as important as the research value of the collection, the interviews, together with this book, provide the Plains' residents with the gift of their collective stories and history.

Among these collective stories are two fascinating chapters which explore the lives of women and of children on the Plains. The reader learns about games played by children, the numerous and exhausting chores children were responsible for, the various schools attended by children, and rites of passage. The experiences of the children growing up the Plains will seem quite foreign as compared with the childhood experiences of most twenty-first century readers. The female perspective is often marginalized in histories. This account, however, includes the female perspective throughout and devotes an entire chapter to three women's experiences on the Plains, each of which was introduced to the Plains through marriage. Their stories disclose the challenges of transitioning from "city life" to life on the Plains. Their stories also provide insight into the formidable roles and responsibilities of women in a rural community. For those that know the Carrisa Plains, this book is a familiar history; for those who are unfamiliar with the Plains, it is a wonderful introduction to the human ecology of this unique area and the not too distant history of its residents.

Time changes everything, and the Carrisa Plains is no exception.

The title of the book alludes to the dissipating memories of the last century. Many of the people and families interviewed for the book have left the Plains, either voluntarily or involuntarily. Technology and global events have forever altered life on the Carrisa Plains, but without exception, the Plains have had a lasting effect on all who spent time there. As Craig states, "The land and the people had become one."

On a recent trip out to the Carrisa Plains, I joined Craig, a BLM archaeologist, and several other volunteers to survey a long forgotten community with only a few hard-to-find relics as evidence of its existence. The eight of us looked for artifacts and debris patterns in an attempt to discern who lived there, when they lived there, and for what purpose. With scant evidence remaining, it was difficult at best to answer any of these questions. The forgotten community, known as the "Georgi Community," remains a mystery that may never be revealed. Fortunately, *Another Place and Time* will preclude the same fate from happening to others of the people who lived and worked there. Craig Deutsche has eloquently preserved the history of the Carrisa Plains through the voices of those who lived there.

Peter Runge
Head, Special Collections and University Archives
Robert E. Kennedy Library
California Polytechnic State University

ANOTHER
PLACE
&
TIME

CHAPTER ONE

Arriving at Night

Beginning of an oral history project

In the Temblor foothills

There was little to see in the beams from the headlights of the car: a dusty gravel road, a low berm along one edge, an occasional mouse scurrying into the nearby grass. The fields beyond were a blank. Even more difficult to imagine was the cultural journey that this visit would begin, a search into the vanishing past of a small community near the Central Coast of California. On that first evening I was intent only on finding my way to one of the visitor campgrounds in the newly designated Car-

rizo Plain National Monument. The purpose of the trip was to offer
some assistance, volunteer service, in removing old barbed wire fencing.
I little suspected that these rusting fences would become a link between
a modern present and the simpler lives of an earlier time. Long journeys
have small beginnings.

A Largely Unknown Valley

What is this place where I had arrived? The valley, known to its residents as the Carrisa Plains, runs fifty miles from northwest to southeast.[1] At its widest it is fifteen miles across, but within its boundaries are
smaller hills, washes, and even a low ridge created by the San Andreas
Fault. The Temblor Mountains lie to the east, and the higher Caliente
Range, rising to 5200 feet, bounds it on the west. Located halfway between the cities of Bakersfield and San Luis Obispo and only a two-hour
drive north of Los Angeles, this valley is largely unknown to the rest
of California. With its principal road largely unpaved, this is a land of
empty space and vast sky.

On later visits I came to know the Carrisa Plains in all seasons. If the
annual rains arrive on schedule, roads in winter will become quagmires,
and hills will bloom with wildflowers in the following spring. Summer
is hot and dry, so by autumn the hills will again be brown. All year long
raptors soar overhead, quail hide in the brush, coyotes hunt in the center
of the plain, and deer walk the low mountains. Human residents will tell
you that the Plains can be the hottest place in California, and it can seem
the coldest. It can be the wettest place, and it can be the driest.

Even on my first visit, I was haunted by relics left from earlier farming and ranching days: an abandoned seed cart, a collapsing grain tank, a
rusted harrow covered with dust. Corrals and loading chutes were visible
from the roads, and in open fields I found water troughs gone dry and
filled only with tumbleweed. Most evocative of all was an abandoned
homestead site. The porch of the house had collapsed, doors were missing, and the roof was falling in. Among the rafters was a collection of
sticks that served as home to a raven, and a similar pile under the sink

had been assembled by a pack rat. Behind the house, I found the overturned body of a truck, the bed of a wagon without wheels, and a scatter of debris from what must have been the shelter for a family cow, for a pig, or for chickens. It was impossible not to wonder about the persons who had once worked and lived there.

What kind of lives had these pioneers led? What kind of persons chose such a place to build their homes? Were they defeated? Did they simply walk away? Photographs of Dust Bowl survivors from the Great Depression came to mind. Or perhaps some were cowboys, not in the John Wayne image, but still riding fence lines and sleeping on the ground. Some of this history can be read in the relics left behind, but most exists only in the memories of these pioneers and their living descendants. A search for this past became a personal quest for me, and over a period of several years, I found and spoke with many of these people. While they answered innumerable questions, still other questions surfaced. Perhaps the value of history is to make us wonder about who and what we are.

Teaming with Jackie Czapla

For Jackie Czapla, the motivation to find stories was initially different. Jackie works at the Visitor Center of the Carrizo Plain National Monument, and she has lived in the Plains for nearly fifteen years. It takes time for a newcomer to become accepted in the small ranching community that still exists at the very north end, but with time she became acquainted with many of this older generation. It became apparent to Jackie that this community was a connected one. All the families were related; any two persons you met would be cousins, or third cousins, or married to someone who had a grandfather that . . . The connections between these people and their experiences on the land became a fascination for her, and so Jackie tentatively began collecting their stories. When other circumstances interfered, she was obliged to put the project aside.

I met Jackie one day at the Visitor Center and insisted that she must resume her search, and I would be eager to hear what she found. She, in turn, insisted that I must be the one to find the earlier settlers and record their memories . . . and so of course nothing happened. Two years later, we talked again and decided that waiting was not possible. The stories would be lost forever if they were not collected soon, and it was clear that no one else was going to carry this out.

We set out to interview whomever we could find that might tell us about life on the Plains in earlier times. These included present ranchers, earlier residents who had moved away, children of homesteaders, hired hands, cattlemen, and sheepherders. We recorded the interviews and transcribed them. For the people we met, the reward, if it might be called that, was a copy of the recorded interview. While these individuals might not consider the recording significant, they recognized that in time their children or grandchildren would wonder, and these records would become part of the family heritage. Beyond simply hearing the stories for ourselves, Jackie and I hoped that these records would be archived in a library or historical society and made available for others. Our wish was that these might be a resource for future writers, historians, or simply for descendants of these families on the Plains. Memories can be fallible, and when stories which we heard were inconsistent, we simply recorded them. There are many histories, and each of us tells our own story. The institutions where the records are now kept and the names of the persons with whom we have spoken are listed in Appendix B of this book.

Detective Game / Treasure Hunt

The search for witnesses became something between a detective game and a treasure hunt. When we interviewed one person, they would tell us of two more people with whom we absolutely must speak. They would remember a name and might tell us the city where they lived. At times someone would volunteer to make contact with the person and provide a reference for us. Sometimes there was nothing more than a hint. In the twenty-first century, it is certainly easier to locate missing persons than in previous times. In certain cases, an Internet search provided a business address. Occasionally a genealogical webpage would identify other family members. The online White Pages became a regular stop as we attempted to find the persons that had been suggested to us. The list of possible people to interview grew and grew, and as we continued, it sometimes seemed that we were getting farther from the end of the project rather than closer.

These searches are described later along with the stories that they uncovered. When the search for specific persons was lengthy, the process itself sometimes provided insight into the families and the community. I have never considered myself a salesperson, but that was what I became. With only a phone number or an address, the next step was to make a contact and persuade the person to have their story recorded. On a telephone call, I estimated that I had three sentences to convince someone that I was not crazy, two minutes to persuade them that the project was interesting, and then five minutes to persuade them to meet and talk with us. I dropped names shamelessly.

> Me: I am Craig Deutsche calling for Don Freeborn to talk about the Carrisa Plains. I was given your name by Gail Edgar who attended the Simmler School with you around 1948. If I have my information correct, your father was Paul Freeborn, and your mother was a sister of Elmer and Walter King.
>
> Don: Gail, Gail, I haven't seen him in forty-five years. He and I were going to our high school class reunion five years ago, but then I was ill and couldn't make it. How is he? Has he been back to see his place at the Saucito?

The conversation continued as I gave him news of his classmates, of the interviews that Jackie and I had conducted, and of the present state of the Monument. In turn, Don recalled that somewhere in his house he had a map showing locations of all the ranches on the north of the Plains in 1950. The recorded interview would follow later, but already two strangers had connected with a common purpose.

I suppose it is human nature to believe that our own personal histories are interesting. When we meet someone who is also interested, and when there is the possibility that our experiences will be saved and become more widely available, this is validating. When a few individuals chose not to speak with us, their reticence could be understood in the context of their lives, and this was sometimes significant in itself. Most persons, when they understood our intentions, were willing to talk and were often enthusiastic. They are to be thanked over and over again for their generosity. I feel as if I had been taken into their family, and I am grateful.

Strangely Familiar

What did I expect to find at the end of the journey? I imagined hearing of lonely struggles and broken dreams, but the facts turned out otherwise. People often spoke of hard work but seldom spoke of hardship. Very few persons walked away empty-handed and defeated. Cowboys spoke about trailing stock east and west, even while taking care of their families. Farmers conducted business with a handshake. High school students boarded five days a week at the school dormitory in Atascadero. Neighbors danced all night long at the Simmler School. One woman who lived at the north end of the Plains baked daily for her neighbors, nursed families that were ill, and helped new brides from the city adjust to their new surroundings. Although many lived in isolated locations, their lives were not lonely.

These were strong persons that I discovered. They laughed and they cried. Some were buried out on the land, and others retired comfortably in town and even in other states. A few have stayed on the Plains, but in most cases their children have moved on. Although in some ways their lives were more difficult than ours, in many ways our own experience reflects theirs. These were our fathers, mothers, and grandparents. With my arrival on the Plains, I had entered into another place and time, but it was also strangely familiar. Welcome now to their story.

[1] "Carrizo" is a Spanish designation for a tall reed that grows in damp ground, and in the late 1800s, this name was adopted for the marshy area at the center of the valley. Early immigrants were from many countries with only rudimentary educations, and so the spoken word led to a number of different spellings which included *Carisa*, *Carriso*, *Carrissa*, and *Carrisa*. The Carrizo Plain National Monument adopted the original Spanish word, but the older ranching families at the north are very definite that their community belongs to the Carrisa Plains. It is a curiosity that the reed grass for which the Monument was named has never been definitely found within the present monument.

CHAPTER TWO

The Earliest Settlers

Land barons and small homesteaders

Mary Morris grave

The first European arrivals on the Carrisa Plains were practical people who came to make their living in whatever way they could. Records of their lives are sparse: a few diaries, occasional homestead records, newspaper accounts, marks they left on the land, and some anecdotes passed down through several generations of family. These stories may be even better for their brevity as more is left to the imagination. If one knows the land, not many details are needed to sense the rhythm of their lives.

My introduction to this earliest history was through newspaper clippings and reports kept in the Bakersfield office of the Bureau of Land Management (BLM). These accounts suggest that cowboys and sheepherders were the first persons of European descent on the Plains. They were almost certainly Spanish and Basque employees who tended cattle and sheep for established ranches on the California coast or in the San Joaquin Valley. It may have been one of these herders who settled and became its first permanent resident, a "J. Garcia" who kept sheep and possibly cattle at what is now the Saucito Ranch. The date given in the BLM records is "around 1850." He is reported to have had an adobe cabin, but little else is known.

More is known about the absentee landowners who bought and held large tracts of land in the early years of the Plains. Much of this information is found in formal records concerning land ownership, purchases and sales, and the legal disputes between two of these landowners. Miller and Lux was the popular name given one of these companies, and the second was the Kern County Land Company, known almost universally as the KCL. It was normal practice for these companies to either lease their lands to others or else to hire cowboys to manage their own livestock.

A third major landholder was James McDonald, a San Francisco businessman who bought land shortly after the Civil War using government script for payment. His holdings were almost entirely at the north of the Plains and reached a maximum of 60,000 acres. A nice story about him related by several persons, although of unknown truthfulness, reports that at one time McDonald decided to travel south from San Francisco for a first visit to his holdings. From the coast at San Luis Obispo, he took a wagon eastward toward the Plains. The land became drier and drier, and the traveling was difficult. While still traveling through the La Panza Range west of the Carrisa Plains, he asked his driver if the land would be any different as he continued onward. The driver said that it was all the same, and McDonald replied, "Then I've seen enough. We'll turn and go back." That may be as close as he ever got.

By the end of the nineteenth century, there had also been attempts at homesteading on the Carrisa. In one interview I was told that there

had been a German community at the north of the Plains near the Temblor Mountains. Steve Beck, a one-time rancher on the Plains, spoke of
finding cisterns, nothing more, in the fields of his family farm. These
were open excavations created to collect rainwater and lined with stones.
For grain farmers of later years, these depressions were a hazard to their
equipment, and rather systematically the pits were filled in. Another of
the present day ranchers recalled hearing of a Dutch community along
Bitterwater Road twenty miles north from the present Highway 58.
Even less is known about these people, and there are no living recollections of how their lands were transferred to later farmers. The decade
between 1890 and 1900 was one of severe drought, and large numbers
of small landowners left the Carrisa in those years. This was undoubt-
edly the fate of these two immigrant communities, the German and the
Dutch.

El Saucito Ranch

One of the earliest year-round residents on the Plains was an employee
and manager of the extensive McDonald estate. Chester Rude Brumley
brought his family west from New York, settled first in San Francisco,
and then in 1875 purchased what became the Saucito Ranch midway in
the Carrisa Plains. Newspaper accounts from that time give glowing, although somewhat trite and overblown accounts of his success as a farmer
and of the magnificent orchards and gardens he planted. Cottonwood
trees planted in those years, although near the end of their lifetime now,
still provide shade in the yard, and a number of cypress trees, non-native
to the Carrisa, grow nearby. The house which was built in 1876 still
stands today.

   This ranch has been an ongoing presence in my own involvement
with the Carrisa Plains. On my very first visit as a volunteer, the Monument Manager took our group to this house and then on a longer hike to
a nearby rock outcropping. When the management plan for the Monument was finally adopted and signed in 2010, the celebration was held
on the lawn in front of the house. Still more recently I had the oppor-

tunity to meet and interview a great, great granddaughter of Chester Brumley. Pam Parsons had become fascinated with her family history, and although much of her knowledge came from archival research, she also could relate a few memories and stories that had been passed down orally. On my part, I was able to tell her something of the more recent history of the ranch. Because the ranch will appear again in later chapters, it is worthwhile giving a more complete description of the setting.

From the ranch house, there are long views eastward across an open field to a sagging fence and an eroded wash. Still another mile farther is the flat surface of Soda Lake, and beyond that you see the Temblor Mountains on the horizon. When I first visited in 2003 and on subsequent visits, I have always admired the quiet beauty of the site. Although ragged, the grass under the trees remains thick; it is green in spring and then brown the rest of the year. Around the house, fallen leaves rustle in wind. Pictures from earlier years show bushes and flowers around the house, and former residents speak of grapevines in the yard. Nearly always barn owls with their round, white faces can be seen moving silently through the trees, and in some years a pair of great horned owls will nest in the tallest of the cottonwoods. Kingbirds, orioles, doves, and blackbirds twitter in the grove when the surrounding fields, like the rest of the Plains, are hot and dry.

The house must have been a delightful home. Surrounded on three sides by porches, it is two stories high with wooden clapboard siding painted white. It is unoccupied today and locked. Through the vacant windows, you see only bare floors and walls. At one time the Monument planned to use the house as an education center for visiting school children, but this plan was abandoned when the costs of restoring it adequately became much greater than could be reasonably expended. The ranch today is sometimes used for special events, but the house itself remains closed.

For many years it was thought that the house was a "kit" construction that had been brought to California around Cape Horn and then carried by wagon from the coast to its present location. In the 1870s, houses of this kind were sold as pre-cut lumber with plans and hardware to be assembled upon arrival. In a recorded interview with the San Luis

Obispo Historical Society, Nellie Brumley, who grew up at El Saucito and was a daughter of Chester Rude Brumley, asserted that this was the case. Discrepancies in this account arose when the Bureau of Land Management set out to stabilize the structure. If this were truly a kit house, it was expected that there would be numbers painted on the studs and boards corresponding to instructions in building plans. Marks of this sort were never found, and even more telling, it was discovered that the studs in the walls were of redwood. It is only in California that redwood grows so the eastern origin was fictional. Memories can be fallible.

Searching through newspaper accounts, genealogy, tax, and census records, Pam Parsons had reconstructed the later history of the Brumley family. In 1886 Chester Rude Brumley bought property in San Luis Obispo and moved there with his wife. Two years later, while out on the ranch, he fell from a horse and died from the injuries. His daughter Nellie married a dentist and became a notable member of society in San Luis Obispo. A second daughter also married, and her grandchildren are now doctors in San Luis Obispo. His son, Chester Jerome Brumley, managed the Saucito Ranch for several years until it was sold in 1896, probably for taxes. His story was ultimately a sad one. Although Chester Jerome had a wife and five children, he essentially abandoned them, drifting from one questionable enterprise to another. He was destitute when he died in the late 1920s, and by that time the Saucito Ranch had passed through several owners and was acquired by a family of *vaqueros* with the name Garcia.

Pam Parsons recounted another story of the Brumley family concerning Indians who visited El Saucito. Its principal source is the same interview which Nellie Brumley recorded for the Historical Society.

> Nellie and her mother were alone at the ranch making cookies when together they saw something strange coming out of the horizon. It turned out to be a group of Indians. The mother told Nellie to stay in the house and then went out and took a pail of cookies. The Indians had really stopped there to get water, but the Brumleys were new and they didn't know anything about Indians so they were probably scared. So anyway, they let the Indians use the water and gave them cookies. You know there

wasn't really communication, and then the Indians rode off. Then a few hours later, one Indian came back by himself; he had left his rifle on the porch. A few days later . . . there were twenty Indians in the first group . . . a few days later eighteen Indians came back, and the story is that there were two openings for sheepherders or vaqueros at some ranch further east. All twenty Indians went to apply for the job, two were hired, and so eighteen came back.

Nellie Brumley was known to be a good story teller, and certainly the account depicts a rather clichéd image of the American West. I was surprised when a similar story appeared in another, entirely unrelated interview.

In the Elkhorn Plain

Thomas McCart was a serendipitous discovery. He walked into the Visitor Center of the Monument one day and commented that the flintlock rifle on display along one of the walls had belonged to his grandfather. What a stunning introduction! Although I was not present, Jackie learned that he lived in San Diego, but his family still owned and sometimes visited 160 acres of land which his grandfather had homestead in the southeastern corner of the Monument. Thomas offered his contact information if we wished to talk with him more about his grandfather, Peter.

I personally met Thomas on a late spring day at his property in the Elkhorn Plain. This is a small dry valley on the southern and eastern edge of the Monument and separated from the greater Carrisa Plains by a low, north-south running ridge. It is certainly the hottest and driest part of the entire Monument. Today there are a few fences and corrals along this valley, and there is at least one line camp that is sometimes used by cowboys that graze cattle. However, there is no sign of any permanent residence, and there are no signs that any of the valley has ever been farmed. It is cattle country with a few water tanks, a few troughs, and miles and miles of bare dirt. Thomas greeted me warmly, and the story of his grandfather began.

Peter McCart arrived in the Carrisa in 1882. He was Canadian and had grown up in a small town north of Detroit. These were difficult times, and Peter's father brought his four sons together, gave each of them a pistol and a horse, and sent them in four different directions to make their fortunes. Peter went west. When he arrived in Bakersfield, he heard stories about good land for homesteading still farther toward the coast. Thomas continued the story of his grandfather:

> For ten cents an acre, he had a chance to buy some of this terrible looking land over in Taft, and he told my grandma what he hated about it. As he walked around, he found these damned tar pieces coming out of the side of the ground, and he said he just couldn't believe that anybody would try to sell the stuff. He continued west heading for San Luis Obispo on the coast. He came here [the Elkhorn Plain] and checked the ground out, and he saw its arid soil. Even though it was damp that year, still it was arid land. He had a grain farming background, and he felt this would be a really good area for dryland grain farming.

Peter had passed by the rich oil fields of Kern County, and he never reached the fertile farmlands of the Cuyama Valley immediately to the west. It was a wet year when he arrived, and the green hills looked like heaven to him. He was unaware of the extremes in climate that have been the history of the Carrisa as far back as anyone knows. Peter filed for a homestead on 160 acres, bought another 160 acres adjacent to this, and took up the life of a farmer and a cattle rancher. During these early years, Peter had fallen in love with Mary Jane Ballantine on a visit to Bakersfield. Her father was a circuit judge, and the family was a pillar of the community. Peter and Mary Jane were married in church, and everybody wished them well as they left for the Elkhorn Plain to begin life together at the homestead. It is easy to imagine her father and family gathered about and quietly congratulating themselves that such a suitable husband had been found. The dry years lay in the future.

At one time, and before the marriage, Peter had worked on the Wheeler Ranch near the Tejon properties in the southern San Joaquin

Valley. He had done well, and as reward Mr. Wheeler had given him five or ten head of cattle. These went with the couple to the Elkhorn Plain, and although Peter had been a grain farmer in Canada, he chose to raise cattle as well. In part, Peter chose both farming and grazing to take a neutral position in the range wars that were spreading across California. Cattlemen and farmers had become enemies, killings were not unknown, and Peter was a cautious bystander. When asked if he was a farmer or rancher, he would reply, "Neither. I am a Canadian." The truth, however, was that Peter had become a naturalized citizen in order to apply for a patent on his homestead. Like farming, raising cattle was also a difficult venture. During his time at the homestead, Peter conducted three drives northward to deliver cattle, and in one year he went as far as San Jose to sell the animals. In another year, he lost 70 percent of his herd to anthrax.

Peter was a gregarious fellow, and with few persons living in the Plains at that time, he must have known nearly all of them. It could not be confirmed precisely, but it seems that he knew the Brumleys who were living then at El Saucito. As the story was handed down to Thomas, when Peter visited the Brumleys, he would bake a pie, bring it for them, and help out with their farm. On one of these visits, the family was badly upset as Indians had come over and tried to intimidate them or scare them. Thomas McCart continued:

> He went back up north and the family told him, "Arm yourself. The Indians are coming." Grandpa didn't believe them. Apparently they [the Indians] did come. They came and tried to intimidate everybody. And here is the confusing part. We don't know if they came here, to this property [in the Elkhorn], or if he saw them at the north end of the Carrisa Plains. But they were drinking, and they got drunk. They were hollering and scared the hell out of everybody, and fell off their horses and got on their horses, and thank God they left . . . He said they hooted and hollered and left.

The details of this story differ from the one told about Mrs. Brumley feeding cookies to the Indians at the Saucito, but the time is about the same, and the nature of these stories is consistent. The 1880s were the last years of the Ghost Dance uprising that had started in Nevada and then spread all across the Western United States. Indeed, the basic story may be correct.

In their first year of marriage, Mary Jane and Peter had a daughter. This was Auntie Florence as Thomas remembered her. Six years later, in the very last year of qualification for the homestead, Mary Jane died during childbirth. The baby also died and was left in an unmarked grave out at the homestead. Mary Jane's body was returned to Bakersfield for burial, a two-day journey by wagon. This must have been a terrible journey and a heartbreaking reception for the family that had seen their daughter travel west as a new bride only a few years before.

Peter returned to the homestead briefly but decided that it was not worth developing and shut it down to return to Bakersfield. He was a good businessman, became a successful mortgage broker, and bought forty acres of land right within the city. Because in those days it was improper for a single man to be raising a daughter alone, Peter had to give Florence up, almost for adoption, to another family. He visited her regularly, and the two remained close all their lives. It also happened that during this period Peter remarried.

> He met my grandmother, Marcella McCart. Her parents were in Los Angeles, I know, and he went down and met her parents and courted her for about a year. Then they got married, and he told her, "I have this beautiful ranch out on the Carrisa Plains. I want to bring you out and show it to you and fire it back up again." Well, she came out here, took one look, and said, "Ha, Ha, that's it. We're going back to Bakersfield."

Two children were born to this second marriage, and although Peter visited his lands in the Elkhorn Plain many times, he never attempted to rebuild his homestead. He and his daughter Florence later opened a successful real estate and insurance business. The family was well off, and ultimately they sold their forty acres in Bakersfield for an astonishing sum of money.

Thomas spoke about hunting trips that his own father took with Peter in later years:

My dad had an airplane that was a trainer with big old bulbous tires, and it was perfect for landing out here. My dad and Grandpa would land here right by the road. They'd come and sit right on this hillside where we are now and tell stories. Grandpa would tell him about the earlier times out here. One time they came out here and spent two nights. Grandpa was incredible. Dad said that with virtually nothing but a pocket knife and his trusty old shotgun, Grandpa had jackrabbit dinner for both of them. He could live off the land out here, and it was just amazing.

Thomas has also returned many times to this same empty hillside in the Elkhorn Plain. He brings his family at least once a year to camp and watch the sky. They have not sold it, nor do they intend to sell. Nothing is grown, and no cattle graze. Perhaps Thomas wonders where the grave of Mary Jane's infant lies. Perhaps Mary Jane Ballantine returns to visit as well.

I have also returned to this corner of the Carrisa Plains a number of times since that interview with Thomas. Once I was there in the spring of a wet year. It was green everywhere, and near the homestead site, a carpet of yellow and gold flowers covered a low swale. From a hill, I looked down and saw the dusty road winding up the valley, and I could picture Peter McCart as he arrived and claimed a home. On a last visit, I also found several recently placed signs that read, "Private Property - No Hunting or Trespassing." I assume that Thomas placed them to convey his ownership and attachment to the land. It is an attachment that is not easily severed.

A Hilltop Grave

West from the Elkhorn, in the main valley of the Carrisa Plains and at the top of a small hill, an iron picket fence surrounds three graves. It is a lonely place, and from here the view extends for miles in all directions. One grave has a headstone reading: "Mary W Morris, Died August 18, 1896, 63 years." The other two burials are unidentified.

Several descendants of Mary and Edmund Morris still live in Central

California. Susan Brown Diefenderfer lives at the north end of the Plains near Soda Lake Road and Highway 58. She is a great, great granddaughter of Mary Morris, and along with two cousins, she is keeper of the family history. As a young child, Susan knew Mary's daughter, Emma, and when Susan was older, she listened to stories told by her Aunt Hazel, granddaughter of Emma. In turn, Susan passed her information on to Jackie and myself. The stories began in Kentucky and Illinois, moved west to Texas, and ultimately came to California.

Mary Wein Nance was born in 1833 in Green County, Kentucky. Her family was reasonably well-to-do and aristocratic, but beyond the names of her parents, very little else is known of her family. It was suspected that the Nance family considered that their daughter married beneath herself. Edmund Morris was born in Springfield, Illinois, in 1832, and he had served in the Civil War on the Confederate side. The circumstances of their meeting are not known, but official records place their marriage in Dallas, Texas in 1853. Together they had seventeen children. One set of twins, born February 3, 1871, died on the following day. A second set of twins born in 1872 lived less than a year. By the time that Mary and Edmund came to California in 1886, another six children had died. Of those seven still living, four accompanied them west. Susan speculates that Mary and Edmund left Texas to put some distance between themselves and their relatives. The Morris family lived two years near San Miguel and then came to the Carrisa Plains. When they saw the lower end of the Plains, it reminded them of Texas, and they decided to stay. Even before the drought years of 1898-99, their difficulties in homesteading in the South Carrisa Plains were considerable.

The homestead site lies along one of the present roads leading to Padrone Spring. Pieces of old glass and crockery were found at the site some years ago, but all that remains today is a scattering of rocks on a small rise outlining the foundation of a cabin. The home was said to have had an oiled dirt floor. There are no indications that the land nearby had ever been used for farming, and given the difficulty of farming in this southern part of the Plain, it is nearly certain that the family depended upon cattle for their living. The nearest surface water is half a mile away at Padrone Spring, and hauling water was surely a part of their lives.

Susan understood that Mary never left the Carrisa during the eight years that she lived there. The male members of the family went to Bakersfield once a year to sell cattle and buy supplies. This would require a trip of two days in each direction, and it would have fallen to Mary to remain behind and watch the two younger girls and feed the animals: chickens, a cow, and maybe a pig. During their years on the Carrisa, Edmund became a postmaster on the Plains. It was called the Goodwin Post Office, although it is certainly unrelated to the present Goodwin Ranch far to the north. Also while the family lived on the Carrisa, one of the children who had stayed behind in Texas came out and joined them. This was Achilles Morris, known to the family as Uncle Pony. If the Morris family had neighbors, nothing is known about them.

What of Mary's death? The circumstances surrounding the event are uncertain. One account relates that Mary and one of the children had taken a wagon west to the coast. On their return, the wagon tipped over, and Mary was killed. An alternate version of this story holds that Mary was not killed in the accident, but died later from the injuries that she had sustained. These reports contradict the family's recollection that she had never left the homestead at all. Family memories report that she had a lump in her breast, and one story claims that "she worked with it enough, and she got it out." Susan Diefenderfer suspects that Mary died of breast cancer, but it is probable that the true cause will never be known.

In spite of the apparent poverty of their circumstances, it is certain that Mary was remembered and honored. Susan has a copy of an elegant announcement of Mary's death. At the top of the page it says: "In Memoriam" and below it is a photo of Mary Wein Nance Morris. She is a beautiful woman, elegantly dressed, and looking directly at the camera. It reads: "In loving memory - Died August 18, 1996, aged 63 years, five months, 25 days." It ends with a short poem.

Farewell my husband, dear, farewell.
Adieu to thee, adieu!
And you my dearly loved ones all,
Farewell, farewell to you.
Though I am gone and you are left

To tread this vale alone,
We'll hope to meet again in Heaven
With Christ before God's throne.

The identities of the other two persons buried on the hilltop are uncertain. One grave, that of an infant, is thought to be that of a grand-child of Mary and Edmund. The other grave, according to one report, is that of a cousin who came out from Texas and died of a burst appendix at age seventeen. Another conjecture holds that it was a negro servant who had accompanied the family west. Beyond the family records or reports, the gravesite itself invites speculation. While the headstone for Mary Morris is prominent, the second grave has only a very small marker with inscribed initials "M.W.M." It resembles a foot-stone of the sort once common in early cemeteries. It seems probable that it had been moved from its original location to the present one. This latter speculation gathers credence from two reports which were related to me independently by persons living today south of the Plains. They stated with certainty that the cemetery site had been vandalized on at least one occasion and maybe even twice. Whatever the facts, the site and the setting are impressive.

The years 1898-1899 were dry years throughout the Plains, and many settlers in both the north and south moved on. The Morris homestead was too difficult for the family to manage, and after Mary died, Edmund sold the homestead, receiving $1.25 per acre. He and one son, Joe, moved to Washington State. The prospect of rain must have drawn them north, but when 130 inches fell a few years later this was apparently way too much of a good thing, and they returned to the California coast where Edmund settled and lived with Emma, one of his daughters. Emma and Edmund are buried at the Estrella Adobe Church near Paso Robles. The son, Joe, is buried in Atascadero. The other two daughters, Mauda and Lydia, are buried in Bakersfield. As Lydia was the youngest of the children, she received the family bible, but the records of her several marriages are confused, and the names of her children are unknown. There is little chance of locating the bible, and with no more threads to follow, the rest is a matter of imagination.

Quiet Heroes

These are not the legends of western homesteaders that are portrayed in popular movies. Their stories were not of dramatic struggles but were instead ones of sustained effort. For one reason or another, these families all left their homes in the Carrisa Plains. Even so, it would be incorrect to say that they had been defeated. In new locations and at later times, nearly all had prospered. Thomas McCart still returns to visit his grandfather's homestead, descendants of the Morris family are living in nearby towns, and members of the Brumley family search out the history of their one-time home on the Plains. Although I had not spoken with the first pioneers myself, their families had been generous in telling the stories. Even with the passage of time, the human side of the early lives was apparent. They had been real people, and the uncertainties in their lives were not unlike our own.

CHAPTER THREE

Grain Farmers

Work and life for dryland farmers

Beck harvester crew

The Carrisa Plains today are nearly empty. In the south, I have seen miles of open space, dried grass, saltbush, and the falling remnants of corrals, fences, sheds, and grain tanks. The people who once worked these fields have moved on. North of the Monument, there are still families living on scattered ranches. Cattle graze where there were once planted fields; and occasionally, rarely, there will be a tractor working a small field along the road. Even these signs are illusory. Many, perhaps most, of these residents are elderly, holding on to land that they had once worked through the seasons. Today few are making a living from farming. As I mentioned earlier, when I thought of speaking with former residents of the Plains, I fully expected to hear of struggles and lonely lives. Indeed, there were these stories, but there was also much more. The interviews which Jackie and I held at the north of the Plains told a more complicated and ultimately a more interesting history.

From the 1920s through the 1970s, this isolated valley was the breadbasket of San Luis Obispo County. In good years, some farmers we spoke with might be called rich; they paid off loans, bought new machinery and cars, put in appliances, bought airplanes, and some even had time for extended family vacations. Of course the dry years brought different circumstances, but bankers knew the farmers and they would carry loans over. When rains came, everything would be right again. The wheat was high quality and was marketed to big milling companies in Los Angeles. The farms, known as ranches to everyone we met, were large. In the planting seasons, the families worked around the clock, and at harvest time additional hands were hired. These were the prosperous years.

It is with these wheat ranchers and their children that Jackie and I began our interviews. Jackie knew many of the families personally, so there was no need to search through land deeds or ancestry records. Jackie and I also hoped that if we were inexperienced at conducting interviews, they would be tolerant of our mistakes. In a number of instances, we talked over coffee and cookies and looked through old family picture albums. Conversations were random, not planned, and the information we collected came in bits and pieces. In reading over transcripts of these early interviews, we often wished that we had asked more or different questions. With later interviews, we would pursue the same questions and hear a different perspective. Although I had expected that we would be hearing a history of ranching on the Plains, the people we met, both in person and through the narratives, became the real story. First though, we might learn how two of the ranches were created.

Land Is Acquired

Hans Peter Beck was born in Denmark sometime around 1870. As a young man, he came to the United States, probably to avoid conscription into the German army. In 1914 his son, Nels Beck, moved from the California coast to the Carrisa Plains where he worked as a hired hand for one of the early ranchers there. East from the Plains, McKittrick was the center of a booming oil field, and there Nels met his wife, Mary Fairbanks. The Fairbanks family had already been on the Plains for two generations, and Mary's mother, known by everyone in the family as Grandma, was legend.

Around 1920, and shortly after being married, Nels bought land near the Temblor Mountains along what is now Highway 58. This plot had belonged to a man named Hubbard, and it included a small mill that processed grain for animal feed. Hubbard had been a blacksmith and then a miller, but Nels was a committed farmer. Later purchases included 2200 acres that had once been part of the McDonald estate and some smaller holdings that had belonged to the earlier German homesteaders. With further purchases and the inclusion of leased land, the Beck family at one time worked a total of 22,000 acres. When Nels and Mary retired to San Luis Obispo in 1945, the farm was taken over by their two sons, Kenneth and Alan. In later years, much of the actual work was done by Kenneth's sons, Greg and Steve. It was Greg with whom Jackie and I spoke at length.

The second ranch in this story has a very different history. It begins with Robert Flint who came west from Ontario, Canada, in about 1850, and it concludes with the distribution of the land among six heirs of the Wreden family in 1941. It was a member of this latter family, Donald Nevins, who related this story to me at his office in Davis, California.

Over a period of years, Robert Flint assembled a huge estate, known as the San Juan Ranch, which extended eastward from the San Juan River to what is now Bitterwater Road. Although these lands were not contiguous, they represented at least 60,000 acres. Robert married late, and when his wife died, their young children were returned to Ontario to be raised there by an aunt. Robert continued ranching in California till he was killed in an accident around 1885. His various properties went to the children who were still very young, and the San Juan Ranch went to a son, also having the name Robert. This son was apparently intoxicated by his new wealth and was known for a party lifestyle and gambling. It was not long till the San Juan Ranch went into foreclosure, and in 1896 it was purchased by a wealthy San Francisco brewer.

Heinrich Wilhelm Klaus Wreden immigrated from Northern Germany to the United States in 1863 to join an older brother who had come ahead of him. It is assumed that they had also chosen America in preference to conscription in the German army. The two brothers, along with several other partners, established the very successful Washington Street Brewery in San Francisco, and eventually Heinrich became a naturalized citizen and anglicized his name to Henry. He married and had a family of six children. For whatever reasons, Henry became interested in land all across California, and after selling his share in the brewery, he bought the Flint estate and moved south to live at its principal headquarters on the San Juan River.

Henry died in 1931, but the ranch continued to operate as a single estate until 1941 when a settlement distributed it among his heirs. The estate was not divided into equal acreages but instead into lots that were perceived to be of equal potential for farming. Although the details were complicated, one of the heirs was a grandson, William Wreden, who became owner of 8500 acres twelve miles north of Highway 58 along Bitterwater Road. He and his family lived in Menlo Park, but two sons, Doug and Bo, spent nearly all their high school summers and holidays on this, the Pinole Ranch. These were the years 1958-1964. In the past nine years, Doug has become one of my good friends, and the story of his ranch will re-appear many times in this book.

Farming through the Seasons

Traditional dryland farming rotates the land on a two-year cycle. There is almost no usable surface water in the Carissa Plains, ground water is highly saline, and the huge water transfer projects of California's great

Central Valley provide nothing west of the Temblor Mountains. Two years are needed for the land to store enough water for one crop, and it is usual for farmers to leave half their land fallow while planting and harvesting the other half. In the next year, the use is reversed. Almost universally the crop was wheat.

Greg Beck, grandson of Nels Beck, had been one of these farmers. Jackie Czapla had already known him for a number of years before I met him. He grew up on the Beck family farm, and after college he worked a number of jobs both on and off the Carrisa Plains. At the time of our interview, wheat farming on the Plains was a failing enterprise, and he was employed as a heavy equipment operator for the California Highway Department. In speaking of his family history, Greg was thoughtful. He had accepted the fact that the way of life he had known as a child was gone. His description of this earlier life is the basis for much of what follows here.

With the conclusion of harvest in August or early September, preparation of the land for the next cycle began. Cattle or sheep would be admitted to the recently harvested fields. The livestock usually belonged to another outfit, a neighbor or perhaps an itinerant sheepherder. The herder paid a small fee for this, and the farmer received the additional benefit of clearing the field. This field would remain fallow for a full year, but still there were problems with weeds to address. Tumbleweed was common, and it was sometimes eliminated by burning. Farmers plowed a line around the field to contain the fire and then set a match. In later years this became more difficult as air-quality regulations set limits on when and how the burning could be done. Turning the weeds under with a disk was an alternative to burning. If this was done promptly after harvest, the tumbleweed could be controlled. If weeds came back in a fallow field the next summer, it was necessary to return again with a light disk to keep them down. Weeds used water, and water was not to be wasted.

If all went well, there would be a few weeks of slack time between harvest and the start of planting in November. This respite was used for equipment repair, for construction of sheds and fences, or for a family vacation. As farms became larger through the years, the Beck family went directly from harvesting one set of fields to planting the next set. Repairs became emergency operations when equipment broke down. There were times when a tractor with a blown engine was towed into the shed at the end of the day so that work could be done all through the night. If it were not out working the next day, this was money lost.

Ideally planting began after the first rains fell but before the ground became so wet as to mire the equipment in mud. Sometimes the seed was drilled into the soil; sometimes it was scattered on the surface and then covered using a springtooth harrow that tilled, or raked, the soil only lightly. Different varieties of grain needed to be planted at particular depths. During planting season, the Beck family worked eighteen hours a day with two shifts of men running the equipment. If the crop was not put in on time, then there would be no harvest the next fall. Without a harvest, the farm was in danger of failing.

Occasionally it was necessary to cultivate the fallow fields again in the spring or summer. The Beck family sometimes used what was called a rod weeder. Greg explained this device as follows:

> A rod weeder has a long, horizontal bar about an inch square and ten feet long. Pulled behind a tractor, it travels a few inches underneath the ground. It is wheel-driven, rotates backwards, and you see the earth moving over the top of it. It basically takes any weeds that are growing there and cuts them off at their taproot and just leaves them sitting there on the top of the field, on top of the ground. This can only be done, of course, if the ground has already been worked to a sufficient depth. You would not be able to do it on hard ground. We tried to knock the summer tumbleweeds down early enough that we didn't have to come back and disk them later. So after the summer went by, we'd get everything set up ready to go plant the ground again.

As noted, the usual crop throughout the Carrisa Plains was wheat. During the years of World War II, this was an essential war commodity. Prices were high and farmers could sell all the grain they could possibly grow. The land had only recently been converted to farming and was rich. Farms were prosperous then and continued so for a number of years after the war. In time, grain markets were saturated, and when a wheat embargo was imposed on Russia during the Cold War, prices fell precipitously. When land bank programs and crop limits were legislated, farmers switched parts of their land to barley. In the north of the Plains, this was successful, but farther south barley grew poorly. Safflower was another crop that was tried for a short while. This was a substitute crop when a particularly wet autumn made it impossible to plant wheat at the usual time. Safflower matured more rapidly than wheat, and so it was sometimes planted late in the season when wheat was no longer an option. Safflower is an oil seed and could be harvested with the same equipment that was used for other grains, but farmers complained that the harvesters became sticky and clogged. Wheat was always the first choice.

The order in which fields were planted or harvested was not accidental. Ideally when work finished on one field, the equipment was simply moved to the adjacent field. There was no sense wasting time moving machinery unnecessary distances. This was the ideal, but it could not always be done in practice. If the next field was lower and too wet, then it could not be planted immediately, and grain planted on hillsides matured at different times than that planted where it was flat. Ultimately the order in which these fields were harvested depended more upon their condition than upon convenience for moving equipment. Having been raised in a city, I had never thought about what was involved in this kind of farming. I was learning a lot.

On the Beck Ranch, the harvest began in early July. Traditionally the family held a barbecue on July 4th, and harvest began the next day. The basic operation was done by an immense machine known, of course, as a "harvester." As the machine crossed and re-crossed the field, standing grain was cut and fed directly into the main body of the machine where the grain heads were separated from the chaff and straw. The harvesters operated twelve hours a day, six or seven days a week, until the harvest was over. Depending upon the size of the ranch, the number of machines available, and the density of the crop, this took two months or more. Sometimes the men celebrated the end of harvest by throwing their straw hats into the machine itself and then wearing the tattered remains to a barbecue that the rancher gave for his hired hands.

The Harvest Crew

The harvesters, manufactured by Holt, Harris, or in later years by John Deere or Allis-Chalmers, were huge machines, and for persons who have not seen them, a description will tell much about summer work on the ranches. In the mid-twentieth century, they were eight or ten feet tall, twenty feet in length, and exclusive of the header which extended out on the right side, they would be eight feet wide. The header was typically eighteen or twenty feet long and included a reel for pushing grain into a cutting bar and a conveyer that brought the cut grain into the main body of the machine. These bodies were wooden and massively heavy. The wheels, machinery, and chains were, of course, metal. From the outside, one saw an astonishing arrangement of gears, belts, chains, and levers that controlled the internal threshing machinery, the position of the header, and the leveling of the machine itself. An engine, usually gasoline, sat at the very front of the machine or else high on a forward deck. The interior was, of course, not easily visible but included screens of various mesh for separating grain from sticks, weed seeds, and straw. Fans blew the lighter materials away, and smaller, heavier materials fell downward in the process. This was a formidable machine both to maintain and to operate.

In the 1920s and earlier, these machines were pulled by horses, and it was usual to have teams of sixteen to twenty animals. In those years, the grain was stored in sacks rather than being loose in bins or tanks, so the early harvesters included a shelf near the ground where one or two men directed grain into burlap sacks and sewed them shut. The sacks were thrown off the machine and later loaded onto flatbed trucks.

From the 1920s through the mid-50s, the harvesters were pulled by tractors, and it also became normal that the threshed grain remained loose and was collected in a bin high on the machine till it could be unloaded into a truck. Each harvester required a crew of three. Alden Loucks, who lived nearly his entire life on the Traver Ranch near the center of the Monument, described the job of tractor driver as follows:

There was always a line that you followed with the tractor . . . And so everything was okay until you get to a corner, and then what are you going to do? Well, you had to get your tractor to start your turn properly so when you got around the corner it would make that corner square. The rest of it was easy. You could mark your windshield on the tractor, and as long as you could look through the windshield and see that last cut edge at the right place, you'd be just fine.

The second person on the crew, known as the "header tender," had the job of adjusting the height of the cutting bar above ground level. It was important to take a suitable length of stalk along with the grain heads so that the threshing went smoothly. Where fields were rough or rocks stuck out of the ground, it was important that the header be high enough that rocks did not damage the cutter and that dirt and rocks did not get carried into the thresher to damage parts there. The header tender sat high on the right side behind a large wheel that looked much like the one used to work rudders on old-time sailing ships.

The third member of the harvest crew was the "separator man" or captain who directed the entire operation. The machinery must not pass too much extraneous material into the grain hopper, but at the same time the threshing must not damage the grain heads or lose grain out the back of the machine with the straw. Any of these errors cost money, either in lost wheat or in grain of lower quality that brought a lower price. The job of the separator man also included maintaining the machinery and supervising repairs. A less obvious responsibility was that of maintaining a level attitude for the entire machine. Where fields were hilly, "side-hill harvesters" were used. These had geared mechanisms that could raise or lower either side of the machine as it was pulled across of a hill. The purpose was to keep the actual threshing screens level even when the ground under it might be sloped. If the threshing floor were tilted, then grain would fall to one side, and the separation of grain from straw failed. The goal, of course, was to produce the maximum profit.

When the storage bin on a harvester became full, it was unloaded into a truck that took this bulk grain from the field to huge tanks elsewhere on the ranch. The "bulk truck" driver was then a fourth person on the harvest crew, although if circumstances were favorable and several machines were working in the same field, he might be able to service more than a single harvester.

Two Brothers

Of the many persons that I met on the Carrisa Plains, Doug Wreden is the one I've known for the longest period of time. He is presently one of two persons responsible for maintenance of equipment and buildings on the National Monument. When I first began removing fences on the Plains, he was the supervisor for our group of volunteers. There were many, many days when we listened to his stories while we ate lunch or simply rested. He is a wonderful story teller, a good friend, and someone I admire.

Although Doug's older brother Bo has lived many years in Berkeley, California, he has retained an interest in the Carrisa Plains and has maintained connections with nearly all the ranching families that he knew during his high school summers working there. I met Bo at the Monument Visitor Center one weekend when he was visiting nearby. He had heard of the oral history project from his brother, and we have spoken together many times since, both in Berkeley and on the Plains. I count him as a personal friend as well.

Without a doubt, Doug was always destined to leave Menlo Park and come to the Carrisa Plains permanently. The journey was not direct, and during lunch times along roads and fields, he spoke of a boarding school in Wisconsin, college drinking escapades, cross-country road trips, and meeting his wife, Cindy. After he became ranch manager on the Pinole in 1968, Doug first farmed wheat, considered working cattle, and then took up raising sheep. When sheep could no longer provide a living, he and his wife became fence contractors installing barbed wire, chain link, and electric fences on ranches all through Central California. Traveling many hours each day to work on different ranches was hard, and when a maintenance position with the Monument became available, he needed only milliseconds to make a decision. The maintenance job includes fixing troughs and tanks, making electrical repairs, fixing some fences and taking down others, putting up signs, welding broken machinery, writing specifications for construction projects, and rescuing visitors who get stuck in the spring mud. Doug detests the paperwork that the government requires, and he claims total incompetence in dealing with computers. These are exactly the jobs that a lifetime of ranching has, and has not, taught him how to do. Doug also laughs when I point out that he is now working for the very same federal government which was once the sworn "enemy" of ranchers on the Plains. Although much of his, and his family's history, was told to me beside his pickup truck in the open, it has also been recorded at his home in a long interview with Jackie and me.

The Work Day

During harvest on the Pinole Ranch, breakfast was at 6:30 AM, and field work normally began between 7:00 or 7:30. In the mid-1950s, at age twelve, Bo Wreden started driving a bulk truck during his summer vacations. Other boys who lived on Carrisa ranches the year around often began still younger, looking through the steering wheel rather than over it. As soon as their legs could reach the clutch pedal, they were ready to learn. Although Bo and another high school friend drove bulk trucks, their duties began even before the harvesters were in motion. Immediately after breakfast, they drove to the field where the harvesters had stopped the day before. It was their job to fuel the tractor with diesel and the on-board engine of the harvester with gasoline. Greasing the bearings on the harvester was their next responsibility. When all this was done, the two returned to ranch headquarters to get the trucks that would be used to carry grain. In odd moments of the day, they would re-supply the fuel storage tanks and grease barrels and then clean up equipment to be ready for the following day.

Driving the bulk truck was a matter of waiting till the bin on a harvester was full and then positioning the truck under the chute to catch the grain. The trucks were old and ran by the grace of God, a good mechanic, and pure luck. The truck that Bo drove had a flat bed which had been outfitted with an old oil field tank on the back to hold the grain. On steep slopes, the truck had difficulties climbing through the fields, and the separator man would berate him for not arriving at the right place and on time. Bo described another of his experiences driving the truck:

> It was overloaded, and it was heavy in the back, so you had to be very careful when you were shifting gears. If you jack rabbit clutched, so it speak, the cab would actually lift off the ground because of the weight of the grain in the rear end. I had an experience once, fortunately it was only once, but it was when we used to drive up to the top of this hill to unload the trucks into the tanks. I let out the clutch. It may, it just may have been too heavy a load anyway. It might have happened anyway, but the whole truck . . . the cab just went up in the air, and the grain poured out the back of the truck. And so it was a big mess, and there was a lot of shoveling to be done.

Another account of driving a bulk truck was given by Jerry Wildman. His family owned the Saucito Ranch from 1941 till 1945, and he began his field work even younger at age ten. He and I spoke about his first year working on that ranch.

Craig: So you have this truck full of grain. You're ten years old, and now heading back to do what?

Jerry: Well, there were three storage tanks on the place. My dad built those on the side of a hill. He carved out a couple of roads, one up above the tank and one below. To unload, you'd go up the upper road and unload it into a hopper that you drove over. The truck had a bottom drop, and it unloaded by gravity.

Craig: But of course that didn't get everything out.

Jerry: As soon as it quit running, you'd crawl inside the truck and push the rest into the hopper.

Craig: And the temperature when you're doing this?

Jerry: Generally stayed around a hundred, a hundred and ten, like that.

Craig: It sounds like slave labor.

Jerry: At that age you didn't notice the heat quite as much I notice it now.

           It seems like I'm a lot more . . . sensitive to heat.

Craig: We all are. Yesterday you mentioned that when grain went into the tanks it didn't fill smoothly.

Jerry: No. The grain would pile up along one edge, and then you'd have to climb into the tank and level it out – put a ladder up to the opening, squeeze in the opening, drop inside there, take a big scoop shovel with you, and just pull the grain away from the edge as it kept falling in.

Craig: Was there a hazard of getting buried as it came in?

Jerry: Not really, but flax was different. My dad tried flax one year out there, and you don't stand in flax. You sink instantly. Flax will just swallow you up, but wheat was all right, especially for a kid that is light weight.

For Bo, one of the pleasant parts of his job was waiting in the truck cab till the time came to empty a harvester. Although the ranch manager had forbidden it, Bo spent this time reading adventure comic books. When he once fell asleep waiting, the manager appeared and lectured him about being paid for doing a job and not for sleeping. In the mid-1950s, a truck driver on the Pinole Ranch earned $8 a day, the tractor driver and the header tender earned $12 dollars a day, and the separator man would clear a whopping $18 dollars a day. Nearly everyone working at the Pinole lived in the bunkhouse, and they were fed three times a day. Any ranch that did not have a good cook was in trouble.

July and August are the hottest months of the year. Temperatures of 100 degrees were normal, and 110 degrees was not uncommon. There was dust, straw, and chaff flying everywhere. With all their moving parts and exposed gear boxes, the machines were astonishingly loud. It was nearly impossible to talk and be heard. To signal the tractor driver, the separator man would pull a cord that rang a bell on the tractor. It was impossible to give instructions by shouting over the noise. The least enviable job was that of the header tender, who sat high over the moving reel where dust and straw were thickest. At the end of the day, the entire crew was covered with debris.

A major torment of working on the harvester came from weeds in the field. Farmers were mixed in their opinions as to which were the worst, but fireweed (genus *Amsinkia*), also known as fiddleneck or Devil's lettuce, was favored in most discussions. Fireweed is notable for the tiny hairs that detach from the stems and work their way into your skin where they break off. They can't be removed. The itching is intolerable, and there is almost nothing that can be done to relieve the torment. When harvesters hit a patch of fireweed, these hairs flew with the dust and got into hair, elbows, knees, everywhere. These along with heat, noise, sun, and long, long days made the work memorable.

Harold Lowe was one of the high school students who worked harvests in 1938 and 1939. Although he was on the La Panza Ranch at the western edge of the Carrisa Plains, his account echoes that of many others. At the end of a day, he and the rest of the crew would jump into the water of a cattle trough. It was cool and helped relieve the itching. Several years later, Harold was fighting in the Pacific theater in the Second World War. His unit was in the jungles of New Guinea with temperatures in the 90s and humidity that reached the same numbers. For seventy-six consecutive days, they lived in foxholes under artillery fire from Japanese troops one hundred yards away. Harold said that it was tough, but whenever he started feeling sorry for himself he thought back to summers harvesting on the Plains – and somehow the war did not seem so bad after all. Perhaps he was exaggerating, but still it gives a picture of field work in the late 30s.

After harvest it was normal for a rancher to set aside some part of the crop to be used as seed for the next planting. Occasionally a rancher might change crops or try a new variety of wheat in a following year, and in this case, it was necessary to buy seed. If harvested grain was to be used for seeding, however, then it had to be "cleaned." This meant that rocks, dirt, sticks, weeds, and weed seeds were to be removed. While the harvester did much of this separation, it was important that planted crops should have as few weed seeds as possible. The county Farm Bureau owned several specialized "grain cleaners" which could work more thoroughly than a harvester in the field. Farmers arranged to have the cleaner brought to their ranch where a paid operator would spend up to a week processing the seed crop. For a short period of time, the Beck family had such a machine of their own, and while this spared them the expense of having someone else clean their seed, it also required a substantial amount of work on their part. Timing was critical as the cleaning had to be finished in the short interval between the end of harvest and the start of planting.

Machinery

To make ranching pay, it became necessary through the years for farms to become larger and larger, and to work the larger acreages the machinery needed to be correspondingly larger. Headers on the harvesters were most commonly eighteen to twenty feet in length, although some were even thirty-six feet long. Disks, harrows, seeders, cultivators, and weeders also became larger. It was not possible to buy disks that were more than twelve or fifteen feet wide, and so "carts" would be pulled behind a single large tractor. These contrivances could be sixty feet across and behind them four or five disks could be attached and pulled side by side. Such a cart could not be bought and was instead constructed in the ranch machine shop. It was essential that ranchers be proficient at welding, both for making repairs and for construction of equipment. One of the special pieces that the Becks had built was a "weed burner," used to burn tumbleweed in the fields in summers before planting. One or several chutes guided cut tumbleweeds into slots where a fire was maintained to finish off the job.

When equipment broke – carts, disks, or cultivators – it was the farmer who made the repairs. Over time, discarded equipment accumulated and could be used for parts. Often pieces were improvised, cut, and welded out of steel scrap that had been stockpiled. Extensive tool sets, small parts cabinets, hoists, grinders, jacks, compressors, cutting torches, and welding outfits were standard on every ranch. Greg Beck served as the principal mechanic on his ranch and spoke about grinding valves, removing engines, and servicing transmissions. On some occasions, a night trip into town would be needed to get parts that were then installed in the wee hours to get a tractor ready for the next day. On rare occasions, a transmission or engine was taken into town for work by a specialized mechanic. This was sufficiently expensive to be painful. Of course, repairs to tanks, fences, and sheds were done on the spot, and if time allowed, even large buildings were constructed without outside help. Self-sufficiency was gospel.

Tractors which pulled the larger pieces of equipment were almost always the caterpillar type. In areas where equipment frequently traveled along paved roads, the damage which these "crawlers" did to pavement was unacceptable, and wheeled tractors were the norm. In the Carrisa Plains, nearly all roads are dirt so treaded tractors with their better traction could be used. When it was occasionally necessary for the Becks to move equipment across pavement, they laid out mats to protect the road surface.

By the 60s there were notable changes in farming equipment. Huge four-wheel-drive articulated tractors were in use, with the result that caterpillar tractors became less common. At about the same time, self-propelled harvesters appeared on the Plains. These could be driven by a single person who simultaneously operated the header and the threshing machinery. With this change, the need for large harvest crews decreased, and only one or two hired hands would be required for most jobs.

Although the changes that occurred in still later years have increased the cost of equipment, they also make field work far more comfortable. My personal experience helping on a cousin's farm in Southern Saskatchewan was plush. This was in the summer of 1980 when I used a large two-wheel drive John Deere tractor to cultivate summer fallow. The enclosed cab featured an upholstered chair, air conditioning, a radio, and a CD player. My workday lasted eight hours only, and my strongest memories are of country-western music and watching hawks circle overhead while they hunted rodents that had been displaced from the fields. My job was simply to steer, but even this is changing.

In the present electronic age, GPS guidance systems are becoming common. When these are engaged, the driver makes one turn around the perimeter of a field and then sets the offset for the succeeding turns, thirty-nine feet and six inches if he is pulling a forty foot disk. The tractor makes the succeeding turns around the field perfectly with nothing for the operator to do unless some irregularity in the field surface appears. Farming in the 1940s was another world entirely.

Hired Hands

In the mid-twentieth century it was rarely possible for a family on the Plains to manage the ranch work on their own, and hired hands were the norm. These were frequently transient crews that worked up and down the valley following seasons and crops. These were sometimes rough characters, and Doug Wreden told about several who worked for him when he managed the Pinole Ranch. These were the years between 1968 and 1980. In his own words:

> There's always some big row. Somebody's going to kill somebody. You've got to remember that the people who worked out here in those days, not all of them, but a great number of them, had had run-ins with the law. This was a place to work and be fed with a roof over your head, and nobody's going to find you. There were all kinds: some of them were college-educated; some were divorced or had just walked away from a wife and family and never showed up again. It was a hiding place, and so you got some rather unsavory characters. There was a guy by the name of Johnny Byers. In my whole life, I've never seen a man so angry with just being alive, just angry at everything. And strange. He'd done time for murder. His wife Bobbie was a cook. He'd beat her up. She'd beat him up. He was a separator man. And after harvest was over, we were cleaning seed again. He stayed around for that, and then they'd take all these sacks that were full of seed, put them in these little sheds, stack them nine or ten high. And Harvey Walker was an old tractor guy, a nice old guy, wore these little wire-frame glasses, and never paid any income tax. IRS finally caught up with him and said, "We're going to attach your wages, Harvey." And Harvey said, "Well, how am I going to buy cigarettes?" "Well, we're going to give you ten bucks a month. You can buy cigarettes, but we're going to take all the rest." He'd never paid income tax in his life.
>
> Well, one day Johnny Byers tried to kill Harvey in the seed shed by

throwing a hundred and forty pound sack as Harvey bent over picking up another one. Johnny's on top throwing one down, just knocked him cold, knocked him out . . . I dragged Harvey out, and he finally woke up, and there were a lot of words going on, but nothing happened, thank God.

Not long after that, I came back to the ranch from Atascadero and there was a sheriff's car out in front. Actually there were two of them. Flashing lights . . . "Oh, oh, who's killing who now?" Bobbie Byers took a hatchet to her husband, Johnny, and cut, almost cut his whole foot off, cut his heel off. She had enough. So the Sheriff was out and took her away, took him away. And we got left with a mess, blood all over the house and had to clean it up. The Sheriff and I were pretty much on a first-name basis.

Doug continued:

And then it wasn't long after I had taken over, when I had a guy working for me named Rick Satre; he had this long gray hair like a fifty year old hippie. He was well acquainted with prison, done a lot of time. He went down to a bar in Shandon one night, and Pat McCornack [a young neighbor to Doug] was at the bar and said, "You're not welcome here, hippie," or something like that. Rick pulled a knife on him and had Pat on the ground with a knife at his throat, and said, "What did you say?" It was pretty humiliating for little Patrick.

About one o'clock that morning, I went to town to pick up my work crew and bring them back to the ranch. Pat's sitting outside with a pistol. I said, "What now. Pat, what the hell are you doing?" and Patrick replied, "Well, Rick, he made me look like a fool in the bar." "Sometimes you are a fool, Pat. Put the damn gun away. I'm going to call your old man, and he's going to come over and get you so fast. You put that gun away, and I won't call, nothing's going to happen."

Later I fired Mr. Satre when he stole my trap wagon and drove to town.

Doug had two things going for him in all this. He had been military police in the Army Reserve, and even more important, he is a very level-headed, easy-going fellow. It seems that grain farming involved more than planting and harvesting.

Farming as a Business

The purpose of all the work was, of course, to produce grain and make a profit. At the end of harvest, most of the ranches stored the crop in large tanks on their farms until the market prices were favorable. If a ranch were badly in need of cash, or if the harvest had been so good that there was insufficient room to store it all, then some grain might be sold immediately. Before the mid-20s, grain was trucked thirty or forty miles over the Temblors to a railhead at McKittrick. When trucks and roads improved, grain was trucked directly to the mills where it was processed – most commonly in Los Angeles.

Grain was sold and sent to market in a variety of ways. A few farmers used large trucks and trailers of their own. More commonly they would contract with a regular hauler to make the delivery for them. Alden Loucks worked only with a particular outfit from Corcoran in the Central Valley to move his grain. The driver, Jake Verboon, was trustworthy, and Alden would have no one else. Some truckers, he reported, would dump part of their load in an out-of-the-way place. After completing the scheduled delivery, the trucker returned to what had been dumped, recovered it, and sold it for his own profit. Sometimes representatives from the milling companies came to the Plains to inspect the crop in the field and sign a contract there. The milling company then sent their own trucks to transport the grain. Some of these buyers even arrived in small planes to carry out their business.

Not all years treated the grain farmers equally. In drought years, profits were negligible, and in the worst years, ranchers might harvest only enough to provide seed for the following season. It was perfectly normal for a rancher to take a bank loan to cover future costs for seed, fuel, and a few other necessities. When the harvest was over and grain was sold, then the loan would be repaid. In dry years, there was nothing to do but go to the bank and take out another loan, go deeper in debt, and hope for the best with the next crop. In most cases, the local banks were cooperative and would loan the capital that was needed.

During the prosperous years, 1940s through 70s, bankers knew the farming families personally and had done business with them for years and even for generations. When the son of an established farmer went to a bank to start his own business, his collateral was his reputation as a smart farmer and hard worker. This could be enough to earn the trust of the bank. Imagining a modern commercial bank operating in this fashion in the twenty-first century can only be a source of humor.

The years 1938 and 1939 were particularly prosperous ones for farmers in the Carrisa Plains. It was in this period that the Pinole Ranch was first planted with wheat. After years as a cattle ranch, the soil was virgin, and with exceptional rainfall, the profits were astonishing: $100,000 in Depression-era dollars. Loans were paid off, two new harvesters were purchased, the buildings were improved, and there was a $7,000 share that went to Eben McMillan, the ranch manager at that time. That period was equally profitable for Lew and Nancy Traver, who leased land near Highway 58. While the exact financial arrangements were not known, the fact that they bought their own ranch farther south two years later is sufficient evidence of their success.

As years passed, the economics of farming changed. Chuck Kuhnle, another rancher living along Bitterwater Road, recalled that in 1950 wheat sold at $3.50 per hundredweight (one hundred pounds), diesel fuel cost 15 cents a gallon, a new harvester could be purchased for $7,000, and a new tractor cost between $10,000 and $15,000. By 2000, these numbers had changed. Wheat sold at about $5.00 a hundredweight, diesel was nearly $3.00 per gallon, and a harvester could cost as much as $250,000. The implications of these figures are clear.

To continue under these conditions, farmers had to work more and more land and produce larger and larger crops. The larger and more efficient equipment helped, but the chances of making a profit were still marginal. The loans needed to buy seed and fuel for the next year became larger and larger, and a dry year with no crop became devastating. The risks in taking out these loans became formidable, and farmers watched the sky carefully for rain, tracked the market for selling prices, and worried if they should risk planting all their land, or try for a more modest harvest with less risk if the crop should fail. For some farmers, the salvation lay in government supports given to remove land from production. Others took part-time work with neighbors or worked in

construction trades. Wives took jobs in town, and children no longer
dreamed of taking over the ranch when their parents retired. The work
was too hard, so instead they went to college, took jobs in mainstream
America, and bought homes in the suburbs. A few families remained,
but by the late 1980s the era of prosperous grain farming in the Carrisa
Plains had come to an end.

Looking Back

In a quiet moment, Greg Beck reflected back on his years on the family
ranch. He had been the principal mechanic for the operation, he had
taken the night shifts on the tractor during planting times, he brought a
wife from the city, and then he had stayed on when the isolation became
too much for her and she left. He and his brother tried an organic grain
business selling for higher prices in urban markets. Ultimately they realized that the business was not going to survive, and when another family
made an offer on their land, they sold. Even then, he stayed on as a ten-
ant living in the family house. The final blow came when he was asked
to leave the house. The land which had been his home was to be divided
and sold as forty acre ranchettes. Greg had once been bitter about the final sale, but with the passage of time he realized that he needed to move
on. Still, he felt the loss:

> A lot of what I learned out there was a love of the land. I calculated I had
> spent over 20,000 hours driving tractor, most of it without a radio, without
> creature comforts, making the first round, and then the rounds after that . . .
> Looking at the different colored soils and the patterns that the disk made
> was a lot of what I enjoyed. When I left, I realized that I had completed an
> aspect of my life.

Perhaps memories of this sort were not only his. Greg spoke of riding a pickup across a field with his father one late afternoon. Clouds
were gathering, and with sunset light, they formed into fantastic patterns in the sky. His dad stopped the truck, and for three minutes they

watched and said nothing. Then they drove on without a word. This was a side of his dad which he had never known before, but the feeling was shared. These were the memories of a Carrisa grain farmer.

CHAPTER FOUR

Cattlemen & Cowboys

Open plains, fences, and water tanks

Jesus and Ida Garcia

In the American imagination, farmers have always been the hardworking citizens that put down roots, raised families, and represented law and order in the West. Cattlemen, and especially the itinerant cowboys, were the heroic figures of legend, some law-abiding and some flirting with the very fringes of civilization. The outlaws of legend were Jesse James and

Joaquin Murietta, while the cinema sheriffs were played by John Wayne and Gary Cooper. Even daily life on the range became romantic in the lyrics of "Red River Valley" and in the voice of Eddy Arnold singing "Cattle Call." The Carrisa Plains had its share of cattlemen, and at one time San Luis Obispo was known as the "Cow County." The corrals, fences, loading chutes, and water troughs, some decaying and some still in use, are the visible reminders of this part of life on the Plains. Indeed, I did hear stories not unlike the ones in the public imagination, but I also heard of family life, daily chores, and economic realities.

In the very early decades of the twentieth century, the Carrisa was open range; farmers were few; and there was no need for fences. Cowboys were known as *vaqueros*. They broke horses, braided *riatas* (a Spanish lasso), and trailed lost steers over ridges and down canyons. Broken bones were not uncommon, and nights were in the open. In dry seasons, cattle were driven west to the coast and east to the Central Valley in search of feed. Stock was sold at the railheads in McKittrick and even San Jose. The work was hard, glamour was occasional, and financial success was never certain.

Vaqueros at El Saucito

The Saucito Ranch on the western side of the Carrisa Plains may have been one of these storied operations. In 1896 it had gone out of the Brumley family, and after several years, it became home to Jesus and Adalida Garcia. Although they first lived on the ranch in 1900, it is uncertain when it was actually purchased. It is definite, however, that the property went out of the Garcia family in 1933. Jesus was born in 1867, died in 1931, and was buried in the Santa Margarita cemetery. Adalida, known to the family as Ida, lived to age ninety-six and was matriarch of the family for many years after Jesus died. They had fourteen children, one of whom was Joe, born in 1903. It was Bill Garcia, Joe's son, who spoke with Jackie and me about the family history.

Bill is one of very few people who actually live within the boundaries of the Monument today. His ranch of about 700 acres is high in the

Temblor Mountains and just below McKittrick Summit. A part of the land was given to his father by Ida, and part was purchased at a later date. The small and rundown house on his property is near the head of a wash and sits under a small group of shade trees. The view out across the Plain extends many miles westward toward Painted Rock and is truly spectacular. Bill and his father, Joe, once ran cattle on this property, but in recent years it has become a weekend retreat where Bill brings his children and keeps his memories.

I first encountered Bill when he spoke at a barbecue held at a public workday on the Monument. He is a strong man, short, with a wonderful drooping mustache and dark skin. In the many times since that first encounter, I have never seen him wear anything but blue jeans, a huge ornate belt buckle, a white straw hat, and a heavy work shirt. He looks like a cowboy, although he works principally in construction in one of the coastal towns nearby. When Bill spoke at the public gathering, it had been a year since one of his lifelong friends, Jon Cooper, had died, and Bill recalled an experience he had shortly after the death. Dust devils were rising over Soda Lake in the summer heat, and in the mirage, Bill saw herds of animals running over the surface. In this vision, his friend appeared among the animals riding in a small jeep which the two of them had often used together. The eulogy was moving. Later in the afternoon, I found Bill, explained that Jackie and I were engaged in collecting histories of families on the Plains, and wondered if we might speak with him some time in the future. He was agreeable, and we left the time indefinite.

Jackie made arrangements for an interview, and we met at the home of Jan Cooper, widow of Jon about whom Bill had spoken. Bill arrived at her house earlier that morning and was helping to put up a trellis for flowers. The Coopers and Garcias had been friends for years, their children grew up together, and the connection was still strong. While the four of us sat and spoke at the kitchen table, Bill brought out several photograph albums from the time his grandparents had lived at El Saucito. These were pictures of cowboys, hunting trips, family gatherings.

Several months later, Jackie and I met with Bill again, this time at his own ranch in the Temblors. When we reached the gate to his property, it was unlocked, and he met us farther on beside his house. Bill had written several essays under the title "From My Front Porch," and we wanted to record and videotape him reading these at his house. We looked out over the Plains, and indeed there were dust devils on Soda Lake below us, but the mirage that Bill had spoken about was absent. It was a warm day, we drank lemonade and looked into the distance, and Bill spoke again about his family's past.

Jesus Garcia and his brother, Guadalupe, came to California from Mexico. Their dream was to live on an extended ranch, a *ranchero*, in the style of the large Mexican landowners. Their horses were fine ones, their saddles and tack were ornate and beautiful, and the ranch house at the Saucito had been built in a grand style years before by Chester Brumley. Guadalupe, known by children and grandchildren in the family as Uncle Lupe, was an entrepreneur, organizing and promoting rodeos across the West and making saddles and bridles that became famous for their fine workmanship. Even in the twenty-first century, horse fanciers who have never heard of the Carrisa Plains are often knowledgeable about this leatherwork. The business was lucrative, and Guadalupe gave some money to his brother Jesus who used it to buy land and cattle.

While Jesus was descended from an older Mexican family, his wife Adalida was the daughter of a Spanish family also having the surname Garcia. Her family had first come to America in the 1700s with the early *Padres* and had worked as carpenters, instructing native craftsmen, building the chain of missions, and then staying on in California. The meeting of Jesus and Adalida was not described, but their wedding picture is a beautiful formal portrait. It is easy to believe that they were Spanish *Grandees* destined to lead a life of luxury on their New World holdings.

Jesus managed the Saucito Ranch, and it supplied the stock, steers, bulls, and horses for the rodeos that Guadalupe organized. In early spring, the animals were trailed across the Temblors to the railroad at Bakersfield, and for the rest of the summer, they travelled from rodeo to rodeo across the West. At the end of the season, they returned to Bakersfield and then to El Saucito where they wintered in preparation for the next rodeo season. The cycle began again with a cattle drive to Bakersfield in the next spring.

Schooling was important in the Garcia family, and with no other possibilities available, Jesus arranged for a teacher to come from Los Angeles, live on the ranch, and instruct the younger children. "Miss Moore" arrived in 1918 just out of school herself. Her full name has been lost. None of the children whom she taught are still alive, and written records about her are sparse. She was a city girl and apparently beautiful.

For Miss Moore, the time spent on the ranch was an adventure. She took a great many photos and also kept an intermittent diary. One of the Garcia girls, Aunt Emma to Bill, was exactly the same age, and they became good friends. There are photos of the two on horseback excursions that show Miss Moore wearing jodhpurs, fashionable riding pants of the time. It is certain that Miss Moore had never ridden before, and the riding apparel had been provided by Emma. Emma herself had gone away to a fashionable school in Los Angeles and fancied herself as being sophisticated. She had learned to drive and had bought a camera herself. Among the pictures were several with the two of them sitting in the family car, and another showing the family riding and picnicking at the nearby Painted Rock (a horseshoe-shaped sandstone outcropping with Indian pictographs on the Carissa Plains). It was not clear where Miss Moore conducted lessons. Other families used her services also, but it was probable that the Saucito served as school for them all.

Miss Moore was an attraction for others of the Garcia family as well. Joe, aged fifteen at the time, and his brother Dan, aged eighteen, were competing for her heart. One would give the postman money to bring flowers out from town, and then the other would pay to have a box of candy delivered. Apparently Miss Moore enjoyed the attention, and the family has a picture of the three of them on their way to a dance. They took a horse-drawn buckboard wagon into Pozo, twenty-five miles to the west across the La Panza Range. The dance went on till midnight when one of the ranchers living nearby would have a midnight buffet. Everyone at the dance got on their horses or buggies and went to the ranch. Then it was back to the dance hall until it was time to drive back to the Plains, where they arrived at dawn. Jesus was not one to excuse ranch help from work simply because they had been up all night. The diary which Miss Moore kept notes, "That mean Mr. Garcia made us all get up and work, wouldn't let us sleep in." Romance on the range ran no more smoothly than it does today.

During the 1920s Jesus was expansive in his dealings. He bought land, used it to leverage loans, and then bought more. The Depression hit, and in 1933 the family lost nearly all of their property. The price paid for cattle was five dollars a head in Los Angeles, and it cost nearly three-fifty each to get them there. Their troubles were compounded by the fact that Jesus had died in 1931. He was diabetic and got gangrene in one foot. It was a minor injury in the first place, but with poor circulation it became infected. He was a stubborn man and refused to get medical help. His foot was amputated, then his leg, and by the time that his thigh was amputated it was too late. His sons were all away promoting rodeos, and when they heard and got back to the home, it was all over. All the family business had been in his head; Jesus never kept records well. There was also some speculation that business deals conducted by the banks, if not actually crooked, had been rigged in a way that made it difficult for people to carry the loans and keep the property. Whatever the details, the Saucito went to the banks, and the Garcia family scattered.

After Jesus died and El Saucito was lost, his widow, Adalida, moved to Pozo where she ran a motel for a few years before she had a house built in Santa Margarita. Joe divorced his wife when Bill was a year old, and there was no way that a single cowboy could raise a child alone. Bill and Joe both went to live with Adalida. Bill said that until he was six years old he thought Ida was his mother. It was a big house where Joe's brothers and sisters went to get married and in some cases to live after a divorce. Ida was a gracious lady and an extraordinary cook for the entire family. Bill could not say enough in praise of her cooking. In his words:

> She spent ninety percent of her time in the kitchen. She preserved, canned, jerked. She did every process of food preservation or cooking you can imagine. My dad would bring home a cow, and she would use every part of that. We'd end up eating . . . I don't know how much. We didn't throw much away. If I told you everything we ate, you'd say, "Oh my goodness," but I

don't remember anybody ever turning anything down that she put in front of you because it had a wonderful flavor, wonderful taste. Her Mexican foods were a specialty.

In 1943, Ida deeded a parcel of land in the Temblors to her son Joe. It came with a curious history. For many years, the Garcia family had trailed cattle to Bakersfield over the Temblors and across some land owned by Clemente Galainena. When he objected, Jesus bought a homestead owned by a German couple, and with this purchase, he surrounded the Galainena lands. There was no choice but to negotiate a deal. It is an irony that nearly sixty years later Bill Garcia and one of the Galainena descendants were still in contention about the boundaries. Joe Garcia and his son Bill were partners running cattle in the Temblors, and this is indeed where Jackie and I held our second interview with Bill.

Joe Garcia may have been one of the sad stories in the Carrisa Plains. He was a cowboy all his life, and although he did own some land, it was never enough to make a living. His son Bill lived with Ida, and Joe took whatever work he could find across the Plains. Bill said that his dad was not much of a father to him, but they did have some good hunting trips together. Hunting was in Joe's blood, and he was good at it. For a good part of the year, he was away hunting with his friends all over California. On the last day of a trip, he'd ask everybody if they had gotten their deer yet, and then he would ask, "Would you like me to get one for you?" No matter how many people said "yes," he would oblige and then come back to say, "Your deer is over in the canyon there," or "Look at the spring behind the hill." Joe would shoot them, gut them out, bleed them, and then send his friends over to bring them back.

Joe was also known as one of the best cowboys on the Plains. Another of the persons that we interviewed said that no one could rope as well as Joe. He could ride full speed after a calf, go off the top of a hill, and while the horse was still in the air throw the rope and bring the calf down. He was always welcome when ranchers were looking for lost cattle or holding brandings . . . but he was never really successful with a ranch of his own.

Another account of life at on the Saucito was written by one of Bill's aunts in 2005. Bill planned a family reunion at the Saucito, but at the last moment the weather became unseasonably cold. Since many of the family were quite old by that time, it was necessary to cancel the reunion. Carmelita knew in advance that she would not be able to attend, and so she wrote the following letter to be read on the occasion.

Dear Billy Joe and Garcia Family,

Your idea of lunch at the Saucito sounds wonderful, however I'm afraid I won't be able to go, but I'm sure you will have a wonderful time. I decided I could write up a few memories I hold dear. I remember one weekend at Saucito we were having a big round-up and barbecue. We set down for dinner, and one of the ladies sat by me, and the tortillas were placed around, and she took one and placed it on her lap for a napkin. I laughed and told her it was to eat, not a napkin. So she laughed with me and said, "Oh gee, I'll remember that. As long as I live, I'll remember that," and she took one bite and said, "Oh, oh, they're good to eat, aren't they." She was my friend forever after that. Many times we took lunch and went to the Painted Rock. From the ranch it was a short ride. We went on horseback a lot of times. We loved climbing on top and sitting on top for hours, eating and telling stories. In the summer when it was hot we would put all our beds outside under the big fig tree. I loved to sleep outside and still do. As you know, I love camping, but it is better now. I need my motor home. The big red barn was also a place where we had a lot of fun playing hide-and-seek and other games we made up. We always seemed to have someone drop in in the afternoon, and mother always set a plate for the extras at the table. I have a lot of beautiful memories of the Saucito. I loved the upstairs where we slept and the cellar where Mom and Dad always kept the food in large sacks and barrels. Candy and cookies were always in barrels too. I guess that's why we all had bad teeth, ha, ha. We canned so much of our food, meat, deer, elk, chicken . . . all our vegetables. We always planted a large garden and had fruit trees all around so we canned and canned. It was so hot sometimes, but we still had to can. It was fun to stack the jars in rows and make the food pretty. I loved to stack them pretty in rows. I could go on but know others will have better stories to tell.

Love to all and have a wonderful day. Wish I could be there. Aunt Carmelita

And I wish I could have been there too.

Dewey Werling: Fifty Years on the Carrisa Plains

Of course there were other cowboys and ranches on the Plains in the same years. One of these ranches was owned by the Goodwin family and was located seven miles north of the Saucito. It was one of several that the Goodwins owned, and although it was originally a family business, it eventually was leased to Dewey Werling and became known throughout the north of the Plains as the Werling Ranch. Let's start at the beginning as told by Dewey's wife, Catherine, and his son, Robert.

James Franklin Goodwin, known as Jimmy, was born in Nebraska in 1855. A year later, his family crossed the prairies in a covered wagon and came to California. He became a banker in San Luis Obispo and was apparently a director of one of the banks in the early years of the twentieth century. This was at a time when oil was being sought and found along the California coast, and Jimmy was not immune to the lure of money. As reported by Catherine Werling, he took a sizable amount of money from the bank and invested it personally in a drilling venture. The loss was discovered, and James was headed for jail when the well came in and money flowed along with the oil. James was able to return the money to the bank, and apparently deals were made that allowed him to remain free. He was then a rich man, and much of his money went into purchases of land and ranches across the central part of California. These included a ranch near Stockton in the Central Valley, a ranch near Pozo in what is now the Los Padres Forest, a ranch near Santa Maria along the coast, a ranch farther south near Lompoc, and lastly their cattle operation in the Plains, which was later to become known as the Werling Ranch.

It is not known when the Goodwins purchased this "Carrizo Ranch," as they called it at the time. However, the house and bunkhouse were definitely built in 1917, and the barn was put up four years later. 1922 was the year when Dewey Werling arrived in California and became a cowboy for the Goodwins. Dewey was born in Colorado in 1904, grew up there, and attended school only through seventh grade. He was known to be good with cattle and horses. One of his employers in Rifle, Colorado, was acquainted with Hank Miller, foreman at the Carrizo Ranch. It was this connection that brought Dewey west, and at the age of eighteen, he became one of the cowhands that helped with the cross-country drives.

Winter and spring rains bring grass in the Carrisa, but when summer arrives forage becomes scarce, and ranchers had to find other places for cattle to feed. One story, not about the Goodwin Ranch, told of a desperate drought year in which cattle were driven east across the Temblors into the San Joaquin Valley and simply turned loose near the Buena Vista Slough to look out for themselves. If they died, it would be no worse than if they had remained west, and if a few lived, then at least something might be salvaged. Even in normal years, the Goodwin cattle had to leave the Plains. They were driven west across what later became the Chimineas Ranch, west to Santa Maria, and then south to a Goodwin ranch near Lompoc. After several months feeding along the coast, the cattle would be driven back to the Carrisa when grass returned there. Dewey was one of the cowboys on this drive.

It was on one of these drives through the Goodwin's Santa Maria Ranch that Dewey met his future wife, Catherine Lee Smith. For reasons that were never explained, she was raised on that ranch, not by her natural parents but by Emmet (Doc) Newton and his wife, Fanny. When the cattle drive went through Santa Maria, Catherine left and rode off with the handsome young cowboy. She and Dewey were married in 1926. Catherine was good with horses and for the next ten years she was one of the regular riders at the Goodwin.

A story from about this time tells of a Los Angeles studio that came out to the Plains to make a cowboy movie somewhere along Seven Mile Road. Robert, Dewey's son, told the story:

Silent, talking movies came out there, and cattle were involved. I'll tone it down, but anyway they came out there, and they was trying to stampede some cattle. And of course they were from the city, and they didn't bring any John Waynes or anybody with them who could ride a horse. This was in the twenties, and he [Dewey] happened to be there, on horseback or something. They had these cattle gathered up, and they had to show a scene where they was stampeding them. He says, "By God, I'll stampede the so-and-sos for you." And so they paid him. He got on his horse, and he carried his six-shooter. He started shooting his gun, and he stampeded them for them.

Dewey was a good employee for the Goodwins, and when Hank Miller retired as foreman on the Carrizo Ranch, Dewey took on the job. Robert, his son, was born in 1931, and when the Goodwins offered Dewey the opportunity in 1934 to lease the Carrizo Ranch, he took it and lived there until 1970. Arrangements for the lease were managed by Guy and Don, sons of Jimmy Goodwin. The papers stipulating five year terms were mailed to Dewey who signed them and sent them back. It was that simple; each party respected the other. Guy would sometimes visit the ranch on the Plains, but more often Dewey and Catherine were guests when Guy and Don stopped at their other family ranch near Pozo. Robert said the visits were like being with family.

The Goodwin/Werling Ranch was nearly 7500 acres, and after Dewey took over in 1934, half was planted in wheat and half was used for cattle. Although cattle are the story here, it is still worth knowing how the farming began. One of the neighboring ranches was run by two brothers named Hanson, and they sometimes came over to visit Dewey and play cards. On one of these visits, they told Dewey, "By God, Dewey, you're not going to make no money punching cows." They said, "You need to farm this place. You've got some good land here." Dewey replied, "Well, I haven't got the money." The two brothers spoke up and said, "We will plow it, we will seed it, we will harvest it, you will sell it, and you pay us off. The rest is yours." They shook hands; nothing was written. This was typical of business done in the 30s and even the 40s. The first crop was a good one. Dewey paid them off and then bought a slightly used 1934 model one-and-a-half ton truck, an old 60 tractor, a disk, a harvester, and made-up his own seed carts. The Werling Ranch was on its way.

Among the jobs that went with raising cattle was that of cleaning out springs. Some were nothing more than wet spots, and to make them useable, they had to be improved: a hole in the ground would be dug to collect water or alternatively the water was piped to a tank or to a cattle trough. Robert described one of these projects:

It would be northwest but mostly north. Along those hills there's a spring up there, and it's still up there, half mile or so. Probably needs to be dug out again, but anyway my dad and Uncle Chuck, his brother, were digging this spring out. They had gone into the old mercantile [store] or something, and they had bought some dynamite. In those days you could buy dynamite, twenty percent, forty percent, sixty percent glycerin, whatever you wanted, and also you could buy strychnine to make your own squirrel poison. But anyway they bought a bunch of sticks of dynamite, whatever percentage it was, and they got in the Model-T, and they came back out to the ranch, and the next day or so they went up there, and they were going to clean that spring. Well, there was cattails in there, and you can not dig a cattail out. It's almost impossible. You need a backhoe, but they didn't have backhoes, so what they did, they planted a few sticks of this dynamite. The Model-T was parked on the hillside, on the right of the canyon. Over here was a big rock, and they were standing behind it kind of for protection. Well they put quite a bit of fuse there and let it burn a little bit to get away from it, you know. And then a bull was coming down the canyon, ca-lump, ca-lump, my dad said. He got down there, and the pockets where they would step, there would be water, and he was going to get a drink of water, so it got a drink of water. They [Dewey and Chuck] had these big old ten gallon Stetsons, and they hollered and waved at him trying to get him out of that spring, and he wouldn't go. He was too thirsty, and all of a sudden, ka-boom, it blew up. My uncle said mud, cattails, rocks, water went way up in the air, and it came down and peppered the bull . . . Uncle Chuck said, "That tail, his tail went straight up in the air and bushed out on the end and he started bawling and kicking mud and . . ."

The bull was not just mad, it was furious. It stamped, it kicked, it threw mud in the air, and it was not about to let Dewey and his brother get back to the truck. They thought about making a run for it. The truck had a starter, but what if it didn't start quickly enough? And the bull was really mad! They hid behind the rock and waited and waited for the animal to cool down, and eventually it wandered away. John Wayne would certainly have had a better plan for all this.

There were several stories about horses on the ranch. One of these is about a horse named Chinote. When Robert Werling was young, it had been given to him by a neighboring rancher named Al Stone. The horse, as Robert described it, was black, and he thought the name meant blackbird. It was old as the hills, at least in its late twenties, a gentle quarter horse and just the animal for kids to ride. Uncle Chuck had a daughter named Curly who wanted to ride Chinote. As she was riding him around the yard, they passed under a clothesline. The horse stooped over slightly, and the line caught Curly under the chin. She didn't think to rein in the animal and started screaming and crying. Somehow the horse knew that something was wrong and stopped. Robert or his mother led the horse out from under the line, but the fact remains that Chinote was part of the family looking out for the kids.

School for children at the north end of the Carrisa Plains was held in a two-room building near the present junction of Soda Lake Road and Highway 58. It was principally attended by children of ranchers and wheat farmers. Robert related several incidents which occurred during his eight years there. This school, usually known as the Simmler School, was at least nine miles from the Werling Ranch, and Robert had to be driven there daily. Roads were dirt, and in one place, the road crossed a large wash. In 1937, when Robert was in first grade, the winter rains had turned the wash into a river. Holly Ickert, a fellow working for Dewey, had a home at Hanford in the San Joaquin Valley. He was on his way there and offered to take Robert up to the school. When they reached the creek, Holly looked at it and said, "Oh I think we can cross all right." As they went through, the fan belt picked up the water, and the engine stalled. Robert opened a door and water came in. Holly laughed, and said, "I can fix that," and then he got out a wrench and loosened the generator so that the fan belt wouldn't kick water on the engine. The engine itself was so hot that it dried almost instantly. Holly got back in, started the truck up, and they were off to the school. On other occasions, when Robert was unable to get home from school, he stayed overnight with neighbors who lived north of the creek.

It is fitting that the last of the stories about Dewey Werling tells again of an encounter with a steer. He was driving at night north of his ranch. The interview transcript reads:

> Robert: It was on Seven Mile Road near the old Pimentel Ranch. Dad had a 35 Dodge, and he run into a steer in the dark, you know. It hit the left front fender and whirled around, and it hit the back door of the 35 Dodge, pretty near a new car, fell through the door, knocked the door in, laying upside down.
>
> Craig: The steer? The steer is now in the car?
>
> Robert: Yes. I'm getting to it. But anyway, at that time Dad was insured with an agent in Bakersfield, so he wanted to get the old Dodge fixed up, painted and everything, so he took it over there. You could still drive it, but it was banged up, and here was this gal in the office. She was talking to my dad, an old cowboy . . . She said, "Well Mr. Werling, you hit this steer," and he said, "Yes, yes, I couldn't see it coming out of the dark. I hit it." And she says, "And it was dark?" My dad said, "Yes, it was dark." She says, "Mr. Werling, if it was dark, how do you know it was a steer?" And he says, "Lady, the animal was upside down, and I had a flashlight."

Like many ranchers on the Carrisa, Dewey worked both cattle and wheat. It was the wheat farming which ultimately failed, and in 1970 the family moved to town for good. Although economic factors were the principal cause, two particularly bad years were the final straw. The year 1969 was extraordinarily wet, making roads impassible and flooding fields. To travel around, Robert put a blade on one of the Werling tractors and moved roads about. This took land out of cultivation and hurt the crop. The following year, there was a hard freeze that killed the crop after it came up. The total wheat harvest salvaged at the end of the year came to sixty tons. In a good times, the yield could be 1000 tons, but sixty was barely enough to provide seed for the following year. Dewey announced that he had seen enough, and it was over. The Goodwins still owned the land, and for a few years, it was leased to Ray Cavanagh, and when Ray left, it was leased to the Beck family. Ultimately The Nature Conservancy bought the land and transferred it to the Bureau of Land Management (BLM) to become part of the Carrizo Plain Natural Area and then, several years later, the Carrizo Plain National Monument. Cattle no longer graze at the Goodwin.

Ranching at the Buckhorn: Grandpa and Don

Ray Cavanagh was on the Goodwin Ranch for only a brief time, but his family had a much longer history of grazing and farming on the Plains. Fred Cavanagh owned two ranches, the Buckhorn and the Trejea, in the La Panza Range west from the Goodwin. He ran cattle there with his two sons, Howard and Gene. Although Jackie and I have spoken with one of Fred's grandchildren, the most vivid description of cowboy life on the Buckhorn was given by Don Messer, an "adopted grandson." Don visited the ranch as a child, worked there throughout his high school years, and remained a close, close friend of Fred Cavanagh even after the ranches were sold. Their relationship was a special one.

For Jackie and myself, meeting Don was a matter of serendipity. The Cavanagh family had been mentioned in several of our early interviews, but we had been unsuccessful finding anyone who knew their history. While Jackie was working in the Visitor Center one day, a lady came in and mentioned that her cousin, Don Messer, had once worked for the family. When we contacted him, Don was glad to hear that the history of the Carrisa Plains was being collected and was happy to speak with us. Although it had been many years since he had worked for Fred Cavanagh, he had kept in touch with the family and had many fond memories from his younger days as a cowboy.

In 1947, when Don was eight years old, his mother took a job as cook at the Buckhorn Ranch. Being the youngest of the family, and having no other place to stay, Don went along. He was already a good rider and had a horse of his own that he rode on the Pismo Dunes along the coast. In Don's words, "arriving on a real cattle ranch was like coming home." After that first year, his mother only cooked for occasional events at the ranch, but Don became a regular visitor. He took a bus from Oceano to Santa Margarita, the mail wagon from there over Pozo Grade, and finally rode to the Buckhorn with Fred Cavanagh. At the end of the weekend, he took the same trip back home. When Don was twelve and the family lived briefly in Walla Walla, Washington, Fred Cavanagh sent money for him to come "home for Christmas." This was an adventure. Alone, he took the Union Pacific down the Columbia River to Portland, switched trains there, and got on the Southern Pacific to Oakland. There he went across the Bay by ferry and took a cab to Union Station where he got another train. When he reached Santa Maria, Fred Cavanagh met him. This was a different kind of world, and independence was characteristic of both Don and the way of life on all the ranches.

Don essentially became part of the Cavanagh family. He visited and worked with them on weekends and vacations. Room, board, and occasional help with extras were his pay. Fred Cavanagh became "Grandpa," and Don was his *"Compadre."* As a child he opened gates, rode with the other cowboys, and ran errands. He graduated to become one of the cowboys and did the same work as any of them: roping, building fences, branding, working hay fields. He was large for his age and did a man's work.

In addition to the two ranches in the La Panza Range, Fred Cavanagh also farmed grain for a short time on the east side of the Plains near the Temblors. The farming was done on leased land, but in Don's first year with Grandpa this came to an end. As a result of confusion or a simple error, Fred was late in signing papers to renew the lease, and when he arrived to complete arrangements, the lease had been granted to another outfit. The farming had been profitable, and its loss was serious. Fred's income now depended upon cattle at the Buckhorn and Trejea.

The mountains west of the Carrisa Plains are not high, but they are rugged, cut by deep canyons and washes. There may be level land on small ridges, and there can be tiny pastures with grass along some of the rivers, but the rest is steep. The slopes are covered with brush, and tracking lost cattle is a long job, hot and dusty. The Buckhorn Ranch is deep in these mountains, twenty miles west of the Simmler School and ten miles beyond the larger La Panza Ranch.

Families in these mountains sometimes went to school or attended functions at Simmler and sometimes traveled west to the coast for business. The Buckhorn itself consisted of a number of smaller plots strung out along a ten mile ridge. The plots had once been homesteads, but with the difficulty of farming and ranching they had failed and been sold. The land actually belonging to the Buckhorn totaled about 7000 acres, and there was an additional 7000 acres of public forest land that were available and permitted for cattle. Don estimated that no more than 250 head were kept, so it was not at all a large operation. If the ranch was not especially profitable, it nevertheless had been a wonderful place to live. Don's words best describe his life there:

Well, when I was there with Grandpa, I slept wherever there was room. I stayed in the big house when there was room in the big house, but when I first went out there I slept in the feed room. In fact when we went up to the Trejea, that was just a cow camp, there was what Grandpa called a Chinese cook wagon that's sitting on the ground, and it was a tack room. I slept on a cot in there. One morning I got up and went to step out the door, and there were rattlesnake tracks. It was all powdery ground because that's where we'd saddle the horses. There was a big rattlesnake track coming or going . . . funny thing was I didn't know whether he was in there now or just left or what . . . Another morning I woke up in the shack at the Trejea, and I was sick to my stomach. My old dog had dragged a dead skunk in and was chewing on it under my bed. Oh, I was sick.

In 1952, Howard Cavanagh was building that dam on the Trejea. They had a big bulldozer, a TD18 which is about the size of a D6, and a carry-all [for moving dirt]. He built the second largest dam in San Luis Obispo County at the time, it may well be yet. It became a real play place, you know. The Cavanaghs and Becks would come up there sometimes on weekends, swimming and fishing. Gene Cavanagh put fish in it, and they had a little boat. In fact he built a boat called Susie Q . . . His daughter Susie lives up in Sacramento, and so he called it Susie Q, and so we had a lot of fun up there.

It was a neat place. Everybody enjoyed it, and the family came out as much as they could, you know.

Hunting was a part of life for the entire family. Howard was known as a wonderful shot, and there were stories of how he could jump from a horse and shoot the moment he hit the ground. He didn't miss. Gene, the second of Fred's sons, was a stalker, and Don claimed that he was like an Indian and could track anything he wanted. Both sons took long hunting trips into the Sierras and even to Colorado.

As Don's words suggest, the Buckhorn Ranch was a common destination for a great many people both from the coast and from the Plains. It was Grandpa's custom to invite friends out during deer season. Game was plentiful, and these were big events. Grandpa was a good cook and loved to barbecue for the guests who stayed over. Some of these were politicians and businessmen from San Luis Obispo, some were farmhands, and one was an oilfield worker from Taft. Grandpa was popular and congenial; anyone could be his friend. Guests brought their contributions to the weekend: crates of produce, cantaloupes, tomatoes, and sometimes even abalone from the coast. They slept wherever there was room. Grandpa was a raconteur and regaled them with stories about the ranch and his life. Having said all this, it should be added that Fred was not a good businessman, and ultimately this was responsible for the loss of the property.

The dam and lake which Howard Cavanagh created on the Trejea were not his only earth moving ventures. Visitors to the Carrisa Plains today know of a road running nearly the full length of the ridge of the Caliente Mountains. About four miles of this route is wide and, if the gate is open, can be easily traveled by almost any vehicle. The last three miles out to Caliente Peak are narrow. At the transition between these sections, there is an old cow camp with a corral for animals and a travel trailer for the cowboys. Howard Cavanagh built and graded this road to help Al Stone, a neighbor, find cattle that were scattered in the canyons along the ridge.

Hunting for lost cattle was a frequent occupation, and Don tells of one of these searches on the Buckhorn:

An interesting story on that . . . Denny Glines had a brahma steer that went wild and just crazy, loco, and Denny put a bell on him so he could find him, but he was like a deer. He [the steer] could sneak through the brush and never ring that bell. We finally decided we're going to get that son-of-a-bitch, and a bunch of cowboys went up there. We found him up on the Chimineas Corner, which is the southeast corner of the Buckhorn right next to the Chimineas Ranch. Well this steer, he had a bunch of cows with him, and that's why they wanted to get rid of him because he was, you know, kept getting his herd and taking off. They were losing cattle, and they were somewhere, but they couldn't find them. So anyway we, we jumped on him, and I was riding Big Red, and I was probably sixteen or seventeen. But we jumped that steer. I was wild. I followed him all the way down the back of that mountain, all the way down Trejea, and I finally roped him down below Trejea Springs and tied him to a tree.

Another of the rogue animals was a steer that Grandpa called "Jerky." In Don's words:

And he [Grandpa] had a plan for him one time, and he always told us, he said, "Now, you watch that steer because if he starts to move, you get out of the way because he'll run right through anything. He'll knock horses down. He's just loco." Well, I watched him a couple times, and he did that. Grandpa used to tell us, "Now when you look at a bunch of cows," he says, "you can see one of them that's got its head up like this. That's the one you watch. And if you see one that's got its head down like that, you've got a problem. The rest of them you can forget about." And that's what Jerky was. Well, Grandpa finally got pissed off, and he decided, you know, he's had enough of that Jerky. So he had a 257, Robert's gun, and we went out with the horse trailer and the jeep . . . We found Jerky sitting over in the Blackfield, this was another one of those homesteads that belonged to the Buckhorn, and Grandpa just pulled up and pulled his gun out and pop, and that was the end of Jerky. And we made jerky out of him.

Eventually, life at the Buckhorn came to an end for Don, and the time came to move on. He was not a Cavanagh by birth, and there was no possibility that he could ever own the ranch. For a short time he worked as hired hand at the Trejea Ranch, and when the job of manager there became vacant, he had hoped to take this on. Although he had been a cowboy for years and knew every gate, fence, and stream, still he was young and was passed up. By this time Don was married with children, and these responsibilities brought him back to the coast and a regular job. By this time, Grandpa's sons had left for other endeavors, and so the Buckhorn was leased to another outfit. The income from the lease was meager, and in 1958, the Buckhorn was sold. Fred moved to town, and an era passed.

A Family Business: The MU Ranch

The Garcias, Werlings, and Cavanaghs were early cattle ranchers in the north of the Plains. At the very south and somewhat later in time, Marcus Rudnick established an extensive operation of a different kind. His Carrisa ranch, purchased in 1950, was a relatively small part of the family business as Marcus also ran two packing plants, a feed lot, a ranch near Weldon in Eastern California, and still another ranch in Arizona. Known as the MU, for Marcus Ulysses Rudnick, the Carrisa ranch was not a small property. It began near Highway 166, extended almost ten miles north to Lawson Spring, and included parts of the both the central plain and the Elkhorn. The total exceeded 60,000 acres, of which 23,000 were deeded and the rest was leased. Although in some places, old furrows from previous farming can still be seen today, the Rudnick investment was entirely in cattle. It was principally a cow-calf operation, which meant that animals were kept year-round. Numbers varied from 500 to 1000 head. When feed was good, the family brought in stockers, cattle that were fed for a single season only and then sold. Several thousand might be kept in the good years. It was big.

Much to our regret, Jackie and I were not able to speak with Marcus Rudnick. He had died several years before we thought of searching out

Carrisa Plains history. Of his eleven children, the oldest was Richard, and it was with him that we first spoke. I found his name in the online White Pages and simply gave him a call. I later realized that I had actually met him a few years earlier at the ranch of a mutual friend living near the community of Weldon. We had shared a beer but thought nothing about the Carrisa Plains. When Jackie and I spoke with Richard at his home in Bakersfield, our conversation was interrupted several times by phone calls from Weldon. One of Richard's grown sons had just fallen from a horse, been injured, and was taken to a hospital. In spite of these anxieties, he was very gracious, and much of the following was related in that interview. More recently I met and spoke with John Rudnick, a younger brother, but John will be introduced later.

The Rudnick family lived in Bakersfield, and the MU was a business rather than a home. Daily chores were done by a resident caretaker, while seasonal work and special jobs were done largely by family who came on weekends or during school vacations. Neighbors or friends helped with brandings and round-ups, while still other jobs might be contracted out.

Richard recalled a time when he and a younger brother, Bennie, helped one of the hired cowboys move cattle from the south end of the MU to a pasture farther north and across from the Traver Ranch. This was in 1953, when Richard was eight or nine years old. It was warm. They had been trailing the cattle for most of the day, and the time came to leave the stock and return home. They were on horseback and were facing a hot and dry ten-mile ride. The cowhand, Roy, was a tough fellow, and so they hadn't brought any water. Richard and Bennie were hungry and thirsty. Before starting their ride home, they stopped at a pasture well, and although they knew that the water was alkali, the boys still took drinks. It was all right at first, but then their mouths dried and became swollen. Richard asked, "Roy, you want to ride over to Traver's house there? I know they have some fresh water. We'll get a drink." "No," he said, "I don't . . . I'm not thirsty. I'll be all right." The two boys worried a bit because even though they used the Traver stubble for feed, still their dad and Fred Traver did not have a smooth relationship. With no other option, they stopped and asked Delma Traver for a drink. She brought them each one glass of water, exactly. They hadn't the nerve to ask for more and were glad for what they got.

When Richard and his brothers were at the MU, they occasionally stayed at the main house with the caretaker, but more commonly they brought bedrolls and tents and slept out at one of the cow camps where they worked. Sometimes they pulled locoweed out of the pastures. This plant, a species of the genus *Astragalus*, is mildly poisonous for cattle and a serious threat to horses. In the spring when the ground was soft, the boys of the family were assigned this job. As they became older, maintenance became part of their ranch work. Although most of the fences were in place when the ranch was purchased, there were always repairs needed. Also, because the south end of the plain is dry, it was always necessary to check on water for the stock. Besides several springs along the base of the Caliente Mountains, there were wells at the main house of the MU, at the Hanline Cow Camp, at the Cochora Camp, and at one or two other locations. Over the years, the family put in miles and miles of pipe to bring water to the pastures where there was feed. Richard estimated that there were fifty miles of this pipe through, around, and under the fields. When a trough went dry, this meant a valve had broken, or what was more trouble, a broken pipe or leak must be found, dug up, and repaired.

Much of the pipe was installed by a fellow named Frank Wicks who lived in Shandon and did odd jobs for the Rudnicks and other ranchers. Richard was both amused and exasperated as he spoke about one of the projects:

> The way he had it figured, he was going to . . . do it in an automated fashion. He had a ditch digger that you could ride on. And so he started this ditch digger, and he'd tie the first section of pipe onto it, and then he had one of his kids at a station glueing another section of pipe on as it came by. This is PVC, inch and a half PVC tubing. Well, what he didn't figure was that the glue he used was a little bit soft, and once you put a few joints of pipe on there, the pipe started pulling . . . the joints started separating, but it didn't separate enough to come apart. But once we got it in the ground, got it under pressure, it would leak. The experiment was nice, but it didn't work for us.

Richard could not count the days that he spent making repairs on this plumbing.

Managing water was a perennial challenge in the dry south of the Carrisa Plains, and a different account was given by Richard's younger brother, John. In 1963 Marcus purchased a second ranch in the Carrisa, and eventually it was John who managed both the MU and this other. This second ranch, located north of Highway 58 and called the San Juan, was one of the six parcels that had originally belonged to Heinrich Wreden. Before telling John's story, he should be introduced.

John lives most of the year in Wyoming and then spends some time in California. He runs cattle in both states and moves them back and forth depending upon weather, availability of forage, and the market. When I phoned him in Wyoming, it was serendipitous that he would soon be coming south, and I might speak with him at the San Juan. The gate to the ranch was locked, but when I arrived he was waiting in a large pickup and led me through to the ranch house. We passed cattle in a corral and pulled up to an old wooden ranch house. Heat and cooking were provided by a wood stove, floor boards creaked, and dirty dishes were sitting on a counter. John had been doing chores since early that morning and was quite willing to take a break. Ranchers always wear blue jeans and large hats, but John was also wearing spurs, both in the truck and in the house. Somehow this all seemed right.

John spoke about putting in a water pipeline from the Cuyama Valley up through the Calientes to the MU pastures. Farmers in the Cuyama had deep wells and were willing to sell water. This was a big deal.

Working with BLM, this project got certified, and I put it in in the 80s. It's a three inch steel pipeline that we threaded, and we used more equipment to get all that done. But it got done, and we engineered it to pump fifty gallons a minute from the Cuyama side to what we call Saddle Tank. From there it would gravity flow to the rest of the ranch, so we felt it was well worth it. It was good quality water, and fifty gallons a minute would have been about four times what we could get with all wells producing at one time.

Still I was a little skeptical. Could we really pump from one station three and a half or four miles through a three inch line without any booster pumping and still get our fifty gallons? I was pretty excited the day I got to turn it on. I went up, and when we started getting water up in the Saddle Tank, I put the bucket under it. I measured it once. I couldn't believe it. I measured it again. How long does it take to fill a five gallon bucket? I did it two or three times. I couldn't believe it. It came out to forty-nine gallons a minute flowing into a tank that would then gravity flow to the rest of the land.

The MU ranch belonged to the Rudnicks, and so I wondered why it was necessary to get a permit from the BLM for the project. John's answer was significant:

We always worked with the BLM when projects went across BLM . . . The MU Ranch is checker-boarded with BLM land, so it's pretty hard to go anywhere without crossing BLM land and even some private ground. So you need their blessing. We increased the water for our ranch, which kind of took the pressure, the burden, off a few very small wells that were very high in mineral content.

As years passed, the ownership and operations changed. In 1980 the Rudnicks sold the MU to Oppenheimer industries, continued ranching with a lease arrangement, and then bought it back. In 1988 it was sold to The Nature Conservancy, who then transferred it to the Bureau of Land Management. John Rudnick was still able to graze on much of the former MU Ranch after 1988 but with a somewhat restrictive lease arrangement. John spoke of a particular incident that told a great deal about ranching in the newer age:

In 1989, I believe, it was . . . I had cattle coming from three different ranches, and they were going to go to the MU. But at that time, things had changed, and we couldn't go on to the MU till December 1st. We were grazing it from December 1st to April 1st. It's hard to buy cattle in December. I had three ranches leased in other states, and I had cattle on those ranches, and with snow coming, the cattle needed to leave those ranches October 1st. Here I've got to put stock on the MU, but I can't get there till December 1st.

What did I do? This is what I did. In the Taft area of California, there's now a prison and houses that are out and away from town, but not too many, still lots and lots of country. So I did what my dad did years ago one time, and I thought about it, "What would he have done?" I talked to the sheepman who had all of that leased. I asked him, "Who controls that ground? Because I've got cattle coming. They're cows and calves." When they're calving, you can't confine them. You have to have them out or it's a disaster. With the lease on the MU at that point, because it had been sold, we could not get on one day early. It had to be December 1st or later, and with only four months on the MU, you don't want to waste any time.

John completed arrangements to keep the cattle near Taft, and they soon arrived by truck from Oregon and Nevada, 650 in all. With no fences on the land, the only way to prevent them from straying was by "day-herding." This meant that six or seven cowboys would be needed day and night for the next sixty days. Fortunately John was able to rent a ten-acre fenced pasture nearby. Using this to confine cattle at night, it became possible for the working crew to get some sleep. As December 1st approached, John began scheduling the two-day drive from Taft, over the Temblors, and on to the Cochora Ranch, which was included in his lease arrangement. In 1989, arrangements for the drive were not simple.

These cattle are ready to go. They're conditioned. We could move them many miles a day. That's not the problem. The problem is making arrangements with oil field companies to work through their infrastructure and not make too many people mad. I wanted to drive them through town, the town of Maricopa, but CalTrans says it takes many months to get permission, so instead of breaking rules and just doing it like maybe they would have done in the old days we got all the permission, and we needed permission from Highway Patrol to cross the road one time, that is Highway 33.

John had found eighteen riders to herd cattle and had put in calls to the CalTrans for permission to cross Highway 33. It all depended upon having a unit from the State Highway Patrol to stop traffic. But there seemed to be no units available, and it was touch and go whether any would arrive. It was further complicated by the fact that December 1st was a Monday, and most of the riders would have to be back at work. At the last moment, everything was cleared, the cattle crossed the road and started up the narrow road through the Temblors. However rain was coming down, and there were only six riders to help.

> And I'm thinking, how am I going to get the six hundred and fifty cows to start up a road that's only two tracks wide to the top. They'll be spread out over a mile by the time you take two or three cows together. How am I going to get them up there without fence, without . . . wandering off. I called a friend, and he had an El Camino pickup, and I told him to bring a bale of hay. He did. He knew enough about chumming cattle to get them to start. Chumming means throw out a little hay and get them to funnel to you and follow your pickup up a narrow part. These cattle were trained well enough so that they came to the hay, got two or three lead cows to catch onto the idea. He moved ahead and put a little hay out. He moved up further, put more hay out. Pretty soon we had the herd started, and it took over an hour and a half for all the cattle to leave the base of Elkhorn Road and actually get on the trail.

Marcus, John's dad, was eighty years old at the time, but he had come along in a pickup truck to watch and help where he could. He and John had not seen each other in forty-five days, but together they drove to the top of the grade to watch. Marcus was nervous. There were just too many things that might have gone wrong, and there might still be problems if the cattle strayed off the road. John was nervous too, but at this point there was nothing more he could do. Then as the cattle reached the top of the grade and started down toward the Elkhorn Plain, Marcus started telling John what he had to do. John related:

> As a young person, I was looking for more appreciation for getting the job done. And so I said to him, "Now you're worried about these cattle getting away. I've been day-herding them for forty-five days. I just got them up the Elkhorn Road with five people. The top hand was the prison warden that rides on the weekend, and you're going to worry about the cattle getting

away." And Marcus Rudnick always has that last word. He said, "Well, you were just lucky." At that time, being lucky wasn't what I wanted to hear, but later on in life as I get older, I really enjoy that moment, because I realize, "What's wrong with being lucky?" and maybe we are lucky. That's absolutely true. We went on to the MU Ranch and were there December 1st.

John and I had been talking for nearly two hours. He had been wearing his spurs the entire time and needed to get back to work. I had a long drive ahead to get back to Los Angeles and would need time to process what I had heard. This was no longer the Wild West. The open range of the Garcia family and the hell-for-leather roping on the Buckhorn Ranch had passed into history and had been replaced by problems of water, forage, and lease agreements. The glamour of the movie westerns had been replaced by realities of family, school, and business. It was all very real and somehow again it was familiar.

CHAPTER FIVE

The Sheepherders

Itinerant sheepmen and a settled rancher

On the Pinole Ranch

Speaking with grain farmers on the Plains was not difficult. Many or most still lived on their family lands, they all knew each other, and they belonged to a strong and connected community. After Jackie and I had spoken with one, another would step forward. Talking with cowboys was more difficult, not because they were reluctant, but because they were mobile. The earlier ones had left, and many of the modern ones lived at some distance from their stock on the Plains. While they knew each other, it was unlikely that they socialized together. Sheepherders were still more difficult to find. In the first half of the twentieth century, herders moved their animals from place to place always looking for better forage. These were immigrants who brought their Old World ways to a new land; they were in the Carrisa but not part of it. In the latter years of the century, some ranchers successfully raised sheep on their own lands, but these were exceptions to the usual practice. Among the early herders, some were French, a few were German, but most commonly they had come from the Basque regions of Spain. Whatever their origin, language and culture made them difficult to find.

The Basque Connection

After several false starts, it was the range manager for the Bakersfield BLM office who was able to give me a phone number for Eric Stewart. His grandfather, Clemente Galainena, had emigrated from Spain in 1900, and although Eric was a third-generation American, he had continued the family business of raising sheep. Once again I was obliged to make a phone call, introduce myself, and ask if an interview would be possible. Indeed, Eric was happy to talk about his family history and gave me directions for reaching his house.

Driving west from McKittrick along Highway 58, you pass a number of oil tanks, some working oil pumps, and more curiously a weather-beaten sign reading "Miller and Lux." Beyond all these, the road climbs past farms and pastures and begins a crossing of the Temblor Mountains. On that climb, I found a dirt road leading a mile up to a ranch house and a compound that is barely visible in the hills.

Leaving the pavement, I passed half a dozen huge, articulated tractors that truly belonged in a surrealistic science fiction movie. Each vehicle had eight, huge, treaded tires standing seven feet high and nearly three feet across. Every vehicle had a huge diesel engine mounted outside the cab, and they were equipped with hydraulic legs that could be extended to the ground to stabilize the machine when it stopped. A much smaller pickup truck identified the caravan with the Vintage Petroleum Company. Huge tractors such as these vibrate the ground, and reflections from subsurface layers are interpreted to give information about possible oil deposits below. Off from the dirt road where the tractors sat, their tracks led straight up a mountainside and back down; it was a serious business. There had been speculation about similar explorations within the Monument, but here it was well underway.

As I pulled into the yard, I was initially greeted by three barking dogs that ran out from a ranch style house. Eric Stewart, a large, jovial man, somewhat beyond middle age but obviously active and healthy, greeted me next. I asked about the oil company, and Eric explained that although he held surface rights on his land, the oil company had subsurface mineral rights which included the right to explore and access whatever they found. Eric clearly hoped that they would find nothing valuable. He had retired only a few years previously. He enjoyed the view from his window, and he valued quiet. We could see several miles off to the east with only a few dirt roads and some cattle on a distant hill. Over a cup of coffee, Eric told of his family's start on the Plains.

Clemente Galainena, Eric's grandfather, was born in 1883 in the Basque region of Spain. He came to California as a teenager, worked sheep near Fresno, and in 1918 was able to buy a ranch on the east side of the Temblor Mountains, the one where I was now standing with Eric. The land had once belonged to the immense Miller and Lux cattle company, and if the story is correct, Clemente purchased it for a total of ten dollars. Shortly after Clemente arrived, his youngest brother, Alejandro, also came to California and leased land in the Carrisa Plains for both farming and sheep. The brothers were no longer employed herders. They had become sheepmen owning their own flocks and even some land. With leased land in still other parts of the Carrisa, the brothers moved sheep seasonally. As with grain farming and cattle ranching, raising and marketing sheep was a business, one that was learned by experience and one that included nuances and intelligence that I had not imagined.

The Cycle of the Seasons

For Eric Stewart in the late 1950s, the year began with wintertime lamb-ing on alfalfa fields in the San Joaquin Valley near Buttonwillow. At that time it was often possible to use these fields for free. After a first har-vest, if a poor second crop grew, this was of little benefit to the farmer. Sheep could clear the field so that there would be no dead straw at the start of the following year. Not only did this arrangement give sheep-men inexpensive forage, it was the highest quality possible and came at exactly the time when ewes needed to be healthy to nurse lambs. In later years, more and more sheep took advantage of the feed, and farmers realized that there was money to be made. Twenty-five dollars an acre became normal rent, but if forage was poor elsewhere and sheep needed feed earlier in the year, this meant that sheep were eating alfalfa that the farmer might have otherwise cut and sold. The prices became steep then, and Eric described the bargaining that went on:

> The sheep rancher: "Hell, it's sure to rain soon. You're never going to make any hay. You won't be able to harvest, so why don't you let us graze, and at least you will make a bit of money." Farmer: "I think I can take a chance on one more crop, but if you are willing to pay seventy dollars an acre, I might consider."

And so the dealing would go on. In one way or another, the Galainena family would use the fields at lambing time.

During these winter months, the ewes were watched carefully to see which were likely to lamb. In the morning, there would be forty or fifty new lambs in the field, and it was essential to see that each had found its mother and was being fed. Twins were fairly common, and it was impor-tant that the mother accept them both and that one did not displace the other. Twin lambs were hobbled with the right front foot of one hobbled to the left front foot of the other. This insured that both would be under their mother at feeding time. Occasionally a ewe was unable to mother both of the twins. She might be underweight and simply would not have enough milk. Also, sometimes a ewe would have only one teat, the second one having been lost in a previous shearing. An orphan lamb would have to be bonded to another ewe, perhaps one that had lost her own offspring. The designated ewe and lamb would be placed together in an enclosure six feet by six feet until they became bonded. In some cases, the skin of a stillborn lamb would be sewed onto the orphan, and the bereaved ewe could then be induced to accept the stranger. Twins were special in another way. As soon as they could be identified, they would be branded as a pair with paint. Other single lambs were not branded. After a few days, the hobbled twins would be freed, but then if a branded lamb was seen to be doing poorly it could be hobbled once more with its twin to guarantee its mother's attention. A lamb that failed to live represented lost money for the owner. In California, the lambing occurred outdoors. In northern states with real winters, lambing occurred in heated sheds, but for the Galainena family the greatest environmental problem was not weather but coyotes.

It was often difficult for a coyote to take down a full grown sheep, but lambs were like candy. During the early years, the sheep were corralled on the fields where they could be watched. Sometimes fences were put up and taken down three times in the season as sheep were moved to new grazing areas. Woven mesh was standard, although electric fences became more common in later years. The fences were also used to separate ewes with lambs from others which had not yet given birth or which had never become pregnant. It was usually easy to identify ewes which had not been bred. With no lambs to feed, they would become bigger and stronger than others. If they failed for several consecutive years, this was money lost, and they would be sold.

As for the new crop of lambs, there was one more task before they went on their way for the summer season. They were branded, their tails were docked, and the males were castrated. The lambs were corralled in pens about thirty feet by thirty feet, while the herder who castrated them was on the outside. He would grab the front legs of the lamb, turn it over, cut the sack, and pull the testicles out with his teeth. Tails on fully grown sheep become messy and a problem, so all the lambs would have their tails docked, that is, cut off. Some herders used a tight band around the tail, and after a few days, the loss of blood supply would cause the tail to simply drop off. The Galainenas, however, used a knife. Eric maintained that it healed faster, there was less chance of infection, and it was not necessary to give tetanus shots. The number of tails piled in the yard at the end of the day provided a count. The tails and testicles were divided among the working crew and the rancher. When I asked about cooking the tails, Eric replied, "You'd roast them. They're mostly fat, but you would roast them with a little rosemary and garlic. They were real sticky, but they were delicious." I couldn't help wondering, "Was this an acquired taste, or was this something everybody loved?" and Eric's reply, "Ahhhh, no, it's an acquired taste, probably." It didn't seem like a taste I was likely to acquire.

After docking the tails, lambs were branded with the band to which they belonged: G1, G2, G3, and so forth, for Galainena band number 1, 2, or 3. In the early summer, each band, ewes and lambs both, would be trailed west across the Temblors for good feed on the Carrisa Plains. Later, as the summer became hot, flocks were moved higher into the Temblors where cooler temperatures maintained the feed longer into the year. Finally, in late autumn, the flock returned to the fields near Buttonwillow to begin the annual cycle again.

The cooler temperatures in the Temblors were important for another reason. When temperatures exceeded 95 degrees, the rams were less virile and breeding was less successful. The bucks were herded separately and then put in with the ewes from May through August. With a five-month gestation period, this meant that lambing occurred October through January. Normally one buck could service fifty ewes. If the flock was on steeper ground, more bucks were used, and if the rancher wanted to have a shorter lambing season, then he would use more rams for a shorter period of time. It was important that births occur at the proper time, and if somehow one of the new lambs was not castrated successfully, then there would problems in the future. Eric reported difficulties when a lamb being castrated had only one testicle. It was never certain if this was an act of God or if it meant that the second testicle hadn't been found. If the latter were the case, then there would be out-of-season lambing next year. I was learning a great deal.

Herders and Flocks

Who were the herders, the men who trailed the sheep across the Temblors, that watched the sheep out on the Carrisa Plains? They were single men, nearly always immigrants hired on three-year contracts. The herders received room and board while they worked for the owner. Rightly or wrongly, their pay was usually withheld until the end of the work period when they were to return home. The rancher then had access to the money during this time and often used it to buy more animals. For the herders, it may have been both good and bad. At least it guaranteed that they would go home with more money in their pockets than when they arrived. Arrangements for this labor were usually made through the Western Range Association. After the workers had been in their home country a short while, they could apply for another visa or green card and return.

The herders, and the sheep ranchers also, kept mostly to themselves. They frequented Basque restaurants in Bakersfield, and living a nomadic life, sheepmen were not part of the farming community at the north of the Plains near Simmler. Predictably their meals included a lot of lamb. Onions, garlic, and potatoes kept well, but other vegetables were rare.

The herders lived with the sheep and traveled with them the whole year. Although horses were commonly used by herders in the northern states, in Central California herding was nearly always done on foot. In early years, herders lived in tents, and in later years, they slept in trailers which traveled with them from pasture to pasture. Normally a camp tender would move the trailers to a new camp while herders were with the sheep, and it was the camp tender who brought them groceries or whatever other supplies they needed. Sometimes the sheep would be corralled at night if there were coyote problems, if there were other bands nearby that might mix, or if there were some probability that they would wander. Eric recalled:

> . . . mostly they [the sheep] would sleep in the open, and they wouldn't trail off or anything unless it was a full moon. But there was one incident when we trailed the sheep from the Carrisa Plains over here [to McKittrick] to

ship the lambs for market. We would ship the lambs and then trail the ewes back over to the Carrisa Plains, all the way across to the Painted Rock area. It was a mistake not to put them in a corral because in three hours they were back over here in McKittrick looking for their lambs. You know, they came right back.

The daily routine:

> They [the herders] would get up in the morning, and you'd go out with the sheep, and you'd kind of give them a direction toward the good feed and this and that, and once you had them off in a direction where they needed to graze, you'd stay and watch them a little bit . . . Often you would hold them up so they weren't wasting feed. You'd get in front of them and hold them back.

It was important not to waste any feed. Left to themselves, the sheep would hurry on to find the best fodder and then trample or leave what wasn't as appealing. It was the herder's job to see that nothing was wasted. In the Carrisa Plains, water was brought to the flocks by truck. Cattle drink ten or more gallons each a day, but sheep need only one or two. The land that Alejandro leased near Painted Rock had two good wells, and when sheep were on the east side of the Plains, a truck might make five or six trips daily to bring water to tanks and troughs near the sheep. They would drink a bit early in the morning, graze for a couple of hours, bed down in the hot part of the day, then drink more and graze in the late afternoon. In cooler weather and sometimes in the Temblors, it was almost unnecessary to truck water. The sheep could get most of what they needed from the green vegetation and from the morning dew on it.

Dogs, Shearing, and Weather

Every sheep camp and every herder had dogs to help. These spent their lives with the sheep and learned their trade as puppies when they followed older dogs. They also had been bred so that herding was nearly instinctive. An arm motion on the right would signal a dog to move around to the right side of the flock, and a motion on the left would send the dogs to that side. A particular yell, a Spanish word, told the dogs to give the flock a turn. The herders also used whistles to direct the dogs, and sometimes the sheep learned the signals and followed them without the dogs. The whistles were made from pieces of stone and could be amazingly loud. Eric once owned such a whistle, but a teacher took it away. In a wonderful bit of understatement, he said, "She wasn't impressed with it at all." In later years, dogs were used to protect sheep from coyotes. These would be mastiffs or other large breeds, and they made the job of the herders much easier – unless the dogs went rogue and attacked the sheep themselves. A single dog would never cause trouble, but Eric insisted that in groups they sometimes became wild, and domestic dogs that went wild were more trouble than coyotes that would only kill for meat. Still later, some herders used electric fences to protect sheep at night. These were mobile and could be put up fairly quickly as they were needed.

In addition to the herders, shearing crews were an essential part of the operation. This was seasonal work, and it required a significant number of men in each crew. A sheep rancher couldn't maintain such a group on his own, and so these crews contracted to do shearing up and down the valley as needed. The season of shearing for the Galainenas depended upon the availability of the crews and took place wherever the sheep were being kept at the time. One band would be sheared in the Carrisa near Painted Rock, the next might be at the base of the Temblors on the east of the Plains, and a third band might even be in the Central Valley. This geography created a peculiar kind of problem with the shearing crew. Eric explained, "They'd want to get paid before they moved. So you finished shearing in the Carrizo, and then they would . . . I'm trying to think of the proper word . . ." I suggested that with extra money burning in their pockets, they would celebrate. "Yeah, and you'd be waiting at the next job and only three shearers out of ten would show up." A smaller crew meant that shearing a full band of 800 could take three days instead of one. The band must be kept in a small area to be ready for shearing, and this in turn meant that feed was depleted and the animals were stressed. Again the significant fact was that it cost the rancher money. Shearing crews were paid by the head and worked fast and worked hard. A good shearer could finish one hundred sheep in a day. With a premium on speed, accidents sometimes occurred, and animals could be nicked by the shears and damaged. The owner watched his sheep, and if too many were injured, then he would try to find another crew for the next season.

All farming depends upon weather, and raising sheep was no exception to this. In a rain year and on wet ground, sheep were susceptible to a fungus that grew on their hooves. The cure required a foot bath and then a search for drier ground. Then, in drought years, forage could become scarce, and the rancher had to make hard choices. Eric would go up and down the Central Valley talking to farmers and looking for fields to rent where there was feed. These were not always alfalfa. Grain stubble was good feed, but almost anything that grew could be used if the situation became serious. Carrots, potatoes, and even fields with cantaloupes had served this purpose. Eric would offer a price, barter, and pray for rain.

Changes through the Years

As with nearly everything else, there have been changes in the sheep business over the years. The herders are still immigrants that come with three-year contracts. Coyotes are still a problem, and sheep are even today moved from pasture to pasture, often on rented land. The changes which have come include the transportation of the sheep and the economics of the operation. Except for a few private parcels, the southern end of the Carrisa is now a national monument and is only occasionally available for grazing. In the north, there are more homes and small private parcels so that it is very awkward and sometimes impossible to drive sheep across the land. They are more commonly moved by truck. While land uses have changed, the marketing of lamb for meat has also changed. It is no longer common for lambs to graze with their mothers for a year before being sold. Feed lots buy the lambs soon after they are born, and their future is an industrial one. After several dry years, Eric Stewart gave up ranching and retired. His ranch, the one purchased by Clemente in 1918, is now being explored for oil. Fifteen miles to the west, several energy companies are seeking permits to build solar electric generating plants. If these are permitted, the companies will be required to buy land and protect habitat for a number of endangered species. Eric believes that this may be his opportunity to raise some cash from his land. It becomes harder and harder to be a gypsy in the twenty-first century.

All Things Are Connected

As Eric and I continued talking, the conversation moved to other topics – neighbors and mutual acquaintances. When I asked if he knew Bill Garcia, Eric chuckled. They owned adjacent pieces of land on the Carrisa side of the Temblors, and Bill had once asked Eric to remove his sheep from his, Bill's, land. Eric insisted that the sheep had not trespassed and were indeed on Eric's property. It was some time till the boundaries of their properties were definitely determined and marked. The irony in the situation is delightful: this was the same land that their grandfathers, Jesus and Clemente, had argued over two generations previously.

Talking with Eric, I mentioned that just the previous night I slept out on Bill's property. When Eric asked more, it evolved that I had not slept on Bill's land, but rather I was on Eric's west pasture. I had stopped at dusk on a dirt road in the foothills of the Temblors, and as I often do, I fixed a quick meal on a camp stove and then rolled my sleeping bag out beside the car. It was dark when I lay down, but a few hours later I woke up with a large moon coming up over the ridge. It was not the moon that woke me but a steady drumming sound that seemed to come from everywhere. For about ten yards in every direction, the ground was clear of grass, and I realized that this was the precinct of a kangaroo rat. One particular species of these rodents is on the federal endangered species list. With a flashlight I saw one hunting along the ground about ten feet from my sleeping bag. It seemed not to care that it was being watched and scampered around the circle diving underground and then coming back up. The moon was so bright that no flashlight was needed, and soon another rat appeared. Kangaroo rats drum on the ground with their large hind legs to mark their territory and to warn of predators. Soon the sound came from still another direction. Finally a rat came within a few inches of my face to see exactly what sort of creature I was. This was a wonderful meeting that I had not expected, and it was an odd coincidence to learn that it happened on Eric's Galainena Ranch.

Although the story of the Van Matre family will appear later, it is strangely related to my interview with Eric Stewart. The first of the homesteads which I found on the Plains, the one which was largely responsible for my interest in the oral histories, belonged to the Van Matres. Jackie and I had been entirely unsuccessful in locating a living family member, but I had reason to believe that Pat McCornack, who appeared previously in a story related to hired hands on the Pinole Ranch, might be able to help. I had a street address for Pat, but I had also been told that he was a rough character, and it might be unwise to arrive at his doorstep with too many questions. Purely on a chance, I asked Eric if he knew Pat McCornack. To my amazement, Eric replied that they were good friends. They ate lunch together every week, and if I liked, Eric would give me a favorable introduction. Two weeks later I phoned Pat McCornack, and we had a delightful conversation. Not only was Pat helpful, but the experience once again proved that the community at the north of the Carrisa Plains was close.

Farmers and Sheepmen

The community was close in other ways as well. As noted, after summer harvest, farmers frequently leased their stubble fields for sheepmen to use. These arrangements went on year after year, and beyond the financial benefits for each, they would often become friends. It was this connection that encouraged Doug Wreden to take up herding on his own lands.

Doug has already been introduced with stories of the Pinole Ranch, and it was he who spoke about the rough characters that sometimes worked there. Doug was the ranch manager, and when grain farming became marginal, he and his wife began looking for other income. Doug supervised groups taking down barbed wire fences on the Carrizo Plains National Monument, and during lunch breaks along roads and beside pastures, he spoke about a horse he once tried to break, about recent work on the Monument, and of troubles he once had with coyotes raiding sheep. Later in a formal interview, he spoke about learning the sheep business, of his successes with it, and finally of the end of the enterprise when it became impossible to make ends meet. It began, however, when he, like nearly all ranchers, rented grain stubble to other sheepmen.

Jake Martin was one of the persons who leased fields, and Doug laughed as he told of arrangements at the Pinole:

> And so they'd bring sheep up, and they would follow the harvesters. Generally we would disk after the sheep left. So if the sheep weren't moving fast enough, you'd almost disk up sheep: they'd be lying down in the stubble. I'd tell Jake, "You'd better be moving the sheep along, Jake. We're disking. We've got two tractors going, and we want to get this stuff covered up." And there was always this conflict because they would move very slowly because they wanted every ounce of feed they'd paid for, and they'd feed it to dust.

Pedro Zalba and Joaquin Asperin were other sheep owners who used the Pinole. They employed Basque herders, and again the herders would be reluctant to leave the stubble any sooner than necessary. Doug would argue, and no matter what he said, they seemed never to understand English. Sign language was not sufficient. In his words: "I finally figured out a trick to making those guys move. You back your truck up to their trailer, jack the hitch up, and start the engine. When they understand that their home is going down the road, then all of a sudden they start speaking excellent English. 'Okay, okay, okay. Tomorrow, tomorrow, okay?' and then they would be gone." *Carumba!* The problem was solved. Doug estimated that in total there were nearly 9000 head that worked their way through the Carrisa in some years.

The First Sheep on the Pinole Ranch

With experience of this kind behind him, it was ironic that Doug would become a sheepman himself. This began when his nine-year-old daughter, Carissa (named after the Plains but spelled differently), joined 4H. She wanted to take a steer to the fair, but that was out of the question for someone so small. She suggested a pig, but Doug said "no." He didn't even like pork, and so how could he like a pig? It had to be a sheep, except that neither he nor his daughter knew anything about them. Shortly afterwards, two wooly little sheep showed up in a pen. A neighbor boy had brought them and proceeded to shear them and teach them "this and that and everything." They kept these sheep for a couple of years, and Doug began thinking, "We need something else besides farming. Why lease the stubble to someone else when you could have sheep of your own? And besides, when the wheat crop failed, you needed something else for cash . . . and the sheep could eat the failed crop even if it couldn't be sold." The result was inevitable.

Carissa got a small flock of Suffolk sheep for her 4H project, and she showed lambs at fairs along the coast. These were spoiled sheep that led pampered lives. Open the gate with tall green grass outside, and they would just lie down and wait for hay and grain. These were not "real sheep," and Doug began to think it was time for some real sheep of his own. He spoke with Pedro Zalba and agreed to buy one hundred ewes. The payment could be deducted from the fee that Pedro paid for running sheep on Doug's stubble.

Learning the Sheep Business

At about the same time, Doug and his wife Cindy were having trouble with a small flock that they already had. There were birthing problems with twins and triplets, and they really didn't know what to do. At a sheep symposium in Fresno, they happened to meet a Montana rancher who had 8000 acres and ran 1000 sheep. Talking afterwards, the rancher said, "Yeah, my mom hires girls from Logan, Utah, every winter to work

in the lambing barn." Doug and Cindy talked it over, and the next winter, Cindy was on a plane to Butte, Montana, to learn how a real sheep
rancher made a living.

It was a tough school. Cindy's plane came in at midnight, and at four
that very morning, she was in the barn struggling with everything she
didn't know. The first week was hard, and Doug said that she cried a lot
over the phone. Art and Marge, the ranchers, were truly fine people, and
Cindy soon became good friends. In Doug's words:

> Art spent all the time out in the lambing barn teaching Cindy all the ins and
> outs and vaccinating . . . and these sheep had quads and quints. They had
> these little Finn sheep mixed in so they were very prolific, and so they'd get
> old Doctor Bill, the veterinarian guy, out there. He'd do a C-section, pull
> five lambs out, cause they're just like scrambled eggs. They're all mixed up.
> You can't go in and sort them out with your hand. So Cindy would assist
> him with that, and she saw the whole process. It cost twenty-five bucks.
> That's what Doctor Bill would charge them. Out here we took a ewe in to
> Los Osos. We had it done. It cost us three hundred and some odd dollars.
> So anyway she became really good friends with Art and Marge. She was
> there six weeks working the lambing in the snow in the winter in Montana.
> She had to bathe in a big washtub in the barn and had to heat the water on
> a fire. And so she said, "I didn't bathe every day." I guess the sheep didn't
> mind.

This was the beginning of the real sheep venture for Doug and Cindy. When she came back to the Carrisa Plains, Art paid her in sheep
rather than cash. A fellow in Coalinga owed Art money, and rather than
collecting the money and then paying Cindy, the fellow in Coalinga gave
Cindy two rams directly. These were to breed the one hundred ewes
from Pete Zalba. Pete thought they were crazy, but the next winter there
were 140 lambs.

> One of those bucks will breed a hundred ewes. And I mean, they just, you'd
> have to pull them off and put them away. They're like a Border Collie
> working. They just don't stop until they die. We took these hundred and

forty some odd lambs, and Pete sent his boys up with a truck, and we hauled them down to California Valley. We made quite a bit of money. But I remember having breakfast with the herder before we put them in the truck, and we had ewe neck stew with a lot of garlic and vegetables. They'd been probably cooking for a week. They just keep adding a little more stuff, and wine, and green salad with vinegar dressing, and French bread, and cheese. And I thought, "It's five-thirty in the morning, and this is kind of weird, but you know, it tastes as good now as it did probably the night before." And that was a new experience. And then we loaded the lambs on, and everybody was happy . . . then we started thinking, "Let's project this out to six hundred ewes or a thousand."

In the next few years, the sheep operation grew. First they bought 600 ewe lambs from a rancher in Utah. Doug and Cindy had breakfast with Doug's parents in San Francisco, and then they flew to Salt Lake City. The rancher picked them up and took them to see the sheep. The deal was made, and Doug and Cindy flew back for dinner with his parents the same night. They asked, "What did you do today?" Doug remembered that his head was spinning.

The lambs were trucked from Utah, and when the were put into a fallow field, the wild oats were so tall that you couldn't even see the animals. They had to jump to even see and find each other, and before the end of the day, the flock had scattered over a thousand acres. It took a full week to get the band together again and put them on a pasture with shorter feed. At the end of the season, the lambs were sold, and the following year, Doug was back in Utah to buy more lambs. This time they were "desert sheep" that had arrived from New Mexico. When lambing time came, Doug and Cindy did it the way she had learned in Montana. They brought the ewes into large pens at night and watched the newborn lambs there. With 600 or 700 sheep, it was exhausting work for the two of them, working alone on four or five hours of sleep a night.

About a year later, they gave up this method and let the ewes give birth out in the fields. Doug would watch to be sure everything was all right and saw that some of the ewes were extraordinary mothers. He watched one put her newborn twins underneath her belly and fight off a golden eagle that was hunting. After that, they began to select sheep for their mothering ability.

Coyotes, Sheep, and Dogs

Always coyotes were a problem for Doug's sheep operation. The solutions which Doug tried included trapping, electric fences, and guard dogs. Doug explained:

> We had the county trapper come out here. The trappers were paid mostly to do skunk work, because of rabies, and to do town work, but they loved to come out here and be in the real wide open for coyotes. We'd have them stay at our little guest house, [as] we called it then, and Cindy'd cook for them. They'd eat with us. Almost became part of the family. And they'd put out snares, and they'd put out leg-hold traps, and then . . .
>
> My son at the time, Matt, my oldest son was about eight or nine, and he really wanted to ride this motorcycle that we used to gather the sheep. He thought, "It's just not fair, Dad, that you get to have fun on the motorcycle all day long." I said, "You don't understand, it's work." And so, "If you'd let me ride the motorcycle, I'd check traps for Don [the county employee], and he wouldn't have to be here every day." And Don was liking the idea. And Don kind of mentored Matt, showed him how to set traps. Showed him how to track, showed him how . . . everything he knew. Matt just loved it. He'd go to school and give a little demonstration [on] how you set a long spring trap for the kids in class . . . and so Matt got to ride the motorcycle, and he got a little 22 to dispatch the coyotes he found in traps, and he'd reset them. Don had a lot more time since he didn't have to come out here all the time. And for Matt this was a full-time [job]. Half the management of those sheep was just keeping them alive.

Doug also tried using dogs to protect the sheep from coyotes. They bought a dog from a rancher near Ridgecrest in the desert, and when she was bred, the litter had thirteen pups. These were Great Pyrenees. The plan may have been a good one, but it didn't work.

My kids, Jacob and Kirsten, were like eight or nine or ten, and [they] fell in love with these dogs. Well, they're not supposed to be so bonded to people. As soon as the kids got home from school, they'd be down in the pen and holding them and sleeping on them and playing with them. "Oh, this is not going good." So, the long and short was the trapper then came out and said, "Doug, I don't know how to tell you this, but your dogs are chewing the sheep up." I said, "Naw, I don't think so."

Later that day, I followed their tracks all over, and oh, no. So I came back and I smelled their breath, and it smelled like mutton. I smelled this other dog, and this other dog, and this other dog. I had to shoot them, four of them. Still had all those puppies. They were in with lambs, and the funny thing was there was one lamb in there that had no ears because the dogs would chew on it. The lambs would try to eat the dog's food, and so the dogs would chew on the lambs, and eventually one lamb had no ears. He's kind of funny looking. None of them ever killed each other, but they kind of got along. And as the puppies got a little older, seven or eight months, we'd put them out in the field, but they would come home, didn't want to stay. So we put an ad in the paper to sell all these Pyrenees puppies. People came from all over California.

At a livestock symposium in Fresno, Doug had seen a demonstration of electric fences. It looked good, and not only did Doug buy fences for his ranch, but he became a dealer and taught other herders how to put them up and use them. He experimented with the fences and worked at it. Four wires instead of three worked best, and the height mattered. Eventually solar panels were used to charge a battery that operated the fence at night. They created forty-acre paddocks, or corrals, that held a thousand sheep. The sheep were confined in one while a second fence was being set up. Then the sheep moved to the second paddock, and the first one was moved to still another location.

Cindy and I did that every day for months. And Pete Zalba would come out. He says, "Keeps the coyotes, keeps the coyotes out." You could see where coyotes started to dig under, and then they got shocked and backed out. You could see where they'd run around those forties and make a trail figuring how to get in there. Because when they get shocked hard enough, they thought the fence was ten feet tall. They could just leap over that in a second. But psychologically . . .

The Final Years

In time, Doug found another system that worked perfectly. There were two large pastures of about 2000 acres, and each had a two-and-a-half acre pen. Wherever the sheep were at five or six o'clock, they were put into the closest pen for the night. The sheep knew they were protected and went in willingly and would just lie down. In the daytime they would forage over a thousand acres, and at sundown they were waiting at the pen. The plan was a good one, but it came too late.

> This was like the eleventh year . . . Wouldn't you know, you finally get it all figured out, and the price just went "pshhh." We hadn't been paying attention, but when I had to take some fence chargers back to Cal Poly, I happened to ask a fellow there, "What's the price of lamb?" "Oh, they're down to forty-two." "Forty-two cents! What's going on?" And so we made it through that year. The next year, it wasn't much better, and in November, I said to Cindy, I said, "Hey, I figure we're only going to make two bucks a head. Are you ready to work your ass off for the next three months for two bucks a head?" "No" "Then it's time to quit."

Before selling, Doug had all the sheep tested for pregnancy. Over 95 percent of them tested positive and this increased their value immensely. A rancher from Nevada came and bought the entire lot at the Dixon sheep auction, and Doug was nearly out of the sheep business. There was still wool from the spring shearing, so Doug and his son drove up to Stockton to the wool co-op. Doug said, "Hey, let's run on over to Dixon and look at those ewes," and they drove over. Doug recalled, "It's like looking at your family, cause you knew all these . . . there's 101, there's 626, and there's . . . and you see them looking . . . they don't seem to belong here. It tore us both up."

This conclusion to Doug's story came as no surprise. Of course I knew that Doug had left the Pinole Ranch some years ago, and I was equally aware that in the twenty-first century almost no sheep are seen on the Carrisa Plains. The practices and economics of agriculture in California had changed, and there was no reason to think that livestock would fare differently than wheat. Much the same fate had fallen on Eric Stewart as well. More impressive than their account of sheep ranching, however, were the two persons who told them. Both had invested a great deal and worked hard, both had adapted to the changes, and both were happy to share their experiences with an outsider. I had been fortunate in my search for sheepmen of the Carrisa Plains.

CHAPTER SIX

A Box of Memories

An earlier generation speaks for itself

Cassette tapes and Soda Lake

"I found these in a file cabinet. You may be interested." Tammy Whitley handed me a small wooden box about five inches wide, ten inches long, and three inches deep. She was the archeologist with the Bakersfield office of the Bureau of Land Management (BLM). Several weeks earlier, I had asked if the BLM archives included an interview conducted some years back with a particular rancher. Tammy apologized that she could not find the recoding I wanted, but perhaps this would be of some interest. In the box were ten or twelve old cassette tapes, some in plastic cases and some open. The names "Ian McMillan," "Ernie Garcia," "Kenneth Beck," and "Angus MacLean" were among those appearing on the fading labels. For a person who had been collecting oral histories of the Carrisa Plains, this was an astonishing find.

The very first homesteaders on the Carrisa Plains had worked the land only briefly, given up, and moved on. The names on these tapes belonged to the next group to arrive, and although most had been dead for years, some of their descendants still lived nearby. Tammy had found the files by accident; they came with no explanation, nothing on them written, and no history. As they were old and in poor condition, it was uncertain if they could even be played. Beyond the difficulty in making these records a part of a public collection, there were the intrinsic questions of who, when, where, and how had they been recorded? I said, "Thank you," and asked if I might keep the collection for a while to see what could be made of it.

Just as the open plains held the fences and windmills that initiated my search for the people and lives on the Carrisa, so here was another and different kind of relic, but one that still pointed to the past. Time had covered many of the artifacts on the ground. Perhaps the dust here could be swept away to find the stories underneath. This was to become a different kind of journey.

You will already know something of the persons appearing in the collection. Ernie Garcia was one of the fourteen children of Jesus Garcia and was uncle to Bill Garcia who has already been introduced. Jackie had met Ernie some years previously when his truck broke down near her home. Although it was a very hot day, she recalled that he would only accept water and rest on the porch of her home. It would be improper for him to enter the house with an unaccompanied woman. Ernie was already very old when Jackie met him, and two years later, he died. The names "Ian McMillan" and "Eben McMillan" were also names that I knew. While they were farmers and ranchers, they were also well-known naturalists and environmental advocates. Angus MacLean was a writer.

One of his books, *The Curse of the Feathered Snake*, recounts fanciful legends and bits of family history from the Plains and from his home on the La Panza Ranch located ten miles west of the Simmler community. Angus had no children, and so there was no possibility of finding any direct descendants. Other interviews in the collection were equally significant: it was a treasure.

Restoring the Tapes

The ranchers in question had grown up in an age when letters were hand-written and were delivered on a bi-weekly schedule. It is an irony that their voices were to become transformed digitally, that the tapes would be electronically enhanced, and that the history of the tapes would finally be discovered using internal clues from the interviews along with a series of Internet searches. The events related in the tapes occurred in the 20s, 30s, and 40s. The interviews were conducted in the 90s, and ultimately the stories were retrieved in the year 2010. How nice that past and present were tangled in yet another dimension.

The tapes were in poor condition, and all of them had background noise that was sometimes louder, sometimes quieter, and which sometimes completely overwhelmed the speaking voices. The difficulties in understanding the conversations were compounded by the fact that all the persons being interviewed were elderly, and most spoke in quiet voices, frequently in asides that the recorder could barely pick up. When several people were present for an interview, they sometimes spoke simultaneously, and no single speaker was intelligible. In 2010 it was even becoming difficult to find a machine that would play cassette tapes; the entire world, it seemed, had gone digital. The collection represented eight interviews, and in the end, it was possible to recover six of these. How much better it would have been to sit and actually talk with these pioneers.

The tapes were played on an old cassette recorder at my home. My computer was placed directly in front of one of the loudspeakers, and its recording program digitized the sounds and stored them. It was then possible to easily play and replay the conversation. Using a graphic equalizer in the computer, I could suppress or enhance various frequency ranges. This removed some, but not all, of the extraneous noise. Nothing could help when a speaker muffled his words, when a cuckoo clock sounded across the room, or someone else started coughing. In spite of all this, reasonable transcriptions could be made by playing difficult passages several times and using the context to fill in words that were lost. What was not possible from listening to the tapes was to find their history or the identity of the woman who had conducted all the interviews.

An Interview with Angus MacLean, Historian of the Plains

The first tape was a conversation with Angus MacLean. He was being interviewed by a woman who was knowledgeable about his family history, about one of his books, and about the Carrisa Plains. Her name never appeared in the recording so that her identity was a first mystery. It was also one of the last questions to be answered in the whole endeavor. The woman was very much interested in the plants and the plant associations which had occupied the Plains in the early years. She also asked about Painted Rock (a horseshoe-shaped sandstone outcropping with Indian pictographs on the Carrisa Plains), about the books that Angus had written, and about his family's history on the Plains. His family had lived on the La Panza Ranch for some time, and several of the stories which Angus had written dealt with the ranch and its surrounding mountains. There had been a cross carved on a tree and a visit by the outlaw Jesse James. The MacLean family had made a number of trips, picnic excursions really, to Painted Rock on the Plains, and his book has several photos of the family on these occasions. The interview discussed the photos and identified the family members in them. Angus's mother had become very interested in photography, and some of her photos were discussed. As for the tape itself and the woman's identity, a few tantalizing hints did appear.

At one point, Angus expressed an interest in revisiting Painted Rock, and the woman invited him to come visit her on the Plains. Later Angus gave the interviewer an autographed copy of his book, *The Curse of the Feathered Snake*. It included a second autograph as well, and he commented, "That other's my sister's autograph. She passed on here just last December. She's the one that did the illustrations." A copy of this book was already on my shelf, and the illustrator was Ione Bowman, apparently the married name of Ione MacLean, his sister. The magic of the Internet then appeared. Of course a search for "Ione Bowman" turned up many leads going nowhere. Most of these referred to her work as an illustrator, not only of that particular book but also of several others which her brother had authored. One of the references led to a San Luis Obispo newspaper that carried obituaries. Ione Bowman had died in December 1989. The recorded interview could then be dated to early in the year 1990. In fact the conversation referred to a particularly nice display of wildflowers outside the window, so spring was the time of the interview. As they talked on, the woman mentioned that she hoped to interview several others about early plant life on the Plains, and she specifically named Kenneth Beck. It was now possible to put at least two of the tapes in a chronological order.

Perhaps as an aside, it should be mentioned that a number of the stories which Angus wrote were about Indians of the central coast region of California, presumably Chumash or their descendants. The taped conversation dwelt at some length on the early cultures, native and pioneer, along the coast. Angus was certain that Spanish peoples had been present for so long, and their interaction with the Indians had been sufficiently intense, that it was no longer possible to speak of separate cultures. There were dark skinned *vaqueros* using Spanish saddles, practicing native herbal remedies, and living and working on ranchos in the hills owned by lighter-skinned men. From his viewpoint, the cultures had blended.

Searching for the Missing Person

The identity of the woman speaking with Angus MacLean remained a mystery. A serendipitous find brought me to the name "Adele Baldwin."

On a library shelf kept by the Bureau of Land Management at the Washburn Ranch, there is a collection of essays, newspaper stories, and letters concerning Carrisa history. Among these papers is a one written by an Adele Baldwin which recounted several legends about Painted Rock. No direct biographical information was given, but the bibliography at the end indicated that she, Adele, had spoken with several of the old ranchers, and among them were Angus MacLean and Kenneth Beck. This was tantalizing, and I made some effort to locate Adele to find out if she had conducted other interviews as well. Her essay indicated that she had lived near the Plains for many years, and this had been the inspiration for her story about Painted Rock. An obvious beginning, obvious in the twenty-first century anyway, was to search the online White Pages, and indeed, a phone number and address appeared. Another Internet search indicated that Adele was interested in California archeology and was employed at the Bakersfield State College in the office responsible for records of archeological sites in the central part of the state. These leads were promising.

The phone number was out of service, and although it seemed a bit intrusive, my only recourse was to simply walk up to the door of her house, introduce myself, and ask. Her address was local, and on a trip between the Carrisa Plains and Bakersfield, I did exactly this. The house was the very last one on a shady street in Dustin Acres several miles east of Taft. The trees were old, the yard was overgrown, the fence sagged, and the house badly needed paint. There was no answer when I knocked. With no other possibility apparent, I knocked on the door of the next neighbor. He was very helpful and indicated that Adele had moved a year previously, but he was willing to give me her cell phone number. As it happened, this number had also gone out of service. A last possibility was to call the historic preservation office where she worked, or had worked, and ask if they could help. As the laws of perversity require, numerous attempts were needed to locate a correct phone number for the preservation office, but once again this provided no real help. Although she had been employed there for many years, Adele no longer worked at the office, and she had left no forwarding information. Another Internet search indicated that she was sixty-four-years-old and that she was listed on Facebook. The date of this posting was unknown. A Facebook search for her name turned up no one older than twenty-five. Every road had come to a dead-end, and it was time to listen again to the tapes for internal evidence about who the interviewer might be.

All of the interviews were conducted by the same woman. It became apparent that she, or someone for whom she worked, was hoping to restore the flora of the Carrisa Plains to what it had resembled before the introduction of farming and ranching. For this project she hoped that the ranchers might be able to provide information about the original flora of the Plains, but in fact the landscape had been largely transformed before any of them were born. It was clear, however, that the woman was more than a casual botanist and that she was familiar with the names of a number of persons who had made early collections of plants in the central part of California. She was professional and more than a few years out of college.

In the taped conversation with Ernie Garcia, the talk drifted to the subject of the Saucito Ranch, where he had grown up as a child. In the recording the woman said, "We are hoping to restore the ranch house to a more stable condition." The use of the pronoun "we," particularly in a conversation which occurred around 1990, suggested that she was working in cooperation with the managing agencies present on the Plains. At that time it was called the Carrizo Plain Natural Area and was administered cooperatively by The Nature Conservancy and the Bureau of Land Management. These clues suggested where I might ask further questions.

Another of the conversations made reference to television and to several television programs. The interviewer indicated that she watched very little TV, but then added, "They've put it on the news . . . Channel Six. Steve's taped it on his VCR." Perhaps her husband was named Steve.

As my curiosity grew, I looked again through the box of tapes and this time paid more attention than before to a small scrap of paper which read, "Duane, these may be of interest to you," and it was signed Kathy. Duane Christian had been an archeologist for the Bureau of Land Management in Bakersfield for many years, and Kathy was a wildlife biologist on the Plains. Kathy and her husband live in what was once the

MU Ranch, now in the south part of the Monument, and perhaps . . .
If Kathy lived in the same house where this unknown woman had once
lived, then that was how the tapes were found, and Kathy might be able
to tell their story. No luck! Kathy is a friend of mine, but she had no
memory of anything at all about the tapes. Not only did she not know
where they had come from, she couldn't remember ever seeing any tapes
or ever delivering them to Duane.

Ernie Garcia, Rancher and Cowboy

Even without knowing the history of the tapes, the interviews were
themselves fascinating and spoke directly about times before the memory of most persons living in the twenty-first century. The Saucito Ranch
was the principal residence for Jesus and Adalida Garcia, but members
of the family had also lived and worked at a number of other locations.
Ernie Garcia described attending elementary school and living with
his brothers and grandmother near Pozo. His older brothers returned
to El Saucito on weekends to work on the ranch, but Ernie was too
young to accompany them. When he was older, Ernie rode horseback
across these same hills of the La Panza Range. He followed along the
faint wagon roads and sometimes took shortcuts traveling cross-country
along ridges and looking down on the Plains from above. Much of the
land was open range, but still there were a number of gates to open and
close along the way. For several years Ernie attended the Carrisa, or
Simmler, School on the Plains, and at another time he attended school
in Bakersfield where the Garcia family owned still another home.

The subject of ranching accidents and medical remedies came up,
and Ernie spoke of these: "My mother would put, like half an onion cut-
side down on a saucer, and put sugar on it, and then put a cup over the
top. Pretty soon the juice would seep out into the saucer, and we would
drink it for a cough." Horehound was good for a cough, and kerosene
served as yet another remedy. Ernie's mother would put some kerosene
on a feather and stick it in his mouth. These may, or may not, have
been as effective as modern treatments, but then no co-pay was required

either. Other remedies and plants that his mother used were mustard plasters, Yerba Buena, Redmaids, and Golondrina. This latter would be boiled and used for bug bites. It was also used as an antiseptic in a cut. Ernie also recalled that his dad had a thin white scar on his forehead as a result of being bucked off a horse. Jesus was a smoker, and of course cigarettes were home-rolled. With blood coming down his face, Jesus had taken a cigarette paper, licked it, and put it over the cut. The bleeding was stopped, and the damage was inconsequential. It was characteristic of cowboys and farmers to handle their own problems. The Surgeon General would not have approved.

Ian McMillan, Rancher and Conservation Advocate

One of the longest interviews in the collection of tapes was with Ian McMillan. His father, Alexander, had created a farm near Shandon, thirty miles north of the Simmler community, and this was where Ian and his brother had grown up. Ian spoke about going to a dance at the Annette schoolhouse as a young man. Ian had driven the family car to the dance along with several neighbors and friends. They danced till daylight, and when they went outside afterwards, the dirt roads were slick, cars were stuck in the yard by the school, and nearly everyone was sliding around in the mud. Ian managed to get his family car on the road, and they all headed south over the grade into Choice Valley. There they became stuck, and so Ian left the car and friends and walked a few miles to a ranch where his brother, Eben, was living. He hitched four horses to a headerbed and started back for his friends. In the interview, Ian explained at some length that a headerbed was a particular kind of cart or wagon that was used to bring grain to a stationary thresher. This was how the harvest was managed at that time. With the sun rising, Ian brought the others to their ranches on the cart behind the horses. It was Sunday morning, and it is probable that the churchgoers in his group never went to bed till afternoon.

This tape also provided information about the interviewer. Ian spoke about a picnic at some rocks, not Painted Rock, but "just behind the house where you live, just north of Soda Lake." This would be the Goodwin property, known then as the Werling Ranch. With a date for the interview sometime after 1990, this might help prod memories if I could find the right person to ask.

Much of the recorded interview concerned changes that had occurred in the flora on the Plains. The exotic, non-native species included brome grasses, filaree, Schismus, and tumbleweed, but Ian could not remember a time when he had not seen these. It had been too late even then to be certain what had originally grown there. One delightful story revolved around a particular species of snapdragon that had been discovered in 1902 by Alice Eastwood on a part of the old McDonald estate. She was a noted botanist and had traveled throughout Central California collecting plants. This particular flower was the first of its kind, a new species. When others later went looking to study this plant, it could not be found. Then, in 1948 Eben McMillan became curious about an unfamiliar flower on his ranch. Neither he nor a botanist that he knew could identify the flower, and so a specimen was sent to John Thomas Howell at Cal Poly State College. When it arrived, Howell lifted three feet vertically off his chair and probably never slept again till he arrived out at the McMillan Ranch to see it for himself. Newspapers carried stories about the "Lost Snapdragon" and its rediscovery.

Ian and his brother Eben were self-taught naturalists. Eben's son, in a later interview, spoke with me of long and intense discussions late into the night when visiting botanists came to the family farm on weekends. In addition to his knowledge of botany, Eben had strong credentials as an ornithologist, and when the economics of his farm became marginal, he produced several wildlife movies and became a traveling lecturer with the National Audubon Society. Outside the more specialized circles of naturalists, Eben was well known as a champion in defense of the California Condor. It is impressive that he may be the only person ever elected to the California Academy of Sciences who never completed high school. The early twentieth century was an age of generalists, and the two McMillan brothers were among them. I can only regret that the interview with Eben was the single one in the collection of tapes that was beyond recovery.

Ian was an avid quail hunter, and the Temblor Range was a favorite place for his family to go. Stories about the number of quail in the hills are still told and are astonishing. The Temblors were also used heavily as range for sheep in the 30s and 40s, and eventually the sheep grazed the shrubs so heavily that no cover remained for the quail. It is even probable that the herders responsible were Clemente and Alejandro Galainena. Ian had planted saltbrush up in the Temblors in an experiment to restore the habitat, but it was only if sheep were fenced out of the area that the brush could survive. He and several others tried everything they could imagine to limit the grazing. They contacted conservation organizations, they contacted other hunters, and they contacted elected representatives, but no one had been interested. They finally gained traction in an unexpected way. Coyotes were, of course, the bane of sheep, and the herders regularly shot all they could and stretched the carcasses along barbed wire fences. Ian took a number of photos of these and ultimately brought the pictures to a woman named Marguerite Smeltzer who lived at the south end of the Plains. She and a friend, both "white-haired old ladies," were outraged. Marguerite was a writer, and both women were members of the Defenders of Wildlife organization. It was intolerable that the sheepherders should be killing wildlife while they continued to overgraze the hills. The two women raised a tornado in the media . . . and the quail habitat gradually recovered.

Henry Twisselman, Rancher and Historian

Perhaps the most notable of the recorded interviews was one with Henry Twisselman. He is, or was, the patriarch of the Twisselman family and is known for his memory and for stories he tells about the Carrisa Plains. He has written two books of history, largely family history, that are well known to residents of the Plains. Henry is also known for having strong opinions on almost any subject but especially on the way the government has managed, or mismanaged, farm lands. The title of one of the books, *Don't Get Me Started*, could be applied to the interview as well. To hear Henry's voice and listen to him recall his early years on the

Carrisa is a privilege.

The Twisselman family held land throughout the north area of the Plains, in the Cuyama Valley, and east of the Temblors as well. Henry grew up on horseback watching cattle, hunting, and helping with family ranching. As a young man, he knew and worked together with Chester Brumley. This would be Chester Jerome Brumley, son of the original rancher at El Saucito. As Henry recalled, Chester had a place of his own somewhere behind what is now the Washburn Ranch, and, of more significance, Chester insisted that he had personally seen Carrizo grass growing in one of the lower canyons of the Caliente Range. This grass, actually a tall, woody reed, is known in the Cuyama Valley, but its presence within the boundaries of the present Monument has never been confirmed. Early explorers reported finding it, but their diaries were so vague that the location is uncertain. Henry was also uncertain, but the description in the tape suggests a location somewhere behind the Wells Ranch. Henry Twisselman has been dead for several years, and so this report may be as close as anyone will ever get to an eyewitness report.

The Search Is Concluded

From listening to the recordings, it was possible to know quite a bit about the woman who conducted the interviews, but never did anyone address her by name. Eventually I knew enough that I could ask questions of people who might have known her in the years between 1990 and 1995. It was time to talk with Kathy again. While she knew nothing about the tapes, she might have known names of persons working for either The Nature Conservancy or the BLM during those years. Kathy suggested a "Nancy Warner" and another name that I no longer recall. Jackie recognized the names and had an email address for the second person who lived somewhere along the coast. All that Jackie knew about Nancy Warner was that she had been with The Nature Conservancy but had moved away from the Plains many years ago and even from Southern California.

Since Jackie had a contact for the second person, I made it my mission to locate Nancy Warner. Again the Internet was the place to look. I reasoned that Nancy Warner would be hard to locate so instead I searched the name "Steve Warner," presumably her husband. The name appeared with heading: "Steve Warner and the Rolling Coyote Band." Coyotes are one thing, but Rolling Coyotes are quite another. I was instructed on how buy their CD, but music was not my mission. I next searched Nancy Warner, and to my surprise, a dozen references appeared.

The sixth entry on the search page indicated that Nancy Warner was a historian living in Washington State. The entry led to a website which indicated that she was interested in local history and that she had lived in several different places around the West. She encouraged people with stories about their families in small rural areas to contact her and provided an email address. This was a real possibility, but there was no date on the website, and there was no assurance that the email address was still in service, much less that this was the person I was really hoping to reach. Of course I sent an email. I hoped to give this person a reason to respond, particularly if she was the voice on the tapes. I mentioned the project, the names of persons interviewed on the tapes, and my estimated dates for the interviews. I explained how I had come to hear the tapes and my interest in the histories. Had she lived at the Werling Ranch during this period? Had she been the person who conducted these interviews? Did she have more information about these persons and about the early years of the Plain? A reply came back, and I had, indeed, found the person I was seeking.

Nancy's husband is not Steve but rather Chuck Warner. He was one of the project directors for The Nature Conservancy at the time when they bought land in the Plains and turned it over to the Bureau of Land Management. Nancy had a contract to collect information and study the early plant habitat on the Plains, and after a year or two, she had written a report on what she had been able to find. She had given a copy of each tape to the Historical Society in San Luis Obispo and had also left copies with The Nature Conservancy. No transcripts had ever been made of these tapes. While there is no certainty, it is likely that the tapes had been left at the Werling Ranch which is still owned by The Nature Conservancy, and that someone, perhaps even Kathy Sharum, had found them and delivered them to the BLM archeologist responsible for the Carrizo Plain.

Preserving the Memories

When I inquired with the San Luis Obispo Historical Society, they could not locate tapes of these interviews. It is likely that the box which was handed to me held the only surviving copies. I hoped that these interviews could be archived along with the others that Jackie and I had collected, but for this to happen it is necessary to obtain written permission from everyone involved or with their direct heirs. Nancy has given this permission, but the other voices represented a problem.

Of the six recovered interviews, five were with persons having descendants still living near the Carrisa Plains, and several of these descendants were persons that Jackie and I had already interviewed. When contacted, these persons offered their permission. It was only Angus MacLean that presented a real challenge. He never married and had no children. His sister, Ione Bowman, has been dead for twenty years, and the name "Bowman" is sufficiently common that an online search is of no help. For that matter, if Ione had daughters, they very probably had different married names. They would have lived at a time when women did not keep their maiden name after marriage. With this realization, the matter of the tapes seemed to have reached an end.

I had always wondered why some people make a hobby of constructing family genealogies, but this experience suggested something of the challenge and satisfaction that may be involved. One clue led to another. And then there was a dead-end, except . . . another reading or another question would open another path and a new discovery. This process was repeated again and again as the picture of earlier times unfolded. The first homestead that I had found in the very center of the open plain had belonged to the Van Matre family. The search for this piece of history was to become the most challenging and also the most satisfying of them all.

CHAPTER SEVEN

Searching for Shadows

The Van Matre Homestead

Fog at Van Matre site

There is a picture on my computer screen that shows low morning sun breaking through a fog. The edges of the picture are dark, and the sky is hazy with faint colors and streaks of light in the clouds. Silhouettes of three wooden harvesters are visible, awkward, angulated, and only partly recognizable as the farm machinery that they are. Toward the right of the picture is the outline of a low building, once a homestead, with roof beams extending beyond the walls. On the ground to the side are hints of wood and several steel objects scattered about but not clearly visible. These are the physical remains from a dream. They speak of an earlier life in a harsh landscape. Their abandonment is part of the mystery.

Who lived here? How did they live? Where have they gone? This site was among the very first that captured me, and as it happened, the occupants here were among the very last to be found. Neighbors knew this as the Van Matre site. The Internet provided a brief history of the family, and a genealogy website listed some names but provided almost no help in locating living descendants. The few clues that initially appeared only deepened the mystery. I'll tell the story in the order that it was uncovered.

Road to the Van Matre Site

It was by accident that I first found the site while exploring dirt roads in the National Monument. The main road passing north and south through the Carrisa Plains is graded gravel. However, when you leave this to approach the Van Matre site, you travel along a dry, winding wash following two rutted tracks. Pieces of farm equipment appear in a field on the right. These are harrows, spring-toothed harrows, named for the rows of semicircular steel teeth that once tilled the ground. Farther along are two huge grain tanks, now collapsing behind a barbed wire enclosure. These sit on immense wooden beams, twelve inches by twelve inches and thirty feet long. Beside these tanks, I once found the remains of an auger that lifted grain from farm trucks and let it fall into the tanks. Beside the auger lay a junction with a moveable flap that could direct the grain either left or right into the intended tank. The auger was rusted and nearly hidden in the weeds.

At a further turn in the road is another collection from the past: a water tank, several crumbling concrete troughs, and most striking of all, a wooden tower twenty feet high with a ladder climbing up one side. Its appearance suggests a windmill, once used to pump water from a well. A short section of steel pipe lying on the ground between this tower and the nearby water tank supports this notion, and still another pipe below the tower going vertically into the ground provides additional evidence. Steel windmills with the large "AeroMotor" insignia did not appear till the 30s; if this was indeed a windmill, it was from early in the twentieth century. Thirty feet away from the tower is a rectangular concrete slab along with several large sheets of corrugated steel. A pipe going vertically downward through the concrete suggests a second well. The steel sheets would have been a shed to cover the well and shelter a mechanical pump. A corral and loading chute leave no doubt that this was all once part of a cattle operation. Half a mile farther south is the Van Matre homestead itself.

The first person who could speak directly about the Van Matre site was Alden Loucks, a neighbor during the years between 1941 and 1971. Alden was raised by his grandparents on the Traver Ranch a mile away to the west. He recalled that the Van Matre family had their principal lands at the north end of the Plains, north of Highway 58 and along Bitterwater Road. The site which I had found was never permanently occupied. It was a temporary camp used seasonally for planting and harvesting grain. Alden recalled that when it was time to work the nearby fields, the Van Matres brought their tractors south for as long as they were needed although the harvesters themselves remained year-round. The Traver family, like most others in that south part of the Plains, centered their marketing, schooling, and social life along Highway 166, in Cuyama, in Maricopa, and in Taft. The principal Van Matre home was to the north of the Simmler community, and as a consequence, Alden never knew them well.

Written Records of the Site

Six months after my first visit, I returned to the site and was struck by the changes that had occurred during the interval. Previously there had been a shed or perhaps a machine shop near the house and in poor condition. On the recent visit, I found a large part of this shed lying on the ground, and some of the steel siding had blown a distance away. When I reported these changes to Tammy Whitley, the BLM archeologist, she replied that the Monument was planning to stabilize some of the structures and that there was a chance that the site could be listed in the National Register of Historic Places. This had been suggested in a report prepared by a consulting firm (SWCA Environmental Consultants) in 2005, but the report also noted that it would be necessary to know more of the history of the site before this could be done.

Among other inventory items in the SWCA report was a truck body to be found fifty yards southeast from the house. By chance this truck also existed in a photo which I had taken two years after the report had been prepared. The vehicle was an ancient Ford, probably dating from the 40s, completely rusted and with the engine and wheels missing. In my photo the vehicle frame sits directly on the ground with no glass in the windows and a scatter of minor trash in the bed. In early 2009, with the SWCA report in hand, I went searching again. This truck should have been an easy find. I looked long and hard, but without a doubt it was gone. In one way or another, this may become the fate of much of the history of these earlier pioneers.

Of more significance, the report noted that one or two pieces of glass in a trash dump could be dated definitively to the 40s, and it further suggested that the house had been built in the 20s, although no basis for this statement was given. It definitely asserted that there had been two additions made to the original house structure. One is an enclosed porch that runs the full length of the east side. The other is a curious structure on the north side which stands a full three feet higher than the main house. No dates or further comments on these additions appeared in the SWCA report.

Interpreting the Relics

Even without written records or recorded conversations, the physical remains tell an interesting story. The taller addition has a nicely paneled interior and has corrugated steel siding on the outside. On the inner walls, green paint contrasts markedly with the bare wood and the rough boards elsewhere in the house. More curious yet is a particular panel on an outside wall of the addition that is entirely unlike its surroundings. This panel, one and a half feet high by four feet wide, is visible from inside with darker, unpainted boards filling in what had once been an opening in that wall. Outside an exactly corresponding section of the steel siding is hinged in a way that allows it to be raised to form an overhanging shelter. There are eyelets on both this outer hinged panel and the wall above it so that a cable can hold it in the open position. On the underside of this raised panel is the word "EXIT" scratched so that it would be most easily read from inside the building. Beside this word is an arrow pointing in the direction of the main house.

No one living in any house needs directions to find the door, and a raised shutter of this sort is entirely out of character with anything else present. It is impossible that this room was ever built as part of a residence. It had almost certainly been a public building which was moved and then added to the original house. It may have been one of the small post offices that once dotted rural California, or more probably it had come from the oil fields in Taft, possibly a paymaster's shack.

Another item of speculation arises from the absence of any visible water source at the homestead site. Water is a scarce resource throughout the Carrisa Plains, and out in the center of the valley, it is often too saline for drinking even when it can be found. The well north of the house must have been suitable only for cattle or otherwise the Van Matres would have built their house there. Surely they had been obliged to haul their drinking water from a more distant source . . . unless of course, I had missed something in my survey. To find the story of the site, its beginning and its end, I would have to find someone who had lived there. It was becoming impossible for me to evade the challenge.

Van Matre History on the Internet

In the age of the Internet, searching for someone is often straightforward, and this seemed an obvious place to begin. The Van Matre name, however, is a very common one in the Netherlands, and the number of immigrants from that country to the United States is far from trivial.

Even the spelling of the name is variable with Van Meter, Van Metre, and Van Matre all occurring. It was necessary to limit the Internet search to California or the Carrizo Plains, and even so, the search was difficult. Ultimately a website dealing with early history of San Luis Obispo County gave a two-page account of Isaac S. Van Matre, who had owned land at the north of the Carrisa Plains.

Isaac was born in Arkansas in 1844. With his father, he had moved to Texas and then in 1868 to California. They had settled briefly near San Diego before moving to Watsonville along the California coast. Isaac farmed at a number of locations in Central California, and although the report is rather confused, it was definite that Isaac owned 280 acres near Creston and a still larger area of land at the north end of the Carrisa Plains near Bitterwater Road.

Isaac Van Matre had five children, one girl and four boys. The Internet history indicated that Isaac and three of his sons, Jennings, Joe, and Henry, worked the original farm along Bitterwater Road, and they eventually worked 4000 acres farther south in the Carrisa Plains. The need for several harvesters at the Van Matre camp was apparent. The fourth of Isaac's sons was Leslie Leonidas, and he in turn had a son by the name of Vincent who became the family historian, compiled an extensive family tree, and entered it on a genealogy website.

Although it did not become apparent till later, it was Jennings, second son of Isaac and known to neighbors as "Jinx," who became the patriarch of the family on the Carrisa Plains. In 1917 he married Barbara Glenn in Atascadero. Jinx was then forty-one, and she was sixteen. Their children in order of birth were Ivy, Vernon, Maynard Duane, and then twin boys born in 1926. The twins were Ernest and Jennings Jr., known to everyone as "Junior." It seemed unlikely that any of these persons would still be alive, but Jackie and I still had hopes of locating one of Junior's four daughters. On the genealogy website they were listed only as "Living Van Matre #1, "Living Van Matre #2," etc. They had all married, but only the surnames of their husbands appeared. We needed more information if there was to be any chance of locating one.

The first of these daughters had marriages to men named "McCornack," "Thompson," and then still a third husband, although the order was not entirely clear. Correspondence on the website included a question from a Dianna Thompson asking, "Who are my ancestors?" Vincent replied that she was a Van Matre, and that Jennings Jr. was her grandfather. Both Vincent and Dianna had listed their email addresses. Yet when I attempted to contact them, one address was out of service and the other sent no reply. In hindsight, it is curious that Dianna's mother, first daughter of Junior, had never given her this information. It hardly needs be pointed out that the name Thompson is so common that a search through the Internet or through telephone White Pages would be nearly useless. There seemed to be no more clues to follow.

Neighbor Recollections of the Van Matre Family

Might current residents of the Carrisa who lived near the original Van Matre home on Bitterwater Road tell something of their story? This was a possibility that held promise. Jackie Czapla and I had been collecting oral histories from ranching and farming families for over a year, and so with no other sources of information, we re-interviewed several people to ask specifically about the Van Matre family. Chuck Kuhnle had lived at the north of the Plains since 1950, and he did have memories of his neighbors.

The principal Van Matre residence was only a short distance from the Kuhnle Ranch. Joe Van Matre, the brother of Jinx, apparently farmed 160 acres slightly north of the rest of his family. Very likely, this was the original homestead that had been granted to Isaac. Jinx, however, was the neighbor that Chuck Kuhnle knew best. Chuck recalled that Barbara, wife of Jinx, was particularly fond of the southern farm, and Chuck believed they referred to that house as the "Bayou." Barbara visited there as often as she could. Why it was called the Bayou was never known; neither Jinx nor Barbara had ever lived in Louisiana.

Knowing how dry the center plain is today, the farming practice which the Van Matre family followed, although unusual, was not entirely odd. Most ranchers in the Carrisa seeded their fields in November and December. This practice was intended to let the crop germinate with the rains which followed during winter months. Jinx did not plant by the calendar but instead waited till the first rains actually fell before putting in seed. This meant that his wheat was sometimes a month behind that of other ranchers, and he thereby took the risk that it would mature late and be burned out by the summer heat before a harvest could begin. Chuck Kuhnle acknowledged that the Van Matres sometimes lived on the edge of poverty.

Jinx and Barbara were something of an odd couple. He was tall and rather opinionated. Apparently he wrote a great many letters that were published in newspapers along the coast. Cloud seeding to produce rain was one of the devils that he fought. Although success was debatable, this practice was tried on the Plains for a short while during the 50s. Jinx maintained that cloud seeding brought rain in the north and west with the result that nothing fell on his land to the south. Barbara read a great deal, was frail in appearance, but was known to everyone as a strong lady and a hard worker.

Chuck related several other bits of information about the family. He confirmed what had been previously suspected, that drinking water had to be imported to the center farm. He recalled visiting the house there and having water dipped out of a huge crockery pot that was used for storage. Its inside surface was layered with green moss, but still this was what was used.

Chuck had only a few recollections of Jennings Jr., but he had distinct memories about Junior's brother, Vernon. "Bud," as this brother was more widely known, was a large man and very quiet. He was amiable and Chuck liked him. His house was across the road from where Chuck lived, and Bud could often be seen sitting in the front yard of the house. Chuck also remembered an incident that had occurred one night on the southern ranch. There had been an intense fog that confounded nearly everything, and a hired man was left working the fields there at night. Bud had become concerned about this hand and drove his pickup down to see if everything was all right. In the dark and the fog, Bud drove through the fields. The search ended with a head-on collision between the truck and the tractor that the hired hand was driving. Neither had seen the other early enough to stop the accident. The truck was totaled.

Nola and Darrell Twisselman were also neighbors of the Van Matres along Bitterwater Road, and they also shared memories of the family. Because Jinx was considerably older, Darrell credits the survival of the farm to his wife Barbara. She was a small woman, and by all accounts she was a force to be reckoned with. Their pickup truck had no jack, and so when flat tires occurred, there had to be another plan to swap out the wheels. Darrell recalled that Barbara carried a couple of cement blocks and a long plank in the truck. Using the blocks as a fulcrum, she would lever the truck off the ground with the board and change tires that way.

Darrell and Nola also spoke about Bud Van Matre in the yard of his house. He was extraordinarily fond of irises and planted bulbs around the house by the hundreds or even thousands. Bud went from one passion to another, and at one time he became involved in building a section of fence near his house. For months he worked on an elaborate and formidable fence. Then he took up still another project before eventually returning to his garden.

The Traver family lived a mile west of the Van Matre camp in the center plain. Although Lew and Nancy Traver had passed away some years ago, Jackie and I were able to interview two of their grandchildren. When I asked Alden if the Van Matre camp had been worked by hired hands, he insisted that most of the work was done by Barbara and Jinx themselves. During harvest season, the sons would help. Alden recollected that Jinx was lanky and severe in appearance. Alden was reminded of the Grant Wood painting called "American Gothic" in which the farmer stands rigidly with a pitchfork held vertically by his side. Karen is a younger cousin of Alden, and she remembered the Van Matres at a later time. As a child, she and Barbara used to walk the fields together, and Karen recalls Barbara finding an arrow point and giving it to her. When Karen met Jinx, it was at the northern homestead site, and she recalled that Jinx had skin cancer and his face was somewhat disfigured. Karen believed that after Jinx died, Barbara lived for a while at the Bayou, although it had deteriorated significantly by that time. An interview with still another neighbor suggested that Junior, fourth son of Jinx and Barbara, drank heavily at some time in his life. All the accounts depended upon memories from the distant past. The memories were sometimes inconsistent and of uncertain reliability.

The Eldest Daughter, Jeanette

Throughout the time that Jackie and I were collecting histories from the Plains, I also continued to volunteer with projects on the Monument, and in the process, I often talked with Doug Wreden. By chance I mentioned how difficult it had been to locate any member of the Van Matre family. To my surprise, Doug said that he had known both Junior and also Junior's first daughter (who I later learned was named Jeanette). She had married one of Doug's friends, Andy McCornack. Although he could not be sure of the details, Doug thought that Junior's daughter had been previously married. After their separation, this husband, if indeed he was that, spent some time in prison. Doug recalled getting a phone call in the middle of the night from Andy asking for help. This first partner had been released from prison and was on his way to reclaim his "wife" and to take revenge on Andy. Would Doug bring a gun and come to help? Of course the sensible answer to this question was "no," but Doug did call the Sheriff, and the showdown was prevented. For some time, the young wife took care of her much older husband, Andy, until he died. Doug was certain that this woman was still alive, but no matter how he tried he could not remember her first name. A search using only the name Thompson, or the other suggested married names, would be hopeless, and even less was known about Junior's other three daughters. The only help Doug could offer was the name Pat McCornack, Andy's son from an earlier marriage. Beyond the fact that he lived in Taft, Doug had no current information for Pat.

In the course of conducting oral history interviews, I later met Eric Stewart, and his stories about herding sheep on the Carrisa have already been related. It was Eric who provided me with Pat's phone number and encouraged me to make a call. The conversation with Pat was delightful. Pat's stepmother, Junior's first daughter, was Jeanette, and she lived in Fresno. He did not know her married name. Her sisters were Cynthia, Charlotte, and Roberta. Pat knew nothing about Roberta, but Charlotte lived somewhere on the coast near Paso Robles, and Cynthia was married and was postmistress in Shandon. With this information, the Internet search resumed.

The genealogy website indicated married surnames of the four daughters, although there was no way to associate a particular name with a particular daughter. Another interview, conducted some time before all this, had suggested that Charlotte worked at the Walmart in Paso Robles. The interviewee added that Charlotte was a rather private person and would very likely decline to speak with us. With some guesswork, I located Charlotte in the telephone White Pages, but the likelihood of meeting her seemed vanishingly small. Nothing whatsoever could be found of a Roberta in California or any of the nearby states.

Making a guess as to Jeanette's married name, I located an address and phone number for her. I would either have to make an unsolicited call or else give up the search. I dialed the number. When a voice answered, I introduced myself and said, "I am hoping to reach Jeanette Van Matre. The subject is history on the Carrisa Plains." There was not an instant of pause, not a word was spoken, and the phone was hung up. In retrospect, I should not have been surprised. Given what I already knew, an unannounced call from a male voice using her childhood name might have been threatening. Although it was history of the homestead site that I was seeking and not family gossip, she could hardly be faulted for wondering why a total stranger had called.

An End to the Search

The last opportunity to find a living Van Matre who had grown up on the Carrisa Plains would be Cynthia who was the postmistress in nearby Shandon. Her name as well as her husband's were available in the White Pages, but the phone had been disconnected. A visit to the Shandon post office would be my only chance to find her. I introduced myself at the counter of the post office and asked if Cynthia was present or still worked there. It was a younger woman who I spoke with, and she replied that Cynthia had moved away several years previously. She had apparently left California, and there was no forwarding address. I relayed this disappointment to Jackie Czapla, and she in turn indicated that Cynthia and her husband had been divorced. It was, she said, a very unpleasant parting, and there were bitter feelings in the family. My last attempt to reach one of the four sisters was to send a fairly lengthy letter to Charlotte explaining my purpose and asking if I might contact her about a possible interview. As I had anticipated, there was no response.

The trail had come to an end, and I had to believe that the story of these lives in the Carrisa would never be fully known. I could only imagine when the family had left and the circumstances of their last years. I inferred that it was probably not a happy story, but then again it may have been a relief to the four children when they moved away. Entirely by accident, I was looking one day at my Internet browser and came across the genealogy website that had initiated the first search. For no particular reason, I checked and found a new communication posted by Dianna Thompson Van Matre. It was dated October 16, 2010, and read:

> Hello all. I just wanted to tell anyone who might look for him that my grandfather Jennings Van Matre [Junior] passed away on Saturday October 9th, 2010. He was well into his nineties and is survived by four living daughters and their children from his first marriage to Geneva Rasmussen. He passed away in Dorris, California, and his ashes have been spread over the Carrisa Plains where he was born. My memories of you will always be fond ones.

I could see no contact information with this posting, and given my previous failures to reach Dianna Thompson, the trail had surely come to an end. While this message was not what I had expected to find, the story had come full circle and finished in the Carrisa Plains. I looked again at my pictures of the house, the machinery, and the outbuildings, but it was their setting which was most impressive. In late summer and autumn, the ground is scorched and nearly bare. Wisps of grass are scattered at intervals; dust rises along a road a mile away; the nearby Temblor Range is dry and brown with gray-green saltbrush in the canyons. It will be hot, over 100 degrees. It is impossible that anything could grow here, much less could there ever be a crop that would support a family. And yet there is a house, a shed that is still standing, and the remains of a collapsing machine shed. Why here? This is open sky country, and in a huge, stark way, it is beautiful. The sunrise and sunset are immense. On dark nights, the stars are everywhere. They are a veil that seems to cover everything and turn the ground white. On clear nights, a rising moon seems to fill the entire eastern sky. When long clouds stretch across the horizon, the moon peeks through, and on the cold winter nights, a halo of weak color surrounds the lunar glow. Jennings Jr. had finally returned to this lonely place. It was unlikely that I would ever know more than this.

CHAPTER EIGHT

Interlude

Reflections about what has been found and where the story goes

Let's reflect for a moment on the ground we have covered so far. I feel compelled to reflect with you because the remaining chapters will be slightly different. When Jackie and I started collecting oral histories, we set out to document how the people had sustained themselves. The land was dry and survival could not have been easy. We asked about how the families had arrived, what led to their departure, and what they had felt about leaving. The relics in the fields and the falling homesteads had led me to expect dramatic stories of a harsh pioneer life. The distance between ranches had spoken to me of lonely struggles. Some of these expectations had been borne out, but there had also been surprises for me.

Peter McCart left his homestead during the dry years of 1898-99, and indeed his closest neighbors were many miles away. The death of his wife, Mary Jane Ballantine, could only have compounded the loneliness. Edmund Morris's family lived through the same dry years. The stories of the death of his wife Mary in 1896 also speak of hard times and a precarious existence. Due to the difficulties, Edmund sold the homestead after her passing and moved with his son to Washington State. Later, the two later returned to the California coast. Mary Morris's hilltop gravesite is largely impressive for its setting – even today there is only one nearby road, and dry grass and brown hills are a dominating presence. Less is known about the early Dutch community to the north of Highway 58 or the German settlers near the Temblor Mountains. That there were no remaining traces of this latter group except for empty cisterns in grain fields has to engage the imagination.

The stories of later years were different, and for me, unexpected. Between 1940 and 1970, grain farming was very successful, farms were large, and families were close. While cattle ranching was not especially profitable, it was sustainable, and in later years, the 70s and beyond, it was carried out in a very businesslike fashion. While most sheepmen were not part of the social life of the Plains, they were nevertheless a part of its economic life – again in the latter twentieth century. During the prosperous years, there was a strong community at Simmler. The decline in this community came for more prosaic reasons than I had initially imagined. There was no overwhelming drought and no Dust Bowl; there were no robber barons and no mercenary railroads. Even the Great Depression had only an indirect effect on the Carrisa Plains. Instead, issues included the rising prices of machinery and diesel fuel, and improvements in transportation leading to competition from other agricultural areas. Opportunities for easier lives in town drew children away.

As I listened to the stories, there were other surprises for me. People spoke of hard work and sometimes of disappointment, but the word "hardship" never appeared. The difficulties which they had were most often taken as a matter of course. Al Wilkinson, a cowboy who worked briefly on the La Panza Ranch, put it this way: "We didn't know no better, and everything worked fine. We were poor. Everybody was poor. We figured no problem." I was also impressed that very few persons spoke of being lonely. Some of this will appear later, but in the mid-century years people spoke about school activities, about dances, about helping neighbors, and about family and hired hands. The small incidents of their daily lives and the personalities who lived on the ranches and farms were more significant than the difficulties.

I could easily identify with Greg Beck as he recalled his hours driving tractor in the field. The stories that Doug Wreden told of his hired help on the Pinole Ranch were delightful, but Doug himself had became a principal character in my story of the Plains. I had found Don Messer to be a charismatic person, both in his kitchen as Jackie and I spoke with him, but also when he told stories of the Buckhorn Ranch – rattlesnakes and skunks, chasing rogue cattle in the canyons, and finally giving up ranch life to earn a living in town. Even people that I had not met, the Van Matres, became real personalities as I searched for their stories and listened to their neighbors. With all due respect to John Wayne and Gary Cooper, the daily lives of real people are often larger than the images of western movie heroes.

The nature of the interviews was changing, and that is reflected in the chapters ahead. Details of dates, land ownership, and precise genealogies had never been central in the search, and as the project continued, interviews became less and less formal. They became conversations about family, about locations of springs, about incidents recalled from childhood, and about the changes which they had seen during their lifetimes. There were at least half a dozen persons that I came to know well and admire. Some important characters in this book are no longer living but were large in the memories of their children. Others were people Jackie and I met and with whom we spoke. You will meet a number of these persons in the chapters that follow. These personal stories give a feeling for time and place that seldom appears in formal history books.

There is one last observation that should be made. A change also had occurred in the process by which people and stories were found. The first interviews had been largely with residents still living at the north end of the Plains. Many of these persons were already listed in Jackie's telephone file. After these persons had been interviewed, it became necessary to search further. In particular, those persons who had sold land to either The Nature Conservancy or to the federal government had moved away. Finding them became a matter of asking for names and for suggestions. It was a mercy that my telephone contract was the one-price-for-everything kind. Less happily it was necessary to pay for gasoline by the mile. I travelled throughout Central and even Northern California, and ultimately some of the most rewarding conversations took place in Oregon, Nevada, and even Wyoming. My own family history has never been recorded and has become irretrievable. In some sense, I was looking to find roots of my own. The stories of childhood games, summers exploring outdoors, and even high school years resonated with my own memories. I was being drawn more and more into the past and into world of the Carrisa Plains.

CHAPTER NINE

The Simmler Community

Isolated but not lonely, bonds between people

At the Farm Bureau, 1950

The community where Highway 58 meets Soda Lake Road at the north end of the Carrisa Plains was once known as Simmler. Today there is little more to see beyond a few decaying farm buildings, a small highway department shed, and an unidentified building with closed shutters and a yard filled with weeds. Cars drive through this intersection at reckless speeds, and I had often thought that lives here must have been lonely. I was to learn that my concerns were unfounded: this had once been the center of a vibrant community.

Jackie already knew some of the families at the north end of the Plains. She belonged to a small congregation that held Sunday services nearby, she attended a local craft fair where neighbors sold projects to be given as Christmas presents, and she sometimes participated in brandings held by one of the nearby ranchers. In our interviews with older residents, we regularly asked about traditions in the earlier Simmler community. At one time, women's groups brought guest speakers from the coast and held sewing events. Men gathered at meetings of the local Farm Bureau. Community card tournaments were sponsored in the winter, dances were held all through the year, and the summers were initiated with a June barbecue. The stories we heard were warm – about neighbors and people rather than about the circumstances of survival. As noted in the last chapter "Interlude," the people that we met, either directly or by report, were becoming the focus of our interviews.

Dances

When early residents were asked about social activities on the Plains, among the first things mentioned were the dances. These were organized by the Farm Bureau in the shuttered building which also served as the elementary school. From the 40s onward, these dances were regular events. One person recalled:

> Somebody would decide at a Farm Bureau meeting, "It's time for a dance." Then a committee would be appointed, a dance committee, and they'd be responsible for getting the music and taking the tabs and the clean-up committee. The orchestra, we'd get one sometimes, typically three piece, piano and maybe a guitar, horn, sometimes a violin . . . We got them out of Paso Robles, McKittrick, Taft.

Neighbors came from miles around, and entire families arrived together. Older children would dance, and the younger ones would run through the hall or play outside. One person recalled that the dance floor was waxed and polished so smoothly that during breaks in the music children would run and then throw themselves on the floor to see how far they could slide. When the evening became late, younger children were put to sleep on blankets in the cloakroom.

The dances went on into the night. Sometime near midnight, the band would take a long break, and the building would empty out. The entire collection of children, adults, and grandparents would drive or ride to a nearby ranch for a dinner that had been organized by the women of the community. After dinner, the dance resumed and continued till 2 AM. This completed the contract with the band, but it was normal then to pass a hat and collect money so the band would continue on for several hours more. People returned home by car, by horse, or by buggy before dawn. They had to be tired, and a number were certainly hung over, but without exception people spoke of going to work or to church the next day on their regular schedule.

A few parents did not bring children to the dances. Greg McMillan, one of the children of Eben McMillan who has already been mentioned, did not attend until he was himself in high school. He assumed this was because his parents did not want him present with the drinking that went on. At some dances people would bring their bottles and leave them marked on a table at the back of the dance room. At all the dances the parking area was a favorite stop. Mostly young men would leave the dance for short periods to visit the trunk of their car outside. This was apparently normal, and the celebrations were not necessarily subdued, but no one ever spoke of accidents or serious trouble either.

Doug Wreden talked about one of these dances that occurred when he was of college age or slightly older. He and Greg McMillan decided that the dance would benefit from a particularly potent tropical punch. It was a magnificent creation with gin, vodka, apple juice, orange juice, and a number of other ingredients all mixed in a twenty gallon washtub. The quantities even required a paddle for stirring. While this was being done, and at the last minute before guests arrived, an older friend, Chuck Kuhnle, joined the two young men and asked, "Have you got citrus stuff in there?" Doug admitted that they had, and Chuck informed them, "You know that will react with that galvanized tub, make everybody sick?" Doug groaned, "Oh, my God. We've got to dump this out?" Doug's story continued: "So we carried it out and dumped the whole thing. But we danced all night, and we just got home about four in the morning. We'd had breakfast down there. We went back to Pinole and just got in bed."

Thirty years later, Doug still sighed as he told about abandoning the plan and pouring everything out on the ground. It all sounded very contemporary to me.

Farm Bureau

A number of other activities were sponsored by the Farm Bureau. Agricultural consultants visited the community to talk about new strains of wheat, about marketing methods, about pesticides or weed control measures, or about alternate crops that might be tried. These were county agricultural agents, or they were instructors from Cal Poly College in San Luis Obispo. A women's group also brought speakers to regular meetings, and these included instruction in sewing, quilting, cooking, or nutrition. Some women held regular sewing or quilting groups at their homes during the year as well. For women, the work on farms was seven days a week and often twelve hours a day. Families were fed, clothes were mended, gardens needed tending, and often small farm chores were a part of their work as well. With some farms separated from each other by miles, taking part in the women's group meetings must have been important for many farm wives.

The Farm Bureau also sponsored Pedro tournaments during the winter months. Pedro is a card game played by four persons and involves bidding and taking tricks. It was popular in the 50s and 60s, and the tournaments continued for some time beyond those years as well. Today older resident on the Plains still gather to play with friends, usually the same friends that they played with many years ago. One of the ladies that Jackie and I interviewed was somewhat proud that she usually won these matches. Her older sister suggested that the victories were not always honorable. The two laughed as they recalled those evenings.

Every year, there is a Pioneer Days celebration in Paso Robles with a parade, picnic, and other events. It was assured that the Carrisa community would sponsor a float in the parade and then picnic together in the afternoon. One year the float had the theme "Saturday Night on the Plains," and featured one of the well-known ranchers in a bathtub aboard the float – not exactly the New Year's Rose Parade, but a home-grown community effort.

At the Simmler School

The Simmler School was another of the bonding institutions for the community. It went well beyond education for the children. The regular events included a Christmas program, drama productions, and graduation. During the 50s and 60s, there might be only twelve children in the school's single classroom. The grade levels went from first through eighth, so it was not unusual for a graduating class to have only one or two students. Still, it was a big event. The entire school participated in the ceremonies, and the entire community attended whether they had a graduating student or not. And it was the same with drama productions and with the Christmas program. Everyone participated; there were parts for all ages.

Attendance at these events should not be a surprise. If Nola and Darrell Twisselman had a daughter in the school, then all of Darrell's six brothers and sisters were present with their children, cousins of the graduate. Nola's mother, Babe King, had three siblings living near the school, and Nola's father was Rowland Cooper with two brothers living no farther than two miles from the school. All these siblings, of course, had families with children of their own. When you realize that there are twelve children in the school, and each of them comes from extended families of this sort, it takes no more explanation to realize that the Christmas program, the Halloween party, and the spring drama production filled the auditorium. The bleachers had been built by one of the parents; the refreshments were supplied by a mothers committee; the garden at the school had been planted and tended by a farmer who lived nearby; and repairs to the building itself . . . details may be complicated but the picture is clear.

Greg Beck spoke about the Halloween party at the school. It was not just for the children but for everyone. All ages came in costumes, and there were prizes for the most imaginative, scariest, best mask, and on and on. Refreshments were essential. Often someone would come to the party and for the entire night no one would know who it was. The costume was complete, and the mystery guest did not speak. *Who was the ghost? Did anyone see him come in a truck? He, or perhaps she, was too big to be one of the children. His shoes look like a man's, but had they been borrowed?* Greg did this one year, but said that since he couldn't talk without giving himself away, it wasn't as much fun as he expected. It was really a game for the children.

Not all entertainments were formally organized of course. Besides the party at the school, Halloween pranks were a part of the autumn season on the Plains. More than one car had been dismantled and then rebuilt on top of a neighbor's grain tank. When Jackie and I asked Greg Beck if he had participated in pranks with his neighbors, he denied it but acknowledged that he had been accused of these on at least one occasion. One morning shortly after Halloween, a neighbor from the Twisselman family came to the Beck farm to see if a missing truck was there. Greg and his brother Steve had often joked with their neighbors, and it had been assumed that of course the truck had been their piece of mischief. The truck was not present, and the neighbor concluded that it had been hidden too carefully for him to find. Several days later, the missing vehicle was found miles away. The steering wheel was missing, and apparently it had been the object of a serious theft. Young men in those days were not so different from young men today.

Volunteer Fire Department

The Volunteer Fire Department was still another bonding institution for the Simmler community. It was under the direction of the CDF, which manages fire fighting in rural areas. The initials stand for Califor-

nia Department of Forestry, but in fact the CDF is a statewide fire fighting organization and is hardly involved in forestry at all. During the 50s,
the CDF stationed someone at Simmler during fire season only. This
changed after 1964 when a huge ranch south of Highway 58 was divided
into two-and-a-half acre lots. This development is now called California
Valley, and it sits between the present Monument on the south and the
Simmler community on the north. To help sales, the developers agreed
to build a fire station if CDF would assign someone with an engine all
year-round. Later volunteers were recruited to allow more persons to
respond to fires and to reduce expenses for the CDF. Initially the Volunteer Fire Department was an experiment as it was uncertain if enough
volunteers would be willing to take the required training.

Greg Beck joined the department when he realized that he had been
helping at fires for years anyway, and that it would be better if he knew
how to do more than drive a tractor or use a gunny sack and shovel.
Greg spoke about this at length.

> I don't know when the rest of the people started meeting, but I remember
> coming on in 1974. Somebody had just resigned or quit or something, so
> there was a vacancy, and I was immediately put on active duty. At that time
> you needed about sixteen hours of safety training.
>
> Originally it was basically a sixteen-hour course, but it kind of changed
> over the years. Back when I started, you were voted on, and then they gave
> you your safety gear, and you were partnered with somebody to keep an eye
> on you if something happened. And you were given a basic first-aid class
> and a little bit of safety training and stuff like that. When I resigned, or
> retired, it had become almost a professional type of fire department. I mean
> it was almost ridiculous. You couldn't call it volunteer anymore.
>
> One of the things we did one time was that they were going to get us
> a new fire engine, but we had to build a garage in order to get it. So we ex-
> panded on the old garage. We pushed it out and made it bigger so we could
> get the new fire engine in there, and that was done on community time and
> labor. Collected money and did fund-raisers and did that.

In the 70s and 80s, even as today, the greater responsibility of the fire department was medical. Fires might be more interesting to some, but more commonly calls were for automobile accidents or for home emergencies and heart attacks. Greg commented that the VFD, volunteer fire department, was seldom called for farm or ranch accidents. If there were such an emergency, the ranchers would put the injured person in a truck and leave for town immediately. Farmers were inherently self-reliant, and furthermore there would have been a significant wait for an ambulance to come out to the Plains. It would simply take the person to the same town where the ranchers were already headed.

Serving with the fire department in one's own community had several unique aspects. When Greg first joined the department, fires in fields were managed in the traditional way: a disk was attached to a tractor which circled the fire and cleared a firebreak. This changed after the federal government purchased conservation lands that eventually became the Carrizo Plains National Monument. On these lands, the damage done to species by mechanized fire suppression was weighed against the damage done by the fire itself. The new protocol would more commonly let the fire burn up to an existing road and then stop it there. A different challenge sometimes arose in giving medical aid to neighbors. Greg said his greatest fear was that he would be called to a house where someone he knew was dying and that he would have to give CPR without success. This had happened to him more than once.

The volunteer fire fighters were sometimes called to accidents along Highway 58 where it passed through the Temblor Mountains or across the Carrisa Plains. Many of these occurred when people drove too fast or under the influence. The highway also produced at least one strange incident that Greg described:

> I went to a wreck up on the . . . well actually we went to a grass fire in the Temblors one time. We got there and found out it had been started because somebody had lit a car on fire and shoved it over the side, and then we found a body inside. We found out later it had been shot in the head so . . .
>
> It was beyond the Kern County line, so it was not the responsibility of our group. But then Kern County decided, well maybe it was in San Luis

[Obispo] County because there's a portion of the Temblors where it jogs back in. It was in San Luis County after all, but San Luis [Obispo] County wasn't going to take the body back until they did a complete autopsy – which is when they found the bullet. Then it became a murder, and I got to testify in a trial because I happened to be the one that went down to check out the car to see if there's anybody in it, and there was.

I honestly can't remember whether I was surprised or not. I think we knew whose car it was, and he'd been missing for a day or two. I honestly can't remember the details now. He was in there. And they tried to burn the evidence is what the deal was, but they did a botched job.

Accidents and Illness

In nearly all the interviews that Jackie and I conducted, we asked about matters of health. On farms where heavy machinery was used under difficult conditions, accidents might be anticipated, and with medical facilities both limited and distant, minor illnesses might become serious. The way in which people dealt with these possibilities tells something significant about their lives.

While some serious accidents did occur, nearly everyone denied that they were common. It is possible that growing up as they did, people were instinctively aware of the hazards, and children working with their parents learned to be careful at an early age. Several persons explained that their father had taught them safety with guns while they were young and expected them to be absolutely responsible. Another person mentioned that his father was very careful to instruct and supervise the high school fellows who came out to work harvest in the summer. But accidents occurred, and one of the more frightening stories that we heard from several people involved the young daughter of a hired hand on the Cooper farm in the mid-60s.

To lift grain to the top of a tank, devices called augers were often used. These have a worm drive, similar to a meat grinder, that pushes the grain up through a long tube. Trucks would unload into a hopper at ground level, and as the hopper was emptied by the auger, the pattern on the surface of the grain must have been fascinating. The child reached into the wheat, and her hand was caught and mangled. She was taken to the hospital by helicopter, but for less serious problems that could still not be treated at home a long car ride to town was the norm.

In 1946 the Saucito Ranch was purchased by Jean Edgar. He had been a practicing veterinarian in Bakersfield during World War II, and with other veterinarians off serving with the military, his large animal practice had become huge and demanding. When the war ended, he brought his family out to the Carrisa Plains looking for gentler life as a rancher. Gail Edgar, his son, recalled several incidents:

> When something came up, it was a trip to Bakersfield. We used to do some pole vaulting at recess in school across a barbecue pit that was dug in the ground. I slipped off of it and came down, and there was a board underneath the leaves with a nail in it, and I pushed it right through my hand here. So somehow or other the school got word back to my dad, and he came and got me and took me into Bakersfield, and the family doctor took care of it. Then one year we were bringing the harvester out from the barn, getting ready for harvest. My brother was four or five years old and was playing with the header wheel. He got his finger caught, and it pulled the fingernail off his little finger. So off they went to Bakersfield. Those were the only two times except for Dad's . . . oh, wait, Mom did have a sciatic nerve problem, and Dad took her to Paso Robles for that, and she stayed in the hospital there for several days, and I would come . . . I would get the bus from Atascadero, where I was in high school, and come down to visit her when she was in the hospital. But those are the only things that I can recall right now that called for medical care that we couldn't do for ourselves.

Gail's assertion that medical problems seldom occurred may have been understated. He told of another incident that occurred in the early years at the Saucito.

> When we moved out there, the word got around that the veterinarian [Gail's father] had bought the Saucito. There was a sheep farmer, Italian guy named Galainena, over on the Temblor Range I believe is where his

headquarters were. And he would bring his sheep over to [the] Carrisa Plains in the early spring when the filaree was really high, and they could graze there down by Soda Lake. There's a little pyramid-shaped hill, and right at the base of that hill was Galainena's camp. It was abandoned during the summer, but when the sheep were out there, they lived at that camp. Anyway, Galainena's sheep were dropping dead, and he knew a veterinarian had come out here, so he came up to our ranch and asked Dad if he'd come have a look and see what's going on. Dad had not brought any veterinarian equipment with him, but he said he'd go down and have a look. And so he posted one of the sheep to send to Oregon or Bakersfield, and Dad didn't even have gloves to wear or anything. The sheep had anthrax, and Dad had a scratch on his arm, on his knuckle here on his hand, and by golly, he got anthrax. This was like 47, right after we moved out there. The family doctor was in Bakersfield, and they saw this big carbuncle, and that guy lanced it, which he shouldn't have done. Dad wound up in the Kern general hospital in isolation, and they didn't know what to do for him. It was just progressing. But Dad had a close friend, state veterinarian that we all knew, so Mom got on the phone and called Ruzy, whatever his name was, and told him what was going on. He said, "I'll take care of it," and he said, "I'm coming down right now." So he came in, came to the health department in Bakersfield, said, "You got a Dr. Jean R. Edgar in here with anthrax?" "Yes." "You got to get him penicillin and lots of it." And you see, penicillin came of its own in World War II as an antibiotic. It had not been used yet to the point that all the bugs had become immune to it. And so that cured Dad. But he was in the hospital for quite a while, and they gave him huge doses of it day and night. And that's what Ruzy told them to do, and that's how they cured him.

In 1952 the Edgar family moved back to Bakersfield, and the Saucito Ranch was sold to Gene and Joyce Bingeman. These were the last of the owners who lived on this ranch before it was sold to the Oppenheimer Corporation. Joyce spoke at some length about their time growing wheat and raising cattle. She also spoke of two serious medical incidents which occurred.

Among the employees working for the Bingemans was an older

Mexican fellow who had been with them for many years. He was driving one of the tractors, and somehow one leg was pinned between caterpillar treads and the body of the tractor. The machine went into a
ditch, it stalled, and Ruiz was trapped. Gene noticed that the tractor had
stopped at an odd angle and went to investigate. He managed to get Ruiz
loose and into his pickup truck. Joyce said that when her husband came
into the house, his face was even whiter than Ruiz's. The leg had been
chewed to the bone, and Gene was nearly ready to pass out just looking
at it. They wrapped the leg in towels, put Ruiz in the pickup, and left for
the hospital in San Luis Obispo. After a lengthy stay, Ruiz came back to
the ranch and was able to work again. "Tough as nails" was the description that Joyce gave.

This emergency had a rather nice side story, and it was not uncommon to hear of similar incidents. While Ruiz was in the hospital, the
Bingeman's oldest daughter Leah became ill with a bad flu and also had
to go to the hospital in San Luis Obispo. By this time, Ruiz was on
crutches. Joyce spoke about the pair in the hospital:

> And he just knew that the nurses weren't going to take care of my little . . .
> she was about four or five at that point, and he'd get these crutches and
> sneak down to the little room where my daughter was so she wouldn't cry
> and be scared because I couldn't be there with her all the time. I had a baby
> at home and men to cook for. And the nurses would catch him in there with
> his crutches and [say,] "You're not supposed to be this far from your bed."
> But he was a good old guy.

The hired men at the Bingeman ranch were really part of the family.

The other major accident which Joyce related involved Gene Bingeman himself. This was a three vehicle accident in 1951 before the family
had purchased the Saucito. Medicine being what it was in those days,
Gene was in traction in the hospital a full six months. In bed, he couldn't
sit up or even turn over. Gene and Joyce had been married for a little less
than a year. They were living on the American Ranch where Gene had
been working as manager. The work crew was a rough lot, and not want-
ing to stay alone with them at the ranch, Joyce moved to town where

she got a job with the telephone company. Eventually when traction was no longer necessary, Gene was put in a body cast. After two or three months, he could use crutches and then eventually a cane. As soon as he was released from the hospital, Gene was back on the ranch. While he could not do field work himself, he was able to resume the job of directing operations there. Ruiz was not the only tough survivor on the Carrisa Plains.

Lottie King

In earlier years, during the 20s and 30s, many of the medical problems on the Plains were managed by Aunt Lottie. She was a nurse, trained in Winnipeg, Canada. When a relative who lived in Shandon became ill, she moved west to care for him. In town she met Walter King, married him, and subsequently moved to the King Ranch at Simmler. In time she became an institution in the community. She won prizes at the county fair for pies and preserves, she made the cakes for weddings, and she was a friend to brides who were newly arrived from the coastal cities. If there was a single person who represented the strength of the community, it was Aunt Lottie.

I had the good fortune to speak with Lottie's son, John Barry King, and Lottie's granddaughter, Sandy Rowlett.

John: She was almost a county doctor. When you heard somebody at three o'clock in the morning coming, or twelve o'clock coming down the driveway, you knew somebody had died or was injured or something. She took care of everybody. She actually had . . . never knew where it was . . . but she had a stash of, I think probably morphine and a few other things that she'd give them to get them to town. And it was stashed somewhere, but we never knew where.

Sandy: All she had to do was call the doctor and say this is what the situation is . . .

John: And he'd say okay. It was Doctor French in San Luis.

Not all off Lottie's prescribed treatments would pass medical muster today. One of these was a dark brown liquid known as "husk." No one could tell just what it was, although one person believed that it was some kind of commercial product. It was used for cuts, scrapes, and minor wounds. Lottie's niece, Elinore Diefenderfer, recalled another tenet of Lottie's practice: "Put it on, wrap it up, and you're cured." Elinore attended the Simmler grammar school around 1930 and spoke of an incident which occurred there:

> I fell off the bars and broke my arm at school. One of the ranchers took me up to my grandmother's who didn't know how to drive a car. Grandpa wasn't there, and the working man was out in the field. My grandmother was about this big, and she goes running out there and gets him. He takes the pickup and drives me over to Aunt Lottie's. She puts me in a cast, and I went back to school.

Some problems were more difficult to manage. In one of the interviews recorded by Nancy Warner in 1990, Ernie Garcia told of an incident from his childhood. As he described the occasion:

> I remember that I got a toe split from there to there and all the way to the bone. My uncle was driving a wagon, and we had hay over there, and I guess we was going to put it up or something, so he was pulling this big header bit behind the wagon, and we kids jumped off and was playing on the tongues. I rolled off the tongue and as the wagon went over me, he run over my foot right there. Boy, it was just laid wide open right to the bone. I couldn't go to school for quite a while. I didn't even get to the doctor. Mrs. King, the Kings, they lived across the road there. And my mother, she didn't have time hardly to doctor me, so that little gal Lottie, she was always coming down helping my mother doctor me up.

There were, of course, situations for which no help was sufficient. Elinore spoke of one of these:

Aunt Lottie never lost one patient until my dad's sister. Lottie got her clear to Santa Margarita, and she died of a heart attack. And Doctor French, he kept her cabinet full of medical things, and he told her, "Don't feel bad about it, Lottie. She could have been on the operating table, and I couldn't have saved her."

One of Lottie's passions was cooking. There were the everyday meals to prepare for the family, and there were the bigger meals to make for the crews that worked harvests in the fall, but these were only the beginning. Sandy recalled spending days helping her grandmother prepare for the county fair. Lottie would enter every category that was offered: canned goods, pickles, chutney, jam, jellies, cakes, pies. Sandy spent days helping in the kitchen and then wrapping everything in cellophane to take to town. Prizes for food at the county fair were one hundred pound bags of sugar. Lottie won nearly three of these every year. This was during World War II, and with sugar rationed during those years, these prizes were wonderful gifts.

Lottie's kitchen had a large baking cupboard with a porcelain shelf where she would roll out pies and breads. She made wedding cakes for neighbors and for friends living in San Luis Obispo. It was too hot to bake during the day, so this was usually done at night. Then she and her son John would put a shelf in the back of their pickup truck and put the layers out on these for the trip to town. There she would assemble the cake and frost it the next day. She baked for neighbors for no reason other than to be a neighbor. Sandy recalled going with her grandmother to make deliveries to an aunt in Santa Margarita and to someone else in Shandon.

Lottie and her husband did not have a great deal of money, but still she was a caregiver for her family and neighbors. Jan Cooper arrived on the Plains as a new bride from the city and was initially alone for much of her time. She recalled:

Well, when I first moved out here, I didn't know anybody, you know, I didn't know anybody. But Aunt Lottie King, she's the one who made our wedding cake, and she would bring pastries, cakes, cookies over here almost every day. She loved to bake, and she knew my husband liked [these], you know. And I'd go over there and visit her, and we'd just sit in her little kitchen.

Later when Lottie was herself alone for periods of time, Sandy sometimes spent every second night at her grandmother's house, and then in the morning Lottie would drive her to school. She credits Lottie with being a formative influence, perhaps the most formative influence, during childhood. She was a part of nearly everyone's life at that time on the Plains.

Neighbors

When Jackie and I spoke with people about their lives on the Plains, again and again they told about simply living with the neighbors and about people who came through. In the Simmler community, cattle ranching had seasonal events that brought neighbors together. Branding calves was one of these, and a rancher would ask neighbors for help in rounding them up, corralling, and branding the animals. Always there was a barbecue given by way of thanks, and the gathering became social as well as a day of work. Several years after Dewey Werling had stopped wheat farming and left the Goodwin Ranch, the Beck family leased that property to keep cattle. Greg's sister-in-law recalled neighbors helping for three full days when they needed to separate calves from their mothers. On another occasion, Joe Garcia needed help getting cattle to town. A neighbor and friend, Bob Lewis, had several trucks that were used for hauling animals, and Joe asked if Bob would help him the next day. Bob replied that he was sorry, but he had other work that needed to be done instead. Later in day, Bob's father arrived and heard the story. He simply said, "Bob, you'd better get your priorities right." The cattle went to town the next day as requested.

Farmers were largely self-sufficient, and they raised much of their own food. During the failing economy of the 30s, the country still needed food, and grain still sold for reasonable prices. Although the Carrisa community was only marginally affected by the Depression, this was not true of the transients who came through. They were looking for jobs and badly needed food. Elinore Diefenderfer said that no one who came to their door in those years was turned away. Her mother set another place at the table, and the stranger was fed. Elinore's explanation: "They were hungry, and so of course we fed them."

Elinore's son, Jerry, recalled difficult times in later years when a group of persons came though the valley looking for work. At that time Jerry had a field that had been planted in potatoes, and harvesting these was labor intensive. The itinerant group was given jobs and fed while working there. Then they moved on farther west, and Jerry gave it no more thought till ten or more years later. He was in a bank in Bakersfield when one of the executives there came up and asked if he was part of the Diefenderfer family on the Plains. The answer, of course, was "yes," and then the executive went on to say that he had been one of the persons who had helped with the potatoes. His family had been desperate, and he had remembered the help and been grateful ever since.

Elinore related another incident from her childhood that also spoke of what it meant to be neighbors. Her parents were reasonably well-to-do, and among the amenities on their farm was a shed with a swamp cooler where they hung beef that had been butchered. After a short absence, the family once came home and found a note on their door. Bill Washburn, a rancher who lived about fifteen miles farther south along Soda Lake Road, had come by. He needed some help on short notice, and when the King family was not home, he had gone to their cooler and taken half a beef. Of course the favor would be repaid, and Elinore thought nothing of the incident except that it told of how neighbors helped each other.

Changes with Time

Listening to these stories, I couldn't help but be impressed with the strength of the community that I had discovered. Again and again people spoke of help they had either given or received from others. Joyce Binge-man spoke about her daughter in the hospital and their hired hand Ruiz.

Several persons spoke of kindnesses done for itinerant travelers during the Depression. Jean Edgar had assisted Clemente Galainena when his sheep had anthrax. Lottie had treated Ernie Garcia's injured foot, she had treated Elinore Diefenderfer when she was injured at school, and she had befriended Jan Cooper. These stories had been related in separate interviews conducted over a period of several years. I was personally astonished to discover that one of my own good friends was the son of the Doctor French in San Luis Obispo from whom Aunt Lottie had received advice and pharmaceuticals. That all the families were related by marriage was so well known as to require no comment at all.

These stories reminded me of a summer I had spent in 1980 working on a cousin's farm in Southern Saskatchewan. We spent some evenings at the hotel bar discussing the merits of the huge rolled hay bales versus the large square stacks. On other evenings the family went to watch the local baseball team in a game with Parkman, ten miles to the east. The game was, of course, followed by beer and food at one of the player's farms. Every Wednesday evening my aunt played bingo at the Legion Hall, and Sunday afternoons were reserved for visiting still other cousins on their farms. As a family member, although somewhat distant, I was included in all this and felt privileged. While this community in Saskatchewan has endured, this has not been true in the Carrisa Plains.

As time went by, the floats, the June barbecue, and even the dances at Simmler became more of a chore than a celebration. The Farm Bureau became a group of two or three elected officers, and participation dwindled. In part, this happened as wheat farming became less profitable. It was also true that cars had improved and better roads made it possible to travel farther. Why go to a dance at the Simmler School, when there are bigger bands in two or three other towns only an hour away? With easier transportation, it became possible for people to live on the Carrisa Plains and commute to other jobs. Many older children and even wives did just this. Some ranches along Highway 58 were sold to become small ranchettes, and newcomers to the Plains moved into these. The school on the Carrisa Plains changed character as well, and enrollment increased with these new residents. Older ranchers were not always pleased with these developments and home schooling became more common. Parent and community involvement in the school decreased. Neighbors are still friends, but the Simmler community is changing. For better or worse, it is entering the twenty-first century.

CHAPTER TEN

Children Growing Up

Chores, play, school, drinking

Simmler School, 1954

My own childhood fell somewhere between country and city, between the days of unstructured playtime and those of Little League and piano lessons. Although I had been permitted to wander unsupervised in our neighborhood, there were also Saturday matinee movies, Cub Scout meetings, and shopping trips downtown. It was difficult to imagine what a child's life was like in a place so far from town as the Carrisa Plains. Always Jackie and I asked about these early childhood years, and many of the stories we heard were truly charming.

We were told about family pets and about games with brothers and sisters. There were chores to do before school, and as children became older, they participated fully in the work of the farms. Boys tinkered with old machinery, learned gun safety from their fathers, and started driving as soon as they could reach the pedals. Girls more commonly learned to cook and helped with the domestic animals. Schools may have been several miles away, and although the arrangements were sometimes difficult, children arrived at school without fail. With no high school on the Plains, children in the south rode buses to Maricopa while those at the north stayed in a school dormitory in Atascadero during the week and then went back home to work at their farm on the weekends.

Several of the most engaging accounts of early childhood centered on the Wells Ranch, the first of the homesteads that I had discovered on the Carrisa Plains. On the October day of that first visit, the homestead seemed like the very end of the world. On later visits in springtime, grass was growing in the yard, and yellow fiddleneck bordered the dirt road that ran nearby. Trees at the north end of the compound had leafed out, and one of them was home to a pair of great horned owls with a brood of chicks. The nearest school is twenty miles away, and the Internet world might as well belong in another galaxy. What could the life of a child have been in such a place?

Children's Games and Chores

Leola Hill, now Leola Hill Wright, spoke in an interview about memories of this ranch. As a child, Leola lived with her parents and four brothers in Maricopa, but during school vacations and on weekends they visited and lived with their grandparents, Hiram Sr. and Hannah Wells. This ranch was the home where she remembers growing up. The land had been first homesteaded in 1917, and the years that Leola recalled were in the 50s. Her memories were happy ones, and although now past retirement age, Leola was exact in her descriptions of those years and was animated in the telling.

The only running water in the house was in the kitchen, and hot water came from the stove. Saturday night baths were rural institutions during those years, and they used a number ten washtub for the entire family. In Leola's words: "That's the way my brothers and I bathed. Mother would bathe us. She'd heat the water, and you know it was one of those communal things. We took turns, and Dad was last because he was the one covered with dirt." In the summer with no place to go swimming, the children found alternatives:

> When Chuck and Lonny and I were little, if it really were hot, we would crawl in the chicken's watering trough and get in a whole lot of trouble for that too. There was always about, oh maybe fifteen inches of water in this tank for the chickens. And Chuck and Lonny and I'd just get in there and lay down. It was wonderful, but it wasn't something that we were supposed to do. We'd start laughing, and of course there'd be an echo. It would give us away, and Mother would be out there in an instant.

Besides Chuck and Lonny, who were younger, Leola had two older brothers. One of these brothers, Bill, was already married when Leola was growing up. Although Bill has since passed away, his wife Joyce spoke about life at the ranch with their son Harvey. Like many others with whom we spoke, Leola and Joyce had stories about snakes:

> Joyce: After we had Harvey, when he could walk and everything, well he went to the outdoor toilet. One day he went out there, and we heard this big scream and everything, and this snake fell down out of the ceiling.
>
> Leola: That was an everyday occurrence. I'm not kidding you . . . I don't like snakes, never have, never will.
>
> Joyce: Fortunately there were no snake accidents.
>
> Leola: No, they were usually gopher snakes. Well, we had pigs, and pigs, you know, are the greatest snake killers in the whole wide world, so we didn't have much, we really . . . but for some reason, the snakes loved that outhouse. I guess they were hiding from the pigs.

Where there are pigs, there are piglets, and Leola recalled:

> I remember one time we had a little pig, and it was being bottle fed, and it was when Harvey was just really little, and they're funny. I don't know if you've ever had any experience with pigs or not, but they're very intelligent. It would get a hold of Harvey's pant leg and just shake it like crazy. And it was chasing Harvey one day, and Harvey ran into the living room with a little pig right behind him. One of my friends from school was there, and she said, "Oh what a cute little puppy." And of course we all just cracked up because of course it was not a puppy. It was a pig, for heaven's sake. But she'd never seen . . . a little, teeny thing.
>
> One of my favorite things when Chuck and Lonny and I were little was with the baby pigs when they're tiny. I could, because I could run . . . well I can't anymore, but I could run really fast then . . . I would put Lonny and Chuck into the . . . there was a hay wagon always in the middle of the barn yard . . . and I'd put the boys up there, and I would go, and I would get a piglet. Of course they'd squeal like crazy, and here'd come mama [pig], and I'd run like crazy and give the boys the piglet and wait. She'd circle around, you know, just waiting for a foot or something, and then when she was over here, I'd run off, and we'd end up with three piglets in the hay wagon. And our mother would come down there and make us give the babies back because the sow was going crazy. But it was wonderful. It was just absolutely . . . never got . . . We never got hurt. We weren't stupid, but the mother pig could have done big time damage, yes, exactly.

Besides pigs, there were chickens and geese to deal with, some on their own farm and some on neighbors'. Here is more from the same interview.

> Leola: Yes, my parents were friends with the Kings. I can remember they had a goose that flogged my baby brother so many times. He was too little to get rid of that sucker, and it would get him. You know, we'd look around like this, and "Okay, Chuck, come on." That thing would come out of nowhere and grab him every time. Oh, Lord. But it was a pet of the family, so there wasn't much to do.

Lonny and I were old enough that we could run away from it, but
Chuck was just a little guy, and it would get him every time.

Craig: That goose obviously knew.

Leola: Oh, of course. If you know anything about geese, they're very good
about figuring out who is the weakest of the bunch and taking advantage of it.

Craig: Well chickens, roosters can be . . .

Leola: Oh, roosters are terrible. We had one in Nevada, not here, that was
my dad's favorite. His name was Charlie for some reason, and it got
every one of us. I mean the boys I'm sure have scars from it. And
one day my dad had gone out to get a chicken for the Sunday dinner, and he pulled a bead on one, and just as he pulled the trigger,
Charlie walked right in front of it, and he nailed his pet. We were
all very happy. Father didn't eat much chicken that time.

Chickens seemed to be a theme with children growing up on the
Plains, probably because gathering eggs was a chore that could be assigned at an early age. Linda Cavanagh Woodard grew up across the
street from the newer Carrisa School in the north. She was the daughter
of Ray Cavanagh and a more distant relative of Fred Cavanagh of the
Buckhorn and Trejea Ranches. Linda spoke of chickens also:

We'd get day-old chickens. We had a big heat thing that would come down,
and it was a special pen just for the new hatched chicks. And when they're
old enough, we'd put them into the regular chicken house. And my job
was to take whatever garbage, whatever slop my mother had, out to the
chickens, take care of the chickens, gather the eggs, whatever. And I had a
rooster, who . . . I called him Hoggy-Menoggy because he would hog all of
the food all of the time. So when I would go in there to feed the chickens
. . . and I probably had forty or fifty of them . . . he would always come,
and I would take the bucket of grain that I had, and I would push it in his
face to get him out of the way, and then I'd sprinkle the grain for the other
chickens.

He didn't like that bucket in his face, and he would jump up and hit it
with his spurs, and then he transferred from the bucket to the person hold-

ing the bucket. And he could jump in the middle of your back, and he would leave bruises. And my dad wanted to kill him a couple of times when my dad had to go into the chicken yard for something, and he nailed my dad. I wouldn't let dad kill it.

We'd have all these cousins from town, and it was my job to entertain them. And they always wanted to do stuff all over the ranch, and invariably it was gather the eggs. Or I would say, "Would you like to gather the eggs?" So I would just stay outside of the pen and send them in. My mother . . . My mother used to be so mad at me because these kids would be crying, and the rooster . . . and oh, my God. It was awful. And one day, because you did have to protect yourself sometimes from this rooster, I would take . . . it was a mop but the stringy part wasn't there, and he came after me, and I swung at him. I hit him in the head, and he just flopped over. I thought I'd killed him. I'm crying, carrying on. I didn't want to do it. My dad goes, "Okay, whatever. He deserved it. Go gather the eggs." And I'm gathering those eggs, and I look up at that door, and there he stands, and he is really ticked off. He died of old age.

Leola also spoke about chores that she and her brother did.

Leola: Well, you know, when you're raised on a farm or ranch your responsibilities get bigger, and the first one is gathering eggs. I hated that. They'd [the hens] look at me, you know, and I knew I was going to get pecked. And my mother and grandmother would say just go in there and put your hand . . . "Mother, I don't want to do this." And boy they'd nail me every time, always did. It was because I was afraid of them. You know, I was really glad when somebody else took over that job, and I could feed the pigs. I had to watch till they're [the hens] off the nest and then run in and grab the eggs and run back out. I hated that. I really and truly did. But that's just part of it.

Craig: And then as you got older, what did your jobs become?

Leola: You got to do the pigs, and then you fed the horses, and you milked cows, cause we always had a milk cow. So you milked the cows. That was all right. I never minded that at all.

Craig: Did you ever graduate to field work? Or moving cattle?

Leola: I was the princess. Oh, I worked with cattle, but I'm the only girl in the whole family so I just got away with murder for the most part. If I wanted to do it, I did it. If I didn't want to do it, it was "don't bother."

Greg Beck also spoke about growing up on his farm:

Well people ask me how I liked that, but it was all I knew. Before television almost, although I remember we did have a television, and I was probably six or seven or eight. And I had to go to bed at seven o'clock. Seven o'clock was exactly when Superman started. I was really upset.

But we had our farming toys, and our construction toys, and we built roads and made farming fields and built houses out of bricks. We had a . . . We built a fort over the back fence of the big house. It started out, we built a platform so we could spy on somebody. We built this platform, and we kind of closed this in and added a room over here, and it became our fort. It stood for years. Pretty good fort builders.

Elinore King Diefenderfer was seven years old in 1930. She grew up on the King Ranch just south of Highway 58 near the Simmler School. Somewhat later her family lived on the American Ranch fifteen miles farther to the south. Jackie spoke with her about farm life in those early years.

Jackie: Elinore, give us an idea of what your daily routine would be, first as a child and then as an adult.

Elinore: Well as a child there was school . . .

Jackie: So you went to school. Did you have any chores you had to do before you went to school?

Elinore: Oh we always helped, with the dishes and cooking . . . In fact my mother had a thyroid operation when I was about fifteen, and we had twenty-five men, and the cook was gone, and I did the cooking. You grew up cooking when you were out here. It's not an easy life. If you had twenty men, you just got the gun and went

out and shot ten or twelve chickens, cut their heads off, cleaned
them, and cooked them. And we always had our own milk.

Jackie: So you had to milk the cows?

Elinore: No, no, we always had a chore man. I don't like milk and can't
stand the smell. We always had a chore man. Maybe not when I
was real little, but down at the American Ranch.

Hunting

It seemed that nearly all the men that we talked with spoke about hunting when they were kids. It was simply the way they grew up. They
began with a 22, but then there would be a shotgun, and finally a deer
rifle. They went out exploring with a buddy, carried their guns, and shot
what they could. There were seasons for deer hunting and for quail, but
rabbits, ground squirrels, feral pigs, and coyotes were year-round. From
the stories we were told, however, I have to suspect that quail hunting
also took place pretty nearly any time that kids took the notion.

On the west side of the Plains and about midway between north and
south in the Monument is the Washburn Ranch. It was assembled by Bill
Washburn during the 30s from a scattering of smaller parcels. Although
Bill Washburn never had biological children of his own, his wife, Marie,
had been previously married and her grandson, Billy Rolfe, always spoke
of the Washburns as his grandparents. Billy spent a great many of his
younger years visiting, living, and then working on the ranch. Hunting
was an important part of his time on the Plains.

Together with a friend that he called "Red," Billy spent endless hours
searching up and down a wash that ran next to the ranch yard. Rabbits
hid in the wash, and squirrels lived in the open fields. Billy was first
given a bolt action 22 and then later a hammerless 22 pump Winchester.
He admitted that the two of them would shoot out the windows of cars
that had been junked just south of the ranch. They played cowboys, and
Eliot Ness was their TV hero. The burrows that ground squirrels make
in fields are a hazard for horses, and both squirrels and rabbits can eat
enough grain to seriously damage a field. Bill Washburn paid a bounty

on these "varmints": a nickel each for rabbits and a dime for each squir-rel. Billy said that he was out in the fields at any time of year, and for the kids it didn't matter that the summer months were intensely hot. With rabbits in the fields, the two boys were out from sunup till sundown.

A variation on this same story was told about the Traver Ranch, ten miles farther south from the Washburn. Alden Loucks was a grandson of Lewis and Nancy Traver and along with his younger brother he grew up on their ranch. He told about quail hunting at Thanksgiving time and about shooting cottontails in the spring. This was for food as well as for sport. It was a grade school friend of Alden's, however, who gave the most vivid descriptions of hunting as a child.

Walter McDermand lived in Maricopa and during the late 40s spent weekends and vacations out with the Travers. Nancy Traver was truly a kind-hearted woman and was quite fond of Walter and his younger brother Harry. She was also a very strong woman who tolerated little nonsense. In particular, Nancy was not fond of the birds that raided her fruit trees. She made a deal with Walter that if he kept the birds out of the tree, she would buy the shells he needed. Walter already had his own gun, a sawed off shotgun, so how could he not accept the offer? But he did refuse, and told Nancy, "I don't want your shells. I've got more." The gun, incidentally, had been run over by a truck and was then given to Walter who sawed off the damaged part of the barrel.

The McDermand family was poor, and they ate what they could find and collect. The two brothers recollected:

Harry: We had lots of potatoes, and us kids would get out and kill rabbits. Then we had meat in the potato soup. We would take one of the dump trucks, and we'd go out at night . . . And we'd get home. We'd clean them and stuff, and the next day my mom would make hot tamales out of them, pressure cook them and take and shred the meat. We didn't know they was supposed to taste bad.

Walter: We had the best mother. We'd come in at two o'clock in the morn-ing, "Mom, we've got a bunch of rabbits." "I'll be right out." She'd get her dress on, and she'd go out, and she'd help us clean them rabbits.

Walter also knew Bill Hill who was running the Wells Ranch in the 40s, and Walter talked about hunting rabbits there at that time. The rabbits that they retrieved were used for food for the hogs.

> Walter: . . . We'd pull off in a field and shut the lights off, and all of us would load our guns, generally shotguns. And then we'd all just set there for a while, and then . . .
> Craig: Turn on the lights?
> Walter: Turn on the lights, jump out, and start shooting, and there were rabbits running into your legs and everything like that . . . well, you could just see where they ate during the night. They'd just take a field and just eat it.
> Craig: Was there significant loss due from the rabbits.
> Walter: Oh, yeah, they'd really destroy the field.
> Craig: It was more than recreation. You were taking care of the farm.

Learning to Drive

Everyone who grew up on the Plains started driving at a young age. They started with tractors in the field or with the Model-A pickup. One of the ranchers recalled that his family put blocks of wood on the pedals so he could reach them. Alden Loucks recalled that in 1946 at the age of nine he first drove with a half-filled sack of barley straw behind his back so that he could reach the pedals. Even then, the gas pedal was hard to reach so he used a hand throttle most of the time. Looking through the steering wheel, not over it, driving seemed to be something that was in his blood.

Between 1983 and 1986, Ken Tack lived on the Traver Ranch. His mother was one of a series of hired hands there. Ken was just over ten years old at the time, and his best friend was Martin Loucks, a nephew of Alden. Together the two boys explored the Plains. Ken said that the rule on the farm was "if you could get it to run, and if you could drive it, then it was yours." It didn't matter if it had brakes; it didn't matter if it had a door. As long as they got home by dinner time, they would have almost complete freedom to go where they chose. And they used their freedom taking motorcycles all over the Plains as well.

The age for a driver's license was fifteen, but at fourteen it was possible to get a permit to drive farm equipment. With such a permit, it was common for kids to use a family truck to get to school. For Ken, the dirt road south from the Traver Ranch to Highway 166 was no problem. From there he drove two miles west to a ranch owned by the Stubblefield family. With a triangle placard which identified the truck as an agricultural vehicle, this distance on pavement was permitted. Ken caught the school bus at the Stubblefield Ranch and rode it the rest of the way to New Cuyama without risking a citation. The plan failed only once when Ken was late for the bus connection, and he drove the full distance himself on Highway 166. There was no accident or citation, but he admitted to a scolding afterwards at home.

Rites of Passage

Besides learning to drive, teenage drinking was part of growing up on the Carrisa Plains. Trips to the parking lot were frequent at the Farm Bureau dances, and for some it was a normal, although not entirely approved, part of the evening. Students from the Plains who boarded at the high school in Atascadero might also drink at the Friday night dances. John Ruskovich was one of those students from the Plains who sometimes went to the dances and then drove home for the weekend. In his words:

> This flatbed out here, that was my senior pickup that I drove home from school. I went back to Aunt Lottie's [where he lived at that time], and I fired up the old crawler, and I was farming. Lottie: "How do you feel?" Me: "Groan." In back of that pickup there's a keg of beer, and there's still beer left in it, and tons of beer cans. Yeah, we crawled home, but it didn't matter, you still went to work. The thought, "Oh, I'm hung over, we don't have to work," that didn't fly out here. You took gobs of coffee and to work you went. The weekends were when we came home, and that was it.

Doug Wreden has been introduced before, and he once spoke of his early summers visiting on the Pinole Ranch. It was a rule on the ranch that no alcohol was permitted, and while this was observed with some care, it did not require that all the hands were dry. After work on the weekends, many of the crew took the ranch truck and drove the fifteen or twenty miles to Simmler. Beer was available, and the crew was not reticent. Doug was about twelve years old, and for something to do, he rode along on one of those occasions. Riding in the back of the truck on the way home, one of the hands realized that there was still a substantial amount of brew aboard and that it would be awkward to hide it on the ranch. The solution was obvious. It had to be consumed on the way, and Doug would have to help out. This was part of growing up on a ranch in Central California.

Doug laughed as he spoke of another occasion, this time involving both retribution as well as sin. Doug insists that it was his friend, Greg McMillan, who led him astray. Greg maintains that it was the reverse. It seems that the two of them decided to visit a young woman that they knew in Shandon. Doug borrowed a truck from the ranch manager, and they brought a six pack of beer for company. Doug can't remember why they thought that the lady would want to see the two of them, but that was moot because her father wouldn't even let her come to the door. They drove back to Greg's ranch with beer flowing and spirits flying. The cattle guard at the entrance to the ranch was a bit rough, and Greg warned Doug to slow down or they would be launched into outer space. They were indeed launched, and the truck turned sideways and nearly rolled, all in one motion. There were skid marks all across the road, and Greg said, "We'd better cover up these tracks. My dad will see this and know what happened." They were too tired and went into the house and collapsed in bed.

The next morning came at six o'clock with a horrible hangover and Greg's mom knocking on the door of their room. She said, "Your father saw the tracks." They said, "Ooooh, nooo." It was Sunday morning, and Greg's mom announced: "And so now you're going to get up and go to church with me." Doug and Greg together: "Ooooh nooo, do we have to?" This was Gladys McMillan. You have to admire her.

The Choice Valley School

For children everywhere, school is a large part of growing up. Children from the Carrisa Plains attended one of three different elementary schools, each small, and each unique by the standards of the later twentieth century. North of Highway 58 was the Choice Valley School, and for eight years, this was a part of the daily routine for Greg McMillan. Although he has appeared in several of the previous stories, it is time now to introduce him more carefully.

I first met Greg near his home about thirty miles north of Highway 58 and not far from town of Shandon. His father, Eben, had been the first manager working for William Wreden on the Pinole Ranch. After an extraordinary harvest in 1939, the share of profits which Eben received allowed him to buy the smaller ranch where Greg now lived. We met beside a corral where he and a cousin had just finished vaccinating eight heifers. They were discussing plans for a small business raising and selling grass-fed beef. Greg had retired from a career in construction and was coming back to his roots as a rancher.

Over lunch, Greg, his wife Linda, and I spoke about schools, children, teaching, and learning. Linda worked with an organization that provided support and tutoring for disadvantaged students, largely belonging to ethnic minorities. I myself had taught at a private college preparatory high school with magnificent facilities – projection TVs, several computer labs, and even a scanning electron microscope in the biology department. By way of contrast, the students which Linda worked with were often the first in their family to finish high school, received almost no encouragement from their homes, and expected to work as clerks or laborers after twelfth grade. The irony in all this appeared immediately when Greg spoke about his own childhood.

Greg and his two brothers had attended the Choice Valley School from grades one through eight. The building was along Bitterwater Road eight miles south of his home. It had been a one-room school with about ten students and a single teacher. Greg could not say enough in praise of the school and of Ellen Newsome, the teacher:

Oh, it was wonderful. I can remember it so plainly. It was a wonderful thing. We did huge gardens. She lived on the site, and so there was a . . . it was called the teacherage. It was like a parsonage, but instead it housed the teacher. She and her husband lived there, and she was related . . .

In fact, Mrs. Newsome belonged to a respected family from the La Panza Ranch. Ellen knew everyone in the community and was related to at least half of them. And she was responsible for everything at the school from seven in the morning till five in the afternoon – cleaning, teaching, making sure kids ate their lunches, and supervising recess. Greg mentioned that many recesses were spent keeping up the yard, pruning roses, and weeding vegetables in the garden.

Recalling the incident when Greg and Doug Wreden had been taken to church after a night out drinking, it was a bit perverse of me to ask what happened when Greg got into trouble at school. His reply was a laugh and denial. If there was any problem, Mrs. Newsome simply called his parents, and after that there was no problem. All the parents had known Ellen before their children ever entered school. She was a pillar of the community, and what she reported was law. Parents supported her without question.

With eight grade levels in one room, it was an extraordinary task to teach every child what they needed to learn and at a level that was individually appropriate. I have no idea how she did this, but the conversation with Greg made it clear that Mrs. Newsome was successful. Another of her pupils with whom Jackie and I spoke was even more vocal in praising this fantastic teacher. He insisted that nearly all of her students at the Choice Valley School eventually went on to high school and then college and did very, very well. Teaching was her life, and she stayed at the school for over thirty years. Linda and I still have things to learn from Ellen Newsome.

School at Simmler

The Simmler School has already been mentioned as one of the binding institutions of the Plains community. In that context, the names of Darrell and Nola Twisselman appeared briefly, and their connections to other families were cited in describing the close nature of the Simmler community. Darrell had attended the Choice Valley elementary school, but Nola had been a student in Simmler. This would have been in the late 40s or early 50s. Nola remembered:

> I remember having to stand up . . . the blackboards are still down there now, and they had a step about this high for the short ones. I was one of them and had to stand on this thing. You had to write the alphabet the full length of that blackboard, have a whole row of A's, big A's, and little A's, and a whole row of B's. That's the way we learned our alphabet and penmanship. You did it on the blackboard, and then you'd have to erase it off for the next person to do it.
>
> I think there were fifteen of us in school at that time. Most of us were probably related except for the Beck and Cavanagh families. The rest were pretty much related except there might have been a few hired hands that had kids too. We had a different teacher every so often, but we only had the one teacher for all the kids. And you always took your lunch to school. The kitchen that's down there now used to be our cloakroom.
>
> My dad used to take us to school in an old pickup. This road wasn't paved. It was a dirt road, and in wintertime there'd be ruts that deep in it [indicating about eight inches]. The water would be clear up to the running boards of the pickup, but he'd drive right down those same ruts. We never got stuck. Get onto the highway and take us on to school. And lots of times the highway would be flooded between here and there. There'd be lots of water like this Carrisa Crick that goes through here and comes out down there a ways. I don't remember ever, ever missing school for the weather. We went to school till June.

When Jackie and I interviewed Elinore Diefenderfer, she spoke not only about cooking for the harvest crew while she was young but also

about going to the Simmler School. It was only a short distance from
the main ranch, and she recalled walking with her sister and crossing the
fence on the steps of a stile. This would have been around 1930. Later
her family lived on the American Ranch fifteen or twenty miles away,
and during those years, her family drove her to school. When she was
older, she and her sister drove themselves. Elinore remembered twenty
or twenty-five kids all in one room and with one teacher. The number
seemed too large, but Elinore listed off the students: The Becks had
three; the Kings had two; the Lewises had four or five: the Kesters had
three; the Van Matres had five; and then there were children of some
of the hired hands. As in Choice Valley, the teacher lived at the school
itself in a house belonging to the school district, and part of her job, in
addition to teaching the children, was doing the janitor work. Unlike at
the Choice Valley School, Elinore recalled that there had been four different teachers in succession during the years she attended.

In 1954 a new elementary school, known as the Carrisa Plains
School, was built on Highway 58 about two miles farther west of the
old Simmler School. Although this Carrisa Plains School was a part of
the Atascadero school district, it was run almost independently by the
families who had children in attendance. These were prosperous years
on the Plains, and with nearly 200,000 acres under cultivation, even a
low tax rate brought in a good deal of money. This prosperity had not
escaped the notice of the rest of the school district, and to the distress
of the Carrisa Plains residents, a call went up to "unify the schools." In
practice, this meant that the tax revenue from the Plains, along with
a significant surplus which had accumulated over the years, would be
transferred to the general fund of the county. This unification would,
of course, require a vote of everyone involved, but the deck was stacked.
The Plains had a far greater tax income than the coastal cities, but the
coastal cities had far more people. Everybody on the Plains voted against
unification. Everyone in the cities voted for it. The result was foreor-
dained, and control of the Carrisa Plains School and its tax revenue went
west. As a sweetener for the deal, the Carrisa community was permitted
to elect one member of the county school board, and for many years this
was Kenneth Beck, father of Greg and Steve.

Driving to School in Maricopa

At the south end of the Carrisa Plains, there was no community institution comparable to the Simmler School. Instead children from the
Wells, Jobe, and Traver Ranches attended elementary school in Maricopa and then later went to Taft or New Cuyama for high school. Most
of the Carrisa Plains lies within San Luis Obispo County, and it might
have been logical for children to travel north to the Simmler School.
Inconveniently, the road from the Traver Ranch to Simmler was dirt
and was frequently impassible during the winter months. Driving south
to Highway 166 required only twelve miles on dirt and was much more
reliable. During World War II, an agreement was reached whereby San
Luis Obispo County paid the Kern County school system to accept these
children in the south. The agreement also paid ranchers an allowance to
drive their children to Highway 166 where they could meet a regular
school bus. People with whom Jackie and I spoke seldom mentioned
the Maricopa School itself, but they all spoke about how they got there.
Riding with neighbors and other children was the community that they
remembered.

Alden Loucks who grew up on the Traver Ranch recalled these journeys. In 1943 his grandfather drove him to school and was paid seven
cents a mile. Initially the children were driven to what was known as
Reyes Station at the intersection of Soda Lake Road and Highway 166.
At that time, New Cuyama had no high school, and so a regular bus ran
from there to Taft through Maricopa. This bus picked up the younger
children at Reyes Station, went directly to Maricopa, and let them off
at the elementary school. A few years later, there were enough children
going to Maricopa to justify a bus for the elementary school itself. It
would pick up five children at Reyes Station and then one or two more
in Brown Canyon south of 166 and perhaps three more from the Hudson family in Klipstein Canyon. With this longer route, Alden had to
leave home at six o'clock every morning. With the responsibility to help
milk the family's cow, he always hoped to get the evening shift so that the
morning did not have to start too early.

For one year at least, this bus route was driven by a woman named

Eileen Edwards who lived on the Hanline Ranch just inside the southern boundary of the present Monument. Her husband, Smokey Edwards, was a hand on the Hanline Ranch. Kathleen Hudson Buttke, who was a child on another of the southern ranches, remembered the pair. Smokey did chores; he was not a cowboy although he had once been a rodeo clown. Eileen was custodian at the Maricopa School as well as the regular bus driver. She was not permitted to drive school children outside of Kern County so she would leave them a mile or two north of Reyes Station and then bring the bus, but not the children, as far as her home. Kathleen spoke of walking the last half mile to her home through mud and winter rain. She never knew Eileen's first name. Kathleen was six years old at the time, and adults were always addressed as Mister or Misses. A few years later, Alden was old enough to drive the children as far as Highway 166, and the rate paid for this had increased to twelve cents a mile.

All the children recalled waiting at Reyes Station on their way to school. This was a gas station, tavern, pickup store, and bus stop run in later years by a remarkable lady named Alice Reyes. She had been a nurse in the military and was a tough, tough customer with a legendary vocabulary. As one person recalled, "Oh, she would, she could cuss a blue streak." Another insisted that she used language that he had never heard even during his four years in the US Marines – a truly remarkable testimonial. Gasoline at her station was expensive. When gasoline prices in Southern California went up, so did prices at Reyes Station. However, when the prices went down in the rest of the state, nothing happened to her prices. Sometimes drivers who were nearly out of gas would have to stop. When they saw the price, they only wanted two gallons to get them as far as Maricopa where it cost less. No deal! Alice told them that they would pay for a full tank, and if they didn't like it, they could push their car the last twelve miles.

Alice had another side as well. Kathleen recalled that one year the bus let the school children off at Reyes Station, but for some reason her father wasn't able to come for her right away. The driver asked if the children could stay at the station till they were picked up. In Kathleen's words:

Alice said, "Oooh, sure, I'll take care of my babies." She loved all of us. She was good to us. She was rough, a rough lady, but she had a heart of gold. I don't remember where she came from, not any more. I was so young when she came, and I was an adult, of course, when she died.

Alden remembered the station differently. He recalled that it was a Standard Station and originally run by Annie and Raphael Reyes. Later it became the Union gas station that Alice managed. It was Annie and Raphael who looked after Alden on his way to school.

Well I was six at that time I think. My grandfather would drop me off, and Annie'd come out and get me and take me up and set me on a bar stool. They had a slot machine over on the side, and if there was anybody in there, I'd be watching them play that slot machine. But usually in the morning it wasn't a problem. It was the evening when I had to wait, cause my grandfather didn't always get there.

Raphael died, and then Annie died. Then the son took over. There was no farming done there at all, with the Reyes. They just had that business. And when the son took over, his wife was the one that everybody knew as Alice. She was . . . she was a World War II nurse out of Chicago, and she'd been through some hard times. She wouldn't mince words with anybody . . . And she always said I'm your second mother. Yeah, she was . . . nothing she wouldn't do for me. She looked out after Jack [Alden's younger brother] and me just like we were her kids. And then Christmas, yeah, I think it was Christmas, this had to have been about 19 . . . I'm going to say like [the] 1950s. Her husband, Raphael, crashed a pickup into a pole over in Cuyama, and it just about made an invalid of him. She ran the station then, and she took care of him. Right up till he died, which was many years later.

The gas station and convenience store has been closed now for many years.

High School in Atascadero

There is no high school on the Carrisa Plains, nor has there ever been one. Kids living at the south end of the Plains drove to Cuyama or Maricopa along Highway 166. Some went farther to Taft, but wherever they went it was a long drive, and families had to find their own way to get kids to school. When children finished eighth grade at the Simmler School in the north, they went on to high school in Atascadero. Even today, this drive to the coast takes more than an hour, and it could only be longer during the golden years on the Plains. The solution for many, many years had children boarding at the school itself. When the dormitory finally closed at the end of the 1990s, it was the last of its kind in California. For many years, however, the high school dormitory was a part of growing up on the Plains.

Elinore King Diefenderfer and her sister Kathleen had lived in the high school dormitory during the 30s, and Kathleen's two daughters lived there in the 50s. The stories that the daughters, Colleen and Marilyn, related were about the school and Plains, but at the same time they were timeless stories of adolescents growing into adulthood.

These were fourteen- and fifteen-year-olds, who lived away from home five days a week. On Sunday afternoon, their parents drove them into town, and on Friday night, they were brought back out to their homes near Simmler. Marilyn said that living away from home for the first time was traumatic, but the saving grace was the company of the others from the Plains who were also living there. Students from Atascadero lived at their homes, so the dorm residents were the cousins and siblings and neighbors they had grown up with. There were separate dormitories for boys and girls, and of course there were dormitory parents. The dorm mother was also the school bus driver and was usually busy so that students had little supervision. It might seem that this was a recipe for trouble, but Colleen insisted that the children from the Plains were too naive to even think about doing something wrong.

Again and again, the people that Jackie and I interviewed spoke of the work ethic that went with growing up on a ranch. From the time they were five years old, the children had chores to do and parents that watched their homework. Their teachers at Simmler were members of the community, and parents supported them. It was accepted law that schoolwork was to be done and behavior was to be acceptable. Beyond this, the school in Atascadero was a busy place from morning to night. The community from the Plains had been transplanted westward.

The two younger sisters talked about driving back and forth to Atascadero:

Colleen: Our dorm mother wanted her time, so she wanted us out of there Friday night and didn't want us back till Sunday, cause she lived there.

Marilyn: Yes, Karen Freeborn's older brother would take us back to school on Sunday afternoon, and we always went to the movies at the old movie theater in Paso that is all closed up now. We always went to the movies on Sunday afternoon . . . I don't think we could go back to the dorm till four o'clock.

Colleen: That was the regulation. And then we would eat oftentimes at this place called Stokies, just a little cafe.

Marilyn: Ice cream parlor.

Coleen: Ice cream, they used to have a banana split, and you got a big pin that said, "I was a pig at Stokies," because the banana split was THIS big, and you couldn't possibly eat it.

Looking fifty years back, the social life for high school students in the 30s, 40s, and 50s seems impossibly naive, but it also had a charm that is now gone. During those years, carloads of boys and girls would come out to the Carrisa Plains for the dances. They lasted from nine till two in the morning and were highlights of the year for the two sisters. Girls stayed at the King's house, and boys stayed at a bunkhouse on another ranch. Many of the high school romances became permanent after graduation.

Marilyn had her first date in ninth grade. The couple remained sweethearts all four years of high school, and immediately after graduation they were married. Forty-five years later they are still together. Colleen also met her husband while in high school. Jackie asked about their dates while they were in school, and the two continued:

Marilyn: Well, one night Colleen, and I, and my husband went to a movie. He wasn't my husband at the time. And my mother called his mother at eleven o'clock, "Well they're not home, they're not home. Is Pat [Marilyn's boyfriend] home?" Pat's mother said, "I don't know if they're home or not." They hadn't heard us come in and just knew we were dead on the highway. Then our mothers went and checked and saw that we were home. We went to movies. There wasn't that much. Football games were big. After-game dances were big. Proms just like anybody else.

Colleen: I had a high school boyfriend for six years.

Craig: Was there the hamburger drive-in with its ritual as well?

Marilyn: Yes there was, Virgil's. It was the only place in town. Everybody met there.

Jackie: Did your boyfriends come out here. You alluded to that.

Colleen: Occasionally yes . . . and he had an old Model-A which he still has, and they would come out here and stop at the cow troughs because it would overheat, but they would make it out here every once in a while. They would come to the dances occasionally.

Marilyn: They were city kids.

In later years, the character of the dormitory and the school in Atascadero changed. Indeed, nearly everything in the Carrisa Plains had changed by the 90s. The school had become a tougher place, and some of the residents in the dormitory were from the town and didn't have the work ethic that living away from parents required. The dormitory was shut down at the end of the 90s, and several explanations for this were given.

Bill and Gail Traver had a son staying at the school in its last two years. Adam Traver had managed quite well during those years, and both his parents agreed that although the discipline problems were real, they could still have been managed if the school had the will. If kids didn't behave, they should have been removed. Instead, the ones that caused trouble were retained, and problems continued. Discipline problems were the reasons given by the school board for the closing, but Bill Traver felt that money was the true cause. The school board wanted the property for other purposes and believed that it would be cheaper to operate a daily bus from the Carrisa Plains than to maintain the living quarters.

Before the dormitory was closed, there were differing opinions about whether children should be away from their parents for so much of the time. Some parents simply felt they needed to see their children every day. Bill and Gail Traver maintained that if children were prepared for living away, they would do well. Children needed to be taught to be responsible for their own studies; they needed to understand priorities about work and play; they had to be able to take care of their room and property; and they had to know that there were consequences if responsibilities were not met. Adam Traver did well while he lived in the dormitory, and it was generally true that the children from ranch families on the Plain were successful. Teachers often commented that those from the Plains were more mature than their peers in the city.

One of Adam's friends from the Plains lived in the dorm, and Adam used to help him with his homework. Adam told him, "Do it now. Do it right. We'll both work now, and then we'll go outside when we're done." The friend did well enough with studies until his mother took him out of the dorm to live at home. She was deaf and really didn't know what her son was doing until his grades hit rock bottom. Some kids took on responsibilities for more than themselves.

Not all teachers at the high school understood that students in the dormitories were in a different situation than the others. Sometimes notes would go home with the stipulation that they must be signed by a parent and returned the next day. For children on the Carrisa Plains, this meant that a parent would have to make a one hundred mile round trip to town and back if the note was to be signed. Gail Traver laughed and described her solution for the problem: Adam was given a stamp with her signature and told to use it wisely. There was never any problem, and no one ever knew. A few parents from the Carrisa were sufficiently unhappy with dormitory living that they made arrangements for children to stay with another family in Atascadero during the week. Ultimately, the school that Elinore, Coleen, and Marilyn had known was to become history.

There is no question that in some ways without the dormitory school is harder for both children and parents on the Plains. The bus into Atascadero requires an hour and a half each way. Perhaps it would be possible to do some homework on the ride or even to sleep, but for students who had motion sickness problems this was three hours a day lost from their lives. The bus left immediately after school in the afternoon, so any sports, or clubs, or even friends became difficult to manage. If children stayed at school for football practice, their parents had to drive to town at 5:30 PM to bring them home long after the bus had left. If there were younger children at home, or if a parent had any other obligations, then there was no recourse but the bus. Gail Traver had a car with 200,000 miles on the odometer, most of them spent commuting to school for and with her kids.

Similar but Different

Thinking back on the stories we had been told, I found that many of them have a familiar ring. In elementary school shortly after World War II, I also built forts and walked to school. At Halloween, my sister and I went trick-or-treating through our neighborhood, and as winter holidays approached, we were all reluctant recruits for school drama productions. Later, in high school, my next door neighbor spent countless hours fooling with his car. The muffler had to have exactly the proper throaty rumble, and if the rear end were lowered, it looked faster and might impress the girls. I had relatively few chores to do at home, but any money for recreation had to be earned delivering newspapers or changing storm windows for neighbors. My own children were less fortunate. They received allowances, but there were fewer meaningful jobs that they could do. Empty fields and lots for unstructured play had become almost non-existent. I sometimes feel lucky to have seen at least something of the earlier times.

CHAPTER ELEVEN

In the Center of the Plains

Three generations on two different ranches

Nancy and Lewis Traver, 1900

Soda Lake Road runs forty miles from Highway 58 at the north to Highway 166 near the southern boundary of the Monument. On a hot summer day, the dusty washboard seems to never end. In winter, there are stretches where rain turns the clay surface to grease. It can be a challenge to simply stay on the road. Midway along this road are two ranches which have special stories. Billy Rolfe spent summers visiting his grandparents at the Washburn Ranch, and his account of hunting squirrels and rabbits with his friend Red has already appeared. Alden Loucks grew up on the Traver Ranch and has spoken of waiting for the school bus at Reyes Station. Today the Washburn Ranch serves as the administrative center of the National Monument, and it is well maintained. In contrast, the Traver Ranch is a group of empty buildings along the road with a collection of old farm machinery in a nearby field. I will begin with the story of the Washburn.

For many years, there was an annual reunion at the Washburn Ranch held by people who had once lived or worked there: hired hands, family members, and a few Monument employees. Jackie Czapla was of these latter persons and arranged that I might also attend to record the conversation. There was a barbecue and potluck on the lawn under old trees, and afterwards Billy Rolfe and an older friend, John Miller, reminisced about their times together on the ranch. This was in 2008, and it was the very first of the oral history interviews that Jackie and I recorded. Quite obviously I was an outsider in the group, but somehow a friend of a friend was welcome. Since that time, I've spoken with Bill Rolfe many times and count him as a personal friend.

The Washburn Ranch

The Washburn, as the ranch is often known, backs up against the Caliente Mountains on the west of the Plains. Bill Washburn worked first at the north of the Plains, and then in the mid-thirties, he acquired the property that was to carry his name. Bill was a cowboy, bow-legged, and in later life walked with a cane. His wife, Marie, had come from Los Angeles, and neither had family connections on the Plains. Their ranch was large and successful, and although they were gracious, they seldom needed to trade machinery, goods, or services with neighbors. The Washburn Ranch was very nearly an institution in its own right. Both Bill and Marie were strong, self-reliant people.

Very little is known of how Bill Washburn came to the Carrisa Plain, although somewhat more is known about Marie. Born Marie Nelson, she and a brother Valentine grew up in the Midwest before moving to California. Marie first married Joseph Rolfe and had a son, Bill Sr. Sometime after separating from Joseph, Marie married Bill Washburn and moved out to the Carrisa Plains. By this time, her son Bill Rolfe Sr. had married, and in turn he had a son, Bill Jr., who as a child went by the name Billy. Although he was Marie's grandson, Billy was not biologically related to Bill Washburn. Billy's parents never lived long in one place, and so it was the Washburn Ranch belonging to his grandparents that he identified as home.

Three people gave accounts of the Washburn family and their ranch. One account was given by John Miller who was a hired hand on the ranch in the late 30s and a life-long friend of the Washburns. Another was given by James Wildharbor. He was son to Earl Wildharbor and, on his mother's side, grandson to Valentine Nelson. James had visited the Washburn Ranch many times with his parents. The third account was given by Billy Rolfe, Marie's grandson.

Marie Washburn

No one could really say how Marie had arrived in Los Angeles. Although she had some medical training, several persons recalled that when she met Bill Washburn, she was working as a seamstress for one of the movie companies in the city. She would have been a single mother at the time raising a child during the Depression years. She was a strong woman and a colorful personality. Some persons were intimidated by her, but those who stayed on the ranch for any length of time found her to be efficient and caring.

The harvest crews on the ranch were large, and Marie fed them. There was a cookhouse behind the living quarters, and that was where she worked and where the hands ate at a long table. Billy recalled one of his grandmother Marie's idiosyncrasies. It was an absolute rule that when the crew came in to breakfast, they must say, "Good morning, Mrs. Washburn." If they didn't say, "Good morning," it was nearly a fatal sin. She could be a little touchy about things like that.

John Miller, a hired man on the ranch, recalled other incidents:

There were a couple of guys she didn't . . . there was a guy'd sit at the table, and he'd go sniff, sniff, sniff. Maybe he had some sort of hay fever. I'll have to admit that it was pretty annoying. His name was Toosie. The guys amongst ourselves, not around him, joked with each other, "Have you got Toosie-itis?" It really did bug her. He'd sniff his nose, and boy she told him off one day.

I was young, and it was hard to get enough to eat. I just worried about eating. You know, I'd complain . . . when I talked to her, I'd say to Marie, "God, I get so hungry about ten o'clock." I'd eaten all the breakfast I could handle. She said, "You see that bowl of pink beans on the table? That's what they're for. You eat a bowl of those, and see if they don't last you till lunch time." That's true. She had those beans on the table every morning.

When John Miller described the meals, it was hard to believe that he could ever be hungry. Breakfast for the hands was: "You name it. Bacon and eggs, ham and eggs, sausage, potatoes, and then her bread." Marie made her own bread, and by report, it could be nearly a meal in itself. At least one person joked that it was twenty pounds to a loaf. It was made with wheat from the ranch that she ground herself.

Although Marie was fully able to live under difficult circumstances, it was also true that she loved nice surroundings. The first house that she and Bill Washburn occupied on the Plains was primitive. As an employee of the Monument, Jackie had once lived at the Washburn Ranch, and she described this first house as no more than a shack. The second house which they built has large windows looking out over the center plain. The stone fireplace is truly elegant, and the kitchen and dining area are proportionately large. It is the master bedroom, however, that is most curious. It has a sunken floor, at least a foot lower than any of the other rooms. Marie had a large and elegant four-poster bed. It was too tall for the bedroom, and rather than shorten the bed or find another, the floor was lowered and the room was enlarged to hold it. John Miller spoke of other furniture and accessories. There were two buffets with beautiful glass doors and panels. The silverware was exquisite, some of it actually gold.

There is no doubt that Marie was the darling of her husband's eye.

Bill bought his wife two huge Percheron draft horses and a very expensive Lincoln Continental. John was certain the two Percheron horses died of old age without ever pulling anything. When I asked about those horses, John said. "I think he just thought, 'Marie'd like to have those.' He was that kind of a guy. I think he'd do anything she'd like."

Even if the horses were ornamental, there was no doubt that the Lincoln was fully functional. Billy recalled:

> After my granddad died, Marie had a huge place on the Hope Ranch near Santa Barbara. She split her time between that and the Big Ranch in the Carrisa. She would drive over Highway 33 which is a terrible twisty road, and I followed her out here one time from Santa Barbara. She drove like a bat out of hell in her big old Lincoln. I don't know how she kept it on the road. I drove a GTO sport car at the time and could just barely stay with her. All of a sudden, she whips off to the side of the road, and I stopped behind her. I asked, "What, What?" and she comes out [and says], "Ooh, sick dog." She had a row of Scottie dogs in the back seat, and at every one of the turns, these short legged dogs, they would roll to one side of the car and then they'd roll to the other side of the car, until finally one of them upchucked.

Bill Washburn

Bill Washburn was a jokester. When he gave young Billy a 22 rifle for hunting, he also gave him advice: "Don't try to make too long a shot or it will strain the barrel." And once when visitors from town wondered why the windmills were placed as they were, with a straight face Bill explained that on the Carrisa there was only enough wind for one windmill per acre. James Wildharbor remembered a time when he and Bill Washburn were wandering around the yard:

> When I was in high school taking all these new courses in math and geometry, he asked me, "Jimmy, what do you think the volume of that harvester is up there?" and pointed to the metal bins that the grain went in to. I said,

"I don't know, probably easy to figure out." He said, "Well figure it out for me. I can't get anybody to figure it." Well it was a trick question. He'd been doing that to everybody, the young kids, and nobody could get the answer, and he knew the answer all along. He knew exactly how many cubic feet that thing would hold, or bushels of grain, or whatever. And so my dad being a machinist, he pulled out his tech measure. We measured that thing all over, every which-a-way. And of course, I never did figure it out.

Bill Washburn loved hunting. The ranch was sufficiently profitable that he could make trips all over North America, and Alaska was a special place that he and Marie visited. Billy spoke about hunting, guns, and trophies:

> My granddad was a heck of a hunter, had gone to Alaska, and the center two rooms in the house were full of trophy heads. He had a Kodiak bear skin, a polar bear skin . . . and several smaller bear skins, a wolf skin, a caribou head, and a moose head. I think he had an antelope head. I'm not sure what else. He had a hunting outfit that he wore that was sealskin. He had snowshoes that were, of course, handmade, and because he was crippled, the guide fixed a snowshoe pad at the bottom of his cane. It was hinged with string going up from the front and the back so that it could walk with same "flexation" that your ankle would have. We kept the trophies for a long time. I don't know where the heads went. We had a lot of bearskins, but over a period of time they started to come apart. We had the polar bear skin right up till fairly recently. My kids grew up climbing around on it. We named it Fred.

Occasionally Billy heard his grandparents in an argument. He said that if his grandfather called her "wooooman," you knew he was mad. Billy reported that if Bill Washburn lost the argument, he would go out to the three-holer and read the Penny's catalogue for hours.

The family always had Scottie dogs at the ranch, and both Billy and John Miller remembered that Bill was very fond of them.

Billy: I remember my granddad giving his Scotties their bath out in the front yard.

John: I never saw him give them a bath, but I know they were all over him. Those little Scotties sure liked him.

Billy: They were good snake dogs. But he had a fifty-five gallon drum out here under the tree. During the summer, the gnats and flies would get around the dogs, and they'd get nasty and dusty, and it was bath time. The dogs would head for the four corners, and eventually he would catch them. He couldn't chase them very well, but he'd corner them. He'd pick them up, and they'd just think the world was coming to an end. He'd just submerge them in this fifty-five gallon drum and wash them around.

Jackie had been told that Bill Washburn knew exactly what to plant, when to plant, and when to harvest. Billy agreed that his grandfather was extremely bright, and he constantly worked with different types of wheat, trying them in different fields, and trying them at different intervals. He grew a special type of red wheat in one of the fields behind the house. Loma Linda Foods used this wheat for a cereal called Ruskets, which was like an early health food. The Washburn Ranch may have been the only place it was grown, and it was a huge source of income.

Managing the ranch was a joint endeavor that Bill and Marie shared. Among the ranch hands, Bill's word was law. It was as if he were the captain of a ship, and no one ever challenged him. Still, if the hired hands had complaints, Billy who worked with a number of them never heard of problems. Billy described his grandfather as the CEO of the company, and Marie was the foreman. She knew absolutely how things were to be done. John Miller said Bill Washburn was the very best to work for. "The only thing, one time I picked up a rock with the harvester. I got told off pretty good cause it cost him a lot of time. There is a fan in the harvester that spins around, and it broke when the rock hit it. We were able to fix it. We weren't down very long. In those days, every minute counted."

Billy Rolfe

The story of the Washburn family would not be complete without mention of Bill Rolfe Sr., Marie's son, and something more about her grandson, Billy. The following material is an edited version of the interview which Jackie and I had with Billy.

My dad was raised out here in California. He went to school in Atascadero, high school anyway. I have a yearbook of his where people wrote things to him like they used to do. Most of them make reference to him cutting school to go duck hunting.

The way he and my mother got together . . . My mother's father [Price Edwards] was a veterinarian in Bakersfield. He was very successful. I think he was the California State Veterinarian or something like that at one point, and he had a large-animal practice. Bill Washburn employed Price Edwards to come out and vaccinate his herd. So we had the very important land owner with the very important veterinarian. My mom [daughter of Price Edwards] and dad [Marie's son] got married in 1944.

My dad was excused from the draft during World War II because a wheat farmer was too important and got diverted from the military. About my dad, apparently he was a very popular guy, a drinker, very generous, a very outgoing guy, and a Golden Gloves boxer. My dad had been an illustrator with Disney at some time before he married my mother. He also had worked in a circus at some point, you know, ground crew type of thing. I don't think he was ever terribly successful financially at anything that he did. Whenever he did get a place, it was co-signed by the Washburns, that sort of thing. But he did buy a new car every year. I know that part.

At the time I was born, I believe he had partnered with Ray Calhoun on a ranch that's at the base of the hills on the other [east] side. My dad built a cinder block house himself, which was the first place they brought me home when I came from the hospital. They hauled in water for it. It had no electricity. My earliest memories are crawling around on the floor and the smell of the Carrisa Plains at night and the smell of the kerosene lanterns that we used. We left there in . . . not long after I was born, before I started kindergarten, and then moved to Delano. That was the end of Dad's connection to the Carrisa Plains other than visiting.

We eventually went from Delano, where he was not doing well farming, over to Paso Robles where he tried raising potatoes. And we didn't do particularly well there, a place where they are now growing some very fine wines, really, really good expensive wine. He would come back out to the Carrisa Plains and stay with the Washburns. I think that he and my mother were having significant discord. I don't know for sure because I was pretty young, but I believe I recall that.

One time he'd been out here with his mom, Marie Washburn. He was going back to Paso Robles with a pickup pulling a horse trailer and went off the road, hit a tree, and killed himself. That would be in 54 when I was eight. After that, there was a falling out between my grandmother and my mother. My mom thought that Marie should bear some blame for this because he and Marie had been drinking. If you hear the other side, he was arguing with his wife, and so you get the usual family turmoil. My grandparents had co-signed on my father's ranch in Paso Robles, and after this, they withdrew their support, so my mother lost that ranch. The Washburns and my mother at that point were not getting along, and for that reason, there's a gap in my involvement with the Plains. In 56 or 57 they started making amends, and I started coming back out.

Three years after the accident, Billy and his mother moved to Bakersfield where he attended high school and a first year of college. Some time later yet, he finished law school. Billy, known today as Bill, had sometimes thought of returning to live and work on the Washburn Ranch in the Carrisa Plains. However, after a remarkable success in his first legal case, he opted for a legal career and a home in Sacramento. When the Washburn Ranch was sold, 160 acres were retained by his grandmother and eventually deeded to him. Today this quarter section with a modest house provides an escape from city life for Billy and his wife. As for Bill Rolfe, Sr., I cannot say that I would have traded places with him, but I wish we could have met. It is a sad story.

One More Story: Earl Wildharbor

The Kern County Land Company, known as the KCL, was one of the large land and cattle operations on the Carrisa Plains. While the company ranched a number of smaller parcels throughout the Plains, they are principally identified with a headquarters area immediately south of the Washburn Ranch. It should be no surprise, therefore, that KCL cowboys were sometimes visitors at the Washburn.

Earl Wildharbor was born in Kentucky in 1917. His parents were Ernest and Minnie Wildharbor, and he came with them to California when he was two or three years old. Earl married Bernice Nelson, niece of Marie Washburn and daughter of Valentine, in 1938. As a young woman Bernice lived on the Washburn Ranch and helped cook for the hired hands. Indeed, she gives Marie credit for teaching her how to cook. Earl was a young cowboy on the neighboring KCL Ranch, and so a mutual interest was nearly inevitable.

James Wildharbor spoke of his dad courting Bernice. They would meet at what was called the West Gate. Earl would be driving the KCL water wagon to be filled at one of the nearby springs, and it would only be a detour of a mile or two to see Bernice. It was never explained how she knew that he was coming, but somehow these matters always work out. On Friday or Saturday nights, there were dances at the Waseola schoolhouse in the Cuyama Valley, twenty or thirty miles away. Once Earl and Bernice went to a dance driving a Model-A Ford over the peak between the two valleys on some kind of old road. Earl may have had the next day off, but certainly Bernice had to help in the kitchen. Cooks never have a day off. This would have been in the late 30s.

After Earl and Bernice were married, they moved to Taft. He worked a year for a railroad in Bakersfield and then got a job in Taft as a machinist with Standard Oil of California. His last years as a full-time cowboy on the Plains were in 1936 and 1938, but in later years, he frequently helped either Bill Washburn or Bernice's parents near Shandon. Earl and Bill Washburn were close friends, and so his work on the Washburn was sometimes paid and sometimes simply to help a friend.

James Wildharbor spoke about one of these occasions:

The only interesting story I know, and my mother used to laugh about it a lot, was Uncle Bill sent him out to one of the line shacks to take care of fences and watch the cattle. And of course he packed up some grub and everything and rode out to the line shack and set everything up before he was supposed to start working. He fired up the stove and put on some biscuits and went outside to chop wood and do other things. Suddenly he noticed smoke from the line shack. Well he burned the line shack down . . . He didn't check the flue. It was full of bird nests. So it burned the line shack down. Mom laughed because Dad saved the biscuits, but he didn't save the house. They never spoke about where the shack was. All I knew was it was a half day's ride from the house wherever that was. It could have been over in the foothills.

James also spoke about visiting the Washburns with his mom and dad when he was a child:

They [his parents] stayed connected with the Washburns quite closely. Every time I'd go out there with Dad in the old truck, he would stop at some of the ranches on the way. There is a little filling station up on the road to Cuyama there, Reyes Station. We'd stop there, get a drink, put some water in the car, and usually there'd be somebody from one of the ranches, and we'd chat for a while and then [drive] on into the Plains area.

My parents stayed connected with the Washburns in a loose kind of way forever and . . . Dad was like a son to him. Dad would go out and help them when they needed it. Every year, it seemed we'd go out there and help butcher a beef or a hog and get half of that and take it home for the rest of the year.

Something more of Earl's relationship with the Washburns appeared as James and his wife Lolly spoke together.

Lolly: [speaking to James] In terms of your dad, your dad was somebody that was always willing to do for other people. I mean, you know, he would put off things for himself to go and help somebody else. He was just that kind of person. And he went through some very tough times when he decided to have that business, and then . . .

James: Dad went into the logging business with his brothers up in
        Northern California, and they went bankrupt. It was hard times
        in the late 40s after the war, and they lost the business and had
        to recover from that. But Lolly's correct. I mean, we made many
        a trip out there to the Plains, to Bill's place bringing out old rig
        wood. My dad would bid on these wooden derricks they had
        in the oil fields around Taft and salvage all the wood off them
        . . . Bill was starting to build the supports for those grain storage
        tanks out there, and my dad had a ton-and-a-half flat bed truck
        that he bought used from Standard Oil. We'd load that thing down
        with those big beams. The beams would go over the fenders in the
        front and hang off the back. We had to crawl in the windows to
        get in the truck, and off we'd go up grocer grade [on Highway 166
        west of Maricopa] and drive out there. He recycled a lot of wood.
        I don't know if he bought it for Bill, or if Bill helped him buy the
        derricks, but whatever it was, we hauled at least four or five loads of
        big timbers out there. You've probably seen them.

The Washburn Ranch Is Sold

Bill Washburn died in 1968. He had no direct descendants. Marie was
no longer young and was in no position to manage the daily work of the
ranch. Her son Bill had been dead for many years, and her grandson
Billy had a successful law practice in Sacramento and was not ready to
leave this to become a second or third generation farmer. It was inevitable that the ranch would be sold. By the early 70s, a number of ranches
on the Carrisa, particularly those toward the south, were in difficult economic straits, and a single buyer appeared. This was the Oppenheimer
Corporation, which bought land and sold stock. When Marie Washburn
sold the property, she withheld 160 acres that lay a mile northwest from
the main ranch house and maintained a home on this property until her
death in 1972. Oppenheimer bought the Washburn Ranch and hired
a manager to run it for them during an interim period. It seemed that

a number of Japanese were interested in the property, and there were speculations that Kobe beef, a particularly high-quality and fatty beef, might be raised on the ranch and marketed by the Japanese.

These possibilities never materialized, and Oppenheimer sold the land to The Nature Conservancy, which in turn transferred it to the Bureau of Land Management. The smaller parcel which Marie Washburn retained was inherited by her grandson Billy and today is a private holding within the Monument.

When Billy was asked about his feelings when the ranch went out of the family, he simply said that it was his grandmother's ranch, not his. "I enjoyed everything I was doing deeply, but I never foresaw myself as heir to the ranch. I was sorry to see my grandmother sell because it was her soul as much as it could ever be to any human being. That was the reason she kept the smaller property." She could never leave.

The Traver Ranch

Ten miles south of the Washburn Ranch along Soda Lake Road, there is today an empty cinder block home, a much older wooden house, and a collection of farm machinery and scattered debris. This was the home of Lew and Nancy Traver for many years after their arrival in 1940. Their grandson, Alden Loucks, has already been introduced, and he spoke at length about growing up on the Plains and about his family's history. When Jackie and I met other former residents from the south of the Plains, the story of the Traver Ranch grew and grew.

Lewis Ernest Traver was born in Wheeler Cove, Iowa, in 1873. When he was one year old, his mother brought the ten children west to San Miguel, California. Lew's father had lost property in the Chicago fire of 1869, moved to Wheeler Cove, and then later returned to Chicago to get his property back. His wife thought he was going back for another woman and moved west to live with her brother who was a blacksmith. Lew grew up in San Miguel, never learned to read or write, and in the late 1880s became a laborer at the Nacimento Ranch north of Paso Robles. It was at this time that he met his wife, Nancy Wright.

Nancy's grandfather had also lived in Iowa, but left after losing a lawsuit. He is reported to have said something like: "When you live in a town where lawyers and judges come in, it's time to move on." He started west on a wagon train and soon became the wagon master. When the wagon train reached the Platte River, the ferryman demanded an extraordinary sum to bring them across. It was too much, so grandfather brought the wagons to another crossing, built his own boat, and took the wagons across on his own. When another group of immigrants arrived, grandfather sold them his boat and then continued west.

Nancy was born in 1876 in Adelaide, California, where she attended school through the eighth grade. Nancy's brother became foreman on the Nacimento Ranch, and it is presumably through him that she met her husband. Nancy Wright and Lew Traver were married in November of 1900.

In 1927 Lew partnered with another fellow and leased two sections of land not far from the Simmler community. This is where Lew and Nancy lived until 1940 when the owner put the land up for sale. Although 1940 had been a very profitable year, fifteen dollars an acre was more than Lew was willing to pay, and so instead he purchased 800 acres farther south in the Plains. For several years the family lived in the small wooden house that came with the land. Together with other lands, either purchased or leased, this became the Traver Ranch.

Lewis and Nancy had three children: Pete, Fred, and a daughter Lola. Pete lived with his parents on the Carissa Plains for a short while and then moved to a ranch of his own near the coast. Fred spent his entire life farming with the family. Lola married and moved to Los Angeles, but in 1941 her husband was killed in an automobile accident, and she returned to the Carissa Plains with her two sons, ages four and one. To help support the family, Lola took a job in a post office on the coast, and the two boys, Alden and Jack, were essentially brought up by their grandparents.

Alden's memory was nearly encyclopedic, and he was extraordinarily generous with his time. Jackie and I spoke with him at length on two occasions at the Visitor Center, and when I reviewed the recordings and discovered unanswered questions, he was quite willing for me to stop at his home along the coast to ask still more. It is largely Alden's account of the Traver family that is given here.

The Travers were dryland farmers and depended principally upon wheat for their income. Their farm included one or two cows for milk, butter, and sometimes cheese. They raised pigs, some to sell and some for themselves, and as on all Carrisa ranches, chickens were a family staple. A well provided water for the animals and for washing, but drinking water was trucked from Lawson Spring about a mile away. Conveniences were few: there was no phone service; electricity was provided by a generator a few hours every day; and an underground cellar provided for food storage. In wet weather, the roads could be impassible, and it was common for the Travers to pull stranded cars out of the ditch with one of their tractors. In later years, they graded the roads themselves as San Luis Obispo County had little interest in this distant valley.

Work on the ranch was hard, the house was primitive at best, and Nancy, known as Grandma to Alden, was not entirely happy with life as it was turning out. Alden believes that it was largely to please her that after about eight years in the small wooden house the family built the cinder block house which stands along Soda Lake Road today. When it was finally occupied, this was truly a grand home, two stories in height if one includes the partially visible basement. Today, with a new galvanized steel roof, it looks strangely out of place in the dry landscape.

Air conditioning was unimaginable during the 40s, and so the construction was planned to maintain heat in the winter and provide cooling in the summer. The kitchen stove heated the house in winter, and when summer came, there were vents to open and let the kitchen heat escape. There were several large bedrooms, an indoor bathroom (almost unheard of in the Plains at the time), and a hall that connected several of the rooms. Because the house is on the side of a small hill, the basement is open on one side and includes a garage. The basement also included a dormitory room that could be used when visitors came but was more commonly used by hired hands who assisted with farm work. The main living room was large, and along one wall was a large stone fireplace with a beautiful mantelpiece.

In his later years, Lew suffered from dementia, and it fell to Nancy to take care of him. She would have been nearly sixty at the time, and so their daughter, Lola, returned from her job in San Luis Obispo to help. Lew died in 1956 at the age of 83, but Nancy Traver remained in the house many years until it became necessary to accept assisted living in town.

Carrizo Grass and a Lost Community

The grandsons Alden and Jack both had motorbikes, and as youngsters, they rode them for hours and hours into the hills and along any trail that they could possibly navigate. Because he had explored so much as a child, and because he lived at the house from 1940 till 1973, Alden knew the land well. His memories ultimately led me on a curious search of my own.

Alden believed there was a stand of Carrizo grass within the boundaries of the National Monument. He was only eight years old at the time, but he remembered riding his motorbike through a low saddle in the Caliente Mountains and finding a spring with a tall grass growing. Alden was reasonably certain that if the spring was still flowing then the grass would be there. Although he could not locate the spring precisely, he gave a good description of its appearance and indicated where to go looking. As this grass has never been found within the boundaries of the National Monument, I was intrigued.

Some months later, I followed Alden's directions and spent half a day looking for the Carrizo grass. The ridge was long and high, and there was only one saddle that fit his description. Beyond this opening was a vertical drop and at its base was a green patch of grass or reeds about two feet high. Carrizo grass is typically eight or ten feet tall and resembles bamboo, but I only saw cattails of a very ordinary sort. It was impossible to descend this dry waterfall, and the roundabout way to reach the bottom would have been a long, long hike. Almost certainly Alden as a child had reached this same point, had assumed that the reeds he saw were Carrizo grass, and then returned home. I was disappointed but not surprised.

Alden also recalled a burial location on the top of a small hill at the south end of the Plains. He had heard, and believed, that at some time in very early years a cowboy had been killed in a cattle stampede, and this grave was his final location. The description that Alden gave was an exact match for the Mary Morris burial that has been described already. There would be no point even mentioning this except to indicate that memories are finite, and reports about specific events and locations may not be always accurate. In contrast to this, however, I was able to find remarkable confirmation for another of Alden's memories.

On several occasions Alden spoke of a "community" in the foothills behind his family ranch. Alden recalled that there were wooden remnants of four buildings in a group and that one was larger and oriented differently than the others. There was nothing in the Monument archives about such a community, nor was I able to find any records of homesteads in the area. One of Alden's friends who knew a great deal of the local history vaguely recalled a "Georgi Community," but that was the sum of what was known. Alden promised to take me to the site "sometime," but other events interfered, and the subject was dropped and nearly forgotten.

About a year later, I visited Alden at his home, and we spoke at great length about an extensive collection of photographs taken at the Traver Ranch between 1941 and 1983. Alden had recently broken an ankle and was unable to walk easily. So when the conversation turned again to the community, I asked if he could sketch a map so that I might go looking on my own. Indeed, the sketch which he produced was very detailed, and the area was familiar to me. He marked the location several hundred yards from the nearest road. Whatever remained there would be so minimal that few persons driving the road today would notice the site. Several weeks later, I was in the Plains with the map and searching.

A few yards off the road near one of the springs, several small and rather odd pieces of wood stood vertically up from the ground. Some were nicely aligned suggesting a fence line, and scraps of barbed wire attached to one of the posts confirmed the explanation. The age was uncertain, but the proximity to the road and the obvious function for managing livestock suggested range improvements that the Rudnick family had constructed in the 50s when they ran cattle in the area. These remains were not what I was seeking.

I spent the next hour walking along the edge of the Caliente foothills. In one or two places, there were juniper stumps that might, or might not, have been aligned as part of a fence. I looked for flat areas that could have been the floor of a cabin, and I looked for unnaturally disturbed ground. Eventually I found a small, highly weathered board lying flat in the grass. Nearby was another, and then a small piece of crockery lay exposed beside a rodent burrow. This was late in the day, and certainly I had found more than a fence or corral.

In the half hour that remained before it was necessary to leave, I was able to confirm that there had been several structures here at one time. Some of the boards were clearly part of a wall that had become detached and fallen over. There was another piece of crockery nearby which might have been a broken sewer pipe, and I also found a strange metal object, the size and shape of a large coffee can. The scatter was not dense, but it extended for some distance, perhaps eighty yards. Of particular interest was a pile of rocks in an area that was otherwise entirely sandy. A few of these rocks were aligned in a way to suggest the edge of a foundation. It was not clear if these remains were from permanent human habitations, if they were part of a line camp used seasonally by cowboys, or if this was merely trash that had accumulated near a few sheds and a corral. I took several photos and wondered whether an experienced archeologist could use them to reach a definite conclusion.

When I described my finds to Alden on another visit, these brought back more memories. He was very certain that in the late 40s, there had been four or five buildings, although they had fallen to the ground even then. He guessed that they dated from the 20s or perhaps even earlier. Alden was also definite that water for the community was piped to the site from a spring about half a mile distant. The low hills north of the site, opposite the Caliente foothills, had a line along their base that had impressed him as a plowline, the furthest extent to which the grain fields had been planted. I expressed some wonder that there was so little left of the site when it was truly off the road and would not be easily seen by passing vehicles. Alden found nothing strange in this: lumber was scarce everywhere on the Plains, and any abandoned structure would surely be scavenged. Alden believed that his brother had once been out there looking for old machinery pieces as well. If the community had existed in the 20s, this would coincide with the existence of another known homestead about a mile and a half to the north. If the buildings were older and dated to 1900, this would be consistent with the dates of the Morris homestead to the south. The possibilities were intriguing.

Two months later, I was part of a group removing un-needed fencing in the Monument, and when the work was over, I brought a friend along to look at this site. On my previous visit, I had made careful notes of the location, so this time there was no need to search. The area with scatter was much larger than I had noticed previously. There were boards with nails, heavier beams, and even planking that could only have been walls of a house or cabin. There was a scatter of broken glass, and some of this had even turned purple indicating an age preceding the 30s. The metal footboard of a bed was found at one location, and sixty yards away we found the headboard. The most significant finds were several sections of rusted iron pipe, ten or fifteen feet long and an inch in diameter. Three of these pieces lay nearly parallel to each other and were separated by thirty or forty yards. They were partly buried in the dirt and pointed directly away from the Caliente foothills. The fourth piece of pipe was fifty yards off. Its orientation was perpendicular to the other three. It was parallel to the edge of the foothills, and it pointed directly toward the spring that Alden had recalled. There were three structures of some kind serviced by running water from the spring. A community at the foot of the Calientes seemed to be more than a story. It truly existed, even if for only a short time.

These physical remains are real and visible, but the probability of finding someone with memories of this settlement or finding family records of the community seems vanishingly small. If no other records are ever found, does this mean that the history is truly gone? We will then have to create the details out of our imaginations.

Nancy Traver

Nancy was born in 1876, married in 1900, and moved to the "Traver Ranch" in 1940. Here the family lived eight years in the wooden cabin, and Nancy cooked on a wood-burning stove. As a child, Alden remembers hearing an explosion early one morning. The stove was "modern" with an internal tank to keep water hot, but apparently the mechanisms failed, steam pressure built up, and the stove exploded. One of the steel lids on the top surface of the stove was embedded in the ceiling. Another had flown out through a window. Nancy was badly shaken but unhurt. Alden said that except for his grandmother's eyeballs, the soot in the stovepipe had turned her black from head to foot. She was both frightened and furious. She made it very, very clear that there would be a new stove, and it would not burn wood. The new model was propane.

Today as you drive along Soda Lake Road through the Plains, you will notice that there is a mile of pavement near the Traver Ranch while the rest of the road, both north and south, is gravel. It was not always this way. Once the road was located farther out in the center of the Plains where the land is lower and wetter. The Travers became tired of the problems in getting to town in winter, and Alden graded the new road to its present location near the house. But the road was dirt, and in dry weather, the dust that cars raised as they came along was a continuing annoyance. One story has it that Nancy was hanging laundry to dry on the line beside the house when several cars came down the road and raised a towering cloud of dust. Of course it settled on the laundry, and she was outraged. She went into San Luis Obispo, stormed into the Supervisors' meeting, and gave them a scalding piece of her mind. An agreement was reached that permitted the road to stay as located, but in turn the county would pave the small section by the house. Alden suggests that this story is a bit exaggerated in its detail, but its direction is correct. I would prefer to believe the original version. You have to admire a woman who could bring the county government to its knees.

There is another story from the ranch that also comes in several versions. It was common throughout the Carrisa that when harvest was over farmers would rent their fields to either cattlemen or sheepherders

for animals to graze on the stubble. Walter McDermand, who sometimes worked for the Travers as a young man, remembered an occasion when the Rudnick family was notably tardy in removing their cattle
from a particular field. As he tells the story, Nancy was once again fed up
and used a shotgun to hurry the animals on their way. Marcus Rudnick,
who was well-known as a difficult personality, arrived and was furious. It
is enough to know that the cattle were much better behaved after that.

Walter McDermand was a high school friend of Alden Loucks and
worked several summers during harvest on the Travers' farm. He was big
and strong and weighed 200 pounds. After high school he and his family
moved to Oregon, and during that time, he became seriously ill. When
the family returned to Maricopa, he was exhausted, without prospects,
and down to 120 pounds. He needed a job and went out to the Traver
Ranch and asked Nancy if she could find work for him. She simply said,
"When do you want to start?" and he moved onto the ranch the next
day. Years later when the subject came up, Nancy told Walter, "Gosh,
son. I didn't need no help, but you looked so poorly and sad that I just
had to take you in and get you fed." Eileen Cropper was another of the
young persons that Nancy and Lew adopted. After a summer cooking at
the ranch, Eileen was homesick, and so she and her husband of one year
returned to their home in Arkansas. The following spring in 1941, they
were back in California on the coast, and the Travers sought them out to
return to the ranch. Eileen could not say enough good about the family.

Walter McDermand was involved in another incident which included Nancy Traver. On one of his trips out from Maricopa to visit the
Travers, he was driving rather swiftly along a section of Soda Lake Road.
As he rounded a curve, another car coming the other way swerved to
avoid him and went high on a side bank. This was Marie Washburn on
her way to town and driving fast as she nearly always did. As there was no
damage, Walter simply continued on without stopping. He stayed over
with the Travers, and the next day Marie stopped to visit. Nancy greeted
her and asked how she was feeling. Marie replied, "Oh my goodness.
I am lucky to be alive. Why just yesterday I was nearly killed by some
young man racing along the road not far from here. I just don't know
what young people are coming to these days." Walter wisely kept his

mouth shut, and Marie didn't recognize the young man who had "nearly killed her." When they were alone later, Nancy asked, "Walter, was that you that Marie Washburn met on the road?" Walter confessed, but all Nancy said was: "I thought so. Please try to drive more carefully in the future." Isn't this the kind of grandmother all of us wish we had?

During the war years, 1940-1945, wheat was an essential commodity, and farming was highly profitable. In the following years of the Cold War, an export embargo and farm price controls made this existence difficult. Costs for fuel, for seed, and for new equipment rose steeply while grain prices actually fell in terms of adjusted dollars. The Traver family stopped planting in 1973, and their land was purchased by the federal government a few years later. Their house still stands, and their fields, scattered in places with old machinery, still show faint plow lines.

I think now of a photo that Alden once showed me: Lew and Nancy at the time of their wedding in 1900. Lew was twenty-seven years old, and she was then twenty-four. Lew's suit is brand new, and his hair is combed perfectly. This may have been the only time in his life when he looked like this. Nancy is dressed perfectly and is looking directly at the camera with eyes as big as saucers. To me, she appears a bit frightened. Perhaps she is trying to see what will lie ahead in the next sixty years. If she had known, would she have accepted that future? We know her story, and it is an impressive one.

Strong People

These were strong people who lived at the center of the Plains. In my own time, I have seen both ranches. At the Washburn, I have watched nesting hawks and listened to the coyote chorus at night. The three-hole outhouse still stands near the old bunkhouse, and weeds are rank in the wash where Billy Rolfe had once hunted rabbits as a child. At the Traver Ranch, I have walked through the abandoned buildings and wondered about machinery that still litters the yard. Beside the wooden house, the one where the Travers had first lived when they arrived, an iron stove sits in the yard. Could it have been the one in Alden's story of his grandmother Nancy? We are all fortunate that Bill Rolfe and Alden Loucks remembered their grandparents so clearly. How much better it would have been to have actually met these older people and listened to the stories of their lives directly.

CHAPTER TWELVE

Two Families in the South

Life on the Hudson and Wells ranches

Early Wells homestead

The north and south of the Carrisa Plains are very different. While wheat farming in the north had been prosperous at one time, the circumstances of ranching were much more difficult in the south. Here less rain fell, grain was less reliable, and in the 70s and 80s, many families were obliged to sell their land and move away. In the south of the Carrisa Plains and also below Highway 166, a few families have remained. With no strong community, however, it was difficult for Jackie and me to find their stories. The Hudson family will appear later, but I will begin with the story of the Wells homestead.

Searching for the Story

The Wells Ranch is far off Soda Lake Road to the west and tucked against the Caliente Mountains. When I visited there, the entry porch was collapsing and windows stood vacant. The yard included a second and smaller building, a root cellar, several truck bodies, a wagon carriage, a large grain tank, and a scatter of wood, barbed wire, and scrap steel. Also in the yard stood a number of delightful trees, which were certainly planted for shade and perhaps for relief from the surrounding monotony. This was where Leola swam in the water trough with her younger brothers and chased piglets through the yard. Leola's stories, however, were the result of the search and interviews described here.

It was Alden Loucks who provided our first clues to the homestead's residents. Alden only knew the family casually but recalled that Hiram and Hannah Wells had arrived on the Plains from somewhere farther to the west. One of their daughters, also named Hannah, had married Bill Hill, and in later years, this couple had assumed management of the ranch. None of these persons were living, but there were five children of Bill and Hannah Hill who might yet be alive. Alden recalled that one of these children was Leola Hill Wright, who lived in Bakersfield, and another was Bill Hill, Jr. Alden Loucks could give us contact information for Joyce Preuitt, who was once married to Bill Jr.

After my conversation with Alden Loucks, I was able to contact Leola by finding her phone number using the online White Pages. She gave me family background and contact information for three of her brothers, Chuck, Lonny, and Larry Hill. Her fourth brother, Bill Jr., was no longer living. When I asked about Joyce, Bill Jr.'s wife, Leola, suggested that I wait some time before calling her as there had been a serious illness in the family. Several months later when I did contact Joyce, she was delighted to talk about her time at the homestead, and she arranged an interview that included Leola. It was a delightful meeting at Joyce's home in Maricopa. Although retired, they both had retained their enthusiasm and energy from much earlier years. Much of what follows comes from their memories and stories.

The Family and the Homestead

Hiram Wells, Sr. and his wife Hannah arrived on the Plains and filed for a homestead in 1917. They had come from the Sisquoc, a rugged country between Santa Barbara and the inland valleys with steep cliffs, sandstone outcroppings, brushy thickets, and streams. Even in the twenty-first century, roads and trails there are primitive, and so in the early 1900s the family had come by mule. After leaving the sandstone county, it is tempting to think that the open plains of the Carrisa were irresistible. In a later interview, Larry, one of Leola's older brothers, laughed at this suggestion. He insisted that the couple must have stopped when a mule lost a shoe. Farming at the homestead was so difficult that he could imagine no other explanation.

Hiram Sr. and Hannah had five children: Hiram Jr., Harvey, Hattie, Hannah, and Hazel. There must have been a reason that all their names began with the letter "H," but it was never explained. It was unclear which of these five children had actually come from the Sisquoc with the couple. The daughter Hannah married Bill Hill, and their children, in descending order of age, were Bill Jr., Larry, Leola, Lonny, and Charlie.

Hiram Sr.'s wife Hannah was a small woman and somewhat severe. She was never mean and always fair, but Leola insisted that when she was angry her eyes could shoot sparks right through you. By one account, she had been a bare-back rider in Buffalo Bill's Wild West Show. Larry insisted that this was nonsense, but that she was a very good rider and worked cattle when the family needed the help. Larry was also quite certain that his grandpa had once worked for the Miller and Lux cattle company in the San Joaquin Valley where he was first a cowboy and then a ranch foreman. He had even participated in a round-up of the last Tule elk when they were corralled and removed from the fields that were being used for hay. Hiram Sr. was easy-going, a character, an unrepentant tease, and a story teller. It was obvious in all the interviews that he was respected and loved. Leola recalled that when she was a child her grandpa had seemed seven feet tall. In looking back, she acknowledged that in reality he was no more than five feet, six inches in height. He was dark skinned with dark brown eyes. Neighbors who knew the family said that in his later years Hiram Sr. had beautiful silver-gray hair and a big handsome mustache.

One of the daughters, Hattie, married Ed Stemper who homesteaded nearby at what was known as Ed Spring. Today the name that appears on maps is "Sempre Spring," an obvious variation on the family name. A second daughter, Hazel, married Homer Bradfield, and they also farmed a short distance from the original Wells Ranch. When I contacted a grandson of Hazel and Homer, he elected not to be interviewed. He was unhappy about the circumstances involved when the Bradfield land had been sold to the federal government. Rightly or wrongly, he believed that the sale had been forced and was not voluntary. The oldest son, Hiram Jr., married Laura Stubblefield who came from a large family living in the Cuyama Valley. He also homesteaded nearby at a spring known then as "Hy Spring," and today as the "Wells Spring." Later Hiram Jr. gave or sold this land to his father and moved west toward Santa Maria and died in 1956. The second son, Harvey, never married and died in 1938.

Concerning the deaths of these brothers, I have been told at least four different stories. One would have Harvey dying from a burst appendix, while another gave the cause of death as an automobile accident on the long grade leading from Maricopa westward to the Plains. Leola and Joyce thought that Hiram Jr. died of injuries in falling from a horse, while Larry recalled that while on horseback he had been struck and terribly injured by an automobile. He had not died at the time, but somehow this accident had figured in his death a few years later. The confusion is compounded by the reported presence of several graves near the Wells homestead where one of these sons was said to be buried. Alden Loucks recalled that sometime in the late 40s or early 50s he had seen two wooden headboards that were almost illegible even at that time. I myself searched the location that Alden indicated and found no trace whatsoever. Another piece of history has been lost.

Farming and Ranching

The Wells homestead and ranch later became known as the Hill Ranch. Hiram Jr. and Harvey were no longer present to work the land, and Hattie and Hazel had married and moved to live with their husbands. It was Bill Hill, married to Hannah, who remained and continued to work with Hiram Sr. Bill and Hannah were helped by two of their sons, Bill Jr. and Larry, when the boys became old enough. Much of the land in this part of the Carrisa was vacant, and until 1938, federal land was available for anyone to graze cattle. After that date, grazing on government land was managed through permits given to private land owners living nearby. However, with essentially no neighbors, the Wells family continued to run cattle all through the nearby hills and up into the Caliente Mountains. Farming was done on land that the family either owned or leased, and in some instances, they simply planted and harvested on nearby fields that were used by no one else. They had at least several thousand acres under cultivation in the good years.

Grain farming was managed by Bill Hill, a hired man named Bob Miller, and Bill's two sons. Larry spoke about planting in October and November with tractors running around the clock. The daytime shift began at seven in the morning and finished at seven in the evening. The night shift worked the next twelve hours. Hannah (Bill's wife) and Hannah (Hiram Sr.'s wife) did the cooking, and when the work shifts changed, the crews had big meals at the house. This was also when minor maintenance was done and when tractors were greased and fueled. Larry spoke in detail about harvesting as well. In the 30s and 40s, grain was sacked and then stored in a large barn where it was piled to the ceiling. I commented that the sacks were certainly heavy, and Larry confirmed that some weighed 160 pounds. Bill Hill, Sr. and Bob Miller would throw them to the top of the piles where Larry and his brother, both young then, could barely roll them over. On several occasions it was mentioned that Bill Sr. was a big, strong man, and this is confirmed in a surviving photo that shows him standing with Hannah in the doorway of their tiny house. In later years, grain was no longer sacked but was handled in bulk. With the intense heat in the south of the Carrisa

Plains, their harvest crew was in the field at 3:00 AM and would stop for the day in early afternoon. The family owned a huge Harris harvester with a thirty-six foot header. This was the largest harvester anyone had ever described, and Larry was clearly proud of the work it could do. For his part, Larry always drove the tractor because he was subject to asthma, and dust on the harvester would virtually disable him.

Hiram Sr. had been a cowboy all his life, and he was the principal manager of cattle operations for the family. For the greater part of the year, animals were simply turned loose in the nearby hills. They found water at Hy Spring, Ed Spring, and several others farther up in the mountains. The cattle were confined only by a fence line along the top ridge of the Calientes and another which separated them from other cattle run by the Rudnick family to the south. These fences had been built by Hiram Sr. during his first years on the Plains, and later they were inspected and maintained by Larry and Bill Jr. When it was time to brand cattle, wean calves, castrate steers, or ship animals to market, the family rode into the hills to find the animals and chase them out of the brush. I had expected that this would be hard, hard work, as it was on the Buckhorn Ranch farther west, but Larry denied that anything special was involved.

The process by which these calves were weaned from their mothers was unlike what had been described by others to whom Jackie and I had spoken. Most other ranchers separated calves from the mothers, and then turned the cows out to pasture while the calves were kept in corrals or separate fields. With few fenced fields, Hiram Sr. would instead put a "blab" over the mouth of the calves and send them back into the hills. This was a leather flap that hung down over the mouth. When a calf lowered its head, the flap was loose and the calf could reach the grass. If it lifted its head to nurse from the mother, the flap was in the way. After a few weeks, the cows would be dry, and the family would conduct another round-up to remove the blab. This was purely business. The romance of the Wild West was not part of their lives.

Although not the principal business of the ranch, the family also managed several hundred hogs. Once again the "Wells Plan" was different from that of other families. For the larger part of the year, the pigs were wild in the nearby hills and ate whatever they could find. This very obviously eliminated the job of rolling grain or fermenting mash, and with pens empty most of the time, maintenance was minor. I laughed a bit at the thought of cowboys on horseback roping and branding pigs, but Larry insisted that there was usually no problem. They simply herded the pigs and held them in the pens long enough to manage whatever was needed. At worst a pig might come crashing out of the brush, and a startled horse would throw its rider to the ground. Events of this sort were of no special significance; they were just part of the job. In dry years when grain crops failed, the family depended upon cattle and pigs to survive – and hoped for better luck in the next year.

In the late 40s or early 50s, the family bought land in Northern Nevada and moved their cattle by train to this new ranch. Water was plentiful, and it was even possible to raise hay there. Farming continued for several years more in the Carrisa, but the cattle were gone. Bill Hill traveled between the two ranches. His son, Bill Jr., was largely responsible for farming at the homestead, and Larry who was always a cowboy at heart moved to Nevada. In the late 50s, the homestead lands in the Carrisa were sold to the Rudnick family.

Hiram Wells, Sr.

Although Hiram Sr. and his wife Hannah lived most of their lives on the Carrisa Plains, their daughter (also Hannah) and her husband (Bill Sr.) alternated between the homestead and a second home in Maricopa. The grandchildren spent weekends, vacations, and summers at the homestead but attended school in town. It was in Maricopa where Bill Jr. met Walter, Harry, and Bob McDermand. These other three boys often visited on the Carrisa Plains, and so Hiram Sr. and his wife appeared frequently in their memories. They and the other children spoke of the elderly couple as Grandpa and Grandma.

Walter McDermand testified to Hiram Sr.'s ability as a sharpshooter:

Grandpa always carried a pistol, and he always kept his boots shined. I remember that. And he was there on the porch, and they had wild roses of some kind, climbing roses on both ends of the porch. And he was polishing his boots, and Grandma said, called him, "Look there. There's a bear." There was a bear standing there looking through the roses at them. And he just kept doing his boots and reached around and got his pistol and shot that bear . . . He was a good shot.

The interview continued:

> Craig: He was also a character I gather from Leola.
> Walter: Oh, he was. He was something else. He was . . . We was walking there, and one time we went deer hunting, me and him, and he had a rifle, an old 30-30, and he says, "Now there's a big deer right around the corner. Get you a couple rocks." Well, I didn't question him. I got me three or four rocks. Around the corner we go, and there's that deer standing and looking at us like that. He says, Throw at it, throw at it." I says, "Why?" He says, "I can't hit him standing." And I threw that rock, and he shot him . . . right in the air.

Bob McDermand remembered that Hiram Sr. carried pistols:

> Grandpa Wells carried two pistols, and they were both 410 pistols in scabbards, and he used them for killing rattlesnakes. He was a good shot. Anyway, there was so many rattlesnakes there that they had to have something to protect themselves.

Bob and his wife JoAnne spoke of another occasion:

> Bob: They opened the back door one day, and the old man, Grandpa, was holding a 45 pistol in a scabbard on his side. Now this is what Bill Jr. told me. And a deer came running across behind the house towards those hills over the top, but it was running across the backyard, and he pulled that pistol and killed that deer, a buck.

JoAnne: That's unbelievable because a pistol drops so much.

Bob: And he stepped it off, Bill did, and he told me it was a hundred steps that he killed that deer . . .

JoAnne: You know how they drop? You shoot a pistol like that, and before it gets there, it's already way down. You have to really allow. So he really was good at it.

Bob: Killed a buck over a hundred paces away with a 45 pistol.

Leola recalled a donkey that belonged to the Wells family and the frustrations it caused. She insisted it was a donkey, not a mule, and just as stubborn as possible. If he didn't want someone riding on him, he found the lowest overhanging branch and ran under it to knock you off. At other times, he would just lie down and refuse to get up. Nothing could get him up against his will. Leola remembered when her younger brother Charlie, five years old at the time, came home crying, "I had to walk. The donkey wouldn't go." Leola continued:

Leola: Well, when grandfather was alive and we had these donkeys, he said that they needed to get some exercise. "So you guys are going to ride the donkeys to move the cattle." Oh, I just was horrified. I tried to get out of that, but they made me go anyway.

Craig: Why did you have the donkeys? Or why did your grandfather have them?

Leola: I don't know. He probably won them in a poker game. I don't know why he had the donkeys.

Craig: You don't ride them for cattle if you can help it.

Leola: Exactly. Well, we did, and it took us probably an hour and a half to get out of the yard because they did not want to go. And finally we got them moving and had the cattle all gathered. There's about twenty-five head of cattle, I guess. Well, my donkey took off right in the middle of them and just pfffft. Well, that sort of thing did not go over well with my grandfather at all. And so he's yelling, "Girl, get that donkey under control." And I had its, I swear to God, its neck, the donkey's head was right here, and he was still running full blast. Well, he finally stopped, and Grandfather came up, and he said, "This better not happen again, girl. I've had enough of this. Look at this. The boys are out trying to move these darn things." It was an absolute nightmare. It was. We got up there, and I think that might have been when Charles had to walk back. I don't know. It was awful though.

The family owned an automobile, but Hiram Sr. never learned to drive. He was not about to learn to do something that had no sense to his way of thinking, or at least that was the excuse he gave. The family bought the car in Bakersfield, and it was Hiram Sr.'s wife Hannah that drove it home. Later Hannah decided that she would teach her husband to drive. As he guided the car up to the gate at the homestead, he pulled back on the steering wheel and hollered, "Whoa." Of course he went right into the gate, and then he declared, "I'm not going to have anything to do with something that doesn't stop when I tell it to." So he never drove again, or at least that is how Leola and Joyce told the story.

In his older years Hiram Sr. fell off a horse and broke his hip. The bones healed poorly, and he walked with a cane, a "knobbly" cane in Leola's words. After the accident, he never rode again. In his last years, Hiram Sr. lived in town with Hannah, Bill Sr., and their children. Every day he would walk from the house where they lived to Capp's Corner nearby where he would have a root beer float. He would take every kid that would go with him and buy ice cream cones for them. Leola was eight at the time.

> Well, Grandfather would walk, and the rest of us would walk about five times farther because we'd run ahead, and then we'd run back, and then we'd run ahead . . . cause he walked very slow with his cane. We'd get up there, and he'd have his root beer float, and we'd have our ice cream, and when he was ready, away we'd go. We'd go back, and he'd do that sometimes daily, or at least three times a week, and there was usually about ten kids. Oh, we were happy to go walking with Grandpa.

Hiram Sr. never drank alcohol, but he drank hot coffee year around. He sometimes drank iced tea, but he preferred hot drinks because he claimed that they kept you cooler. And year-around he wore long johns, Levi's, a flannel shirt, a leather jacket, and his hat. After sixty some years of married life together, Hiram and Hannah died within three months of each other, each eighty-eight years old. Hiram was buried in his hat and leather jacket.

Hudson Family Arrives in the Carrisa

The Hudson family was also well known at the south of the Plains. Cliff Hudson was a cowboy whose name had appeared in several interviews, but for quite some time Jackie and I had been unsuccessful in learning more of his story. For reasons entirely unrelated to the history project and quite by accident, I met Kathleen Buttke at a meeting in the Carrisa Plains School. As a child, she had lived several years at the MU Ranch, and Clifford Hudson had been her father. Rick (Leo Jr.) Hudson was a second member of the family that I met, and he is of the same current generation of Hudson family members as Kathleen. It was Alden Loucks who provided the introduction to Rick. It was a matter of luck that Rick had become the Hudson family historian. After half a dozen phone calls and several deferred interviews, I met Rick at his home in Taft.

Rick never knew his mother, as she had died in childbirth when he was born. Rick's father, Leo Cedric Hudson, apparently held Rick somehow responsible for this death, and so the two were always very distant. Rick's father essentially disappeared from his life, and like many other children on the Carrisa Plains, he was brought up by his grandparents.

Rick's grandfather was Percy Floyd Hudson, one of eight children in a family that arrived in the Cuyama Valley in the 1890s. Previously the Hudsons had lived farther west near Los Osos, near Guadalupe, and in Tepusquet Canyon near Santa Maria. They were all educators, and it was no accident that Percy should complete high school. The extended Hudson family settled and worked a large ranch east of Cerro Noreste Road and south of Highway 166.

Youngest of nine children, Rick's grandmother was born Lourena Stubblefield in the year 1884. Two years later, the family moved into a mud and lath adobe house along Highway 166 several miles west of Soda Lake Road. Parts of this adobe still stand to mark the family homestead. It had one window in the kitchen area, one window over the door, and its few rooms were separated by cloth partitions. Lourena finished fourth grade at a country school and then returned home to help her mother run the family ranch as a cowgirl. Her father was sometimes at home and sometimes away. He was an adventurous sort, a gold miner, and none of the family really knew where he went in the absent years.

Percy and Lourena most probably met at one of the social functions in the Cuyama Valley. They were married in 1907 and then lived on the Hudson Ranch. Rick described the "estate" where his grandparents lived and worked:

> The rest of the Hudsons owned that same piece of land with him . . . plus he [Percy] owned several hundred acres that were his own. So he had plenty of land. He had about two hundred head of cattle, I think, and it was sometimes twenty-five hogs. We had a hog pasture, and we'd turn those hogs out in the oak trees, and they'd eat the acorns and whatnot. My grandmother, bless her heart, she was a cowgirl. When she married my grandfather, her dowry was twenty-three head of Hereford cattle, three horses, her saddles and bridles, and a box with some quilts and stuff in it.

Life on the Hudson Ranch

Rick described his life as a five-year-old living on the ranch: "He milks cows, feeds chickens, gathers eggs, cleans corrals, and works right alongside Grandma and Grandpa." The family kept several hundred chickens for eggs and sold them to markets in Maricopa and Taft. They also had a cow for milk and cream. Lourena made cheese, and it was Rick's job to turn the crank when they made butter. Before getting a hand crank model, they had a dasher churn that Rick still keeps, a memento from his grandmother. As for the food that they had on the ranch:

We had a lot of cattle, and we had pigs, probably had thirty, forty pigs sometimes. We'd butcher pigs, and my grandfather had a smokehouse. He used to smoke meats and cure meats. Down at the Klipstein headquarters, there were olive trees down there. We used to go down and pick olives and cure olives. And all summer long we spent . . . we had about five acres of garden, and we probably had, I'd say, a good half acre of grapes, a grape vineyard. Granddad worked the garden.

We had an orchard. We had apple trees, pear trees, peach trees, plum trees, prune trees. You name it, we had all kinds of fruit. We had the grape vineyard with Concord grapes and Thompson grapes and Muscat grapes. And we had a berry arbor. It was blackberries and other types of berries that grew up over this arbor. And we always had to keep those trimmed. We had a big arbor around the north side of the house that was just covered with grapevines.

I asked how food was preserved.

And under that, under that arbor just below the kitchen, there was a cellar under the house, and across from that cellar was what we called the wet safe [an evaporative cooler]. Well, everything was in sealed containers. We used to get coffee in jars, and we used these gallon coffee jars to keep milk, and butter, and cheese, and stuff, and lock it in there, and then of course eggs . . . We would can all summer long, and we'd fill that room with canned goods right out of the garden and whatever we would pick from the arbor.

The way we preserved meat mainly was . . . we would kill an animal, and we would dress it up. My grandmother would make, she'd make these carcass sacks out of cheesecloth. We'd take these carcass sacks and put them over the carcass, and then we'd wrap it up in a canvas, and we'd put it away . . . in a porch room where we kept food and stuff. There was shelves in there. At night we'd take that carcass out of the porch room, and we'd hang it up in a tree, cause at night it got cold up there. And so it would get cool during the night, and in the morning about daybreak, sunup, you'd go get it out of the tree, and you'd wrap it up in the canvas, and you'd put it back in the porch room. And at night you'd take it back out, and you'd hang the carcass up in the tree again, and then you'd cut off of it. As you needed meat you'd cut off of it. Maricopa had a locker plant, and we'd use that locker plant a lot to put meat in also.

No supermarkets for the Hudson family! They were remarkably self-sufficient. Lourena was the cook, and baking was her special pride. She made what she called Old English Wedding Cake. This was a kind of fruit cake that she made for Christmas time. She would make the loaves in the summer, wrap them in cheesecloth, put them in tins, and let them soak in brandy. They stayed up in a cupboard until Christmas when she would pull them down and give them for presents. Mincemeat was another of Lourena's extended cooking projects. With less ceremony, she made fourteen loaves of bread every week with yeast that propagated all year long. Rick also remembered pies, cakes, and a cookie jar that was never empty. Baking was done first on a wood stove and then later on a propane model. When I remarked that with such a pantry it must have been hard for him to leave, the tone of our conversation changed. "That was a good life. My grandparents were up in their, about seventy when I was born, so as I grew older they got to where they couldn't do a lot. Well I was there, and I was young, and I was strong, and I could do the work. Granddad would expect me to do a lot of things."

Before telling of later years, there is more to recall from Rick's youth. I wondered whether it was lonely living far from town and having no one of his own age around. This had never occurred to him. Their house was a center for the entire community. Relatives and neighbors were always at the table to eat at Aunt Lou's house. There was a heavy snowfall at Thanksgiving one year, and the guests could not get their cars up the road to the house. The entire family went down the road, unloaded the cars, and brought the party up to the ranch for the meal. When I asked how many were there, Rick stopped to think, and then continued.

Rick: They [Percy and Lourena] had six children, and their spouses, and they had seventeen grandchildren, plus there were always other people that would come in.

Craig: Your grandmother was cooking for days.

Rick: Yeah, she cooked all the time. She would spend ten to fourteen hours a day in that kitchen, stoking that old wood stove or later propane. That's what she did. She just cooked all the time. And her kitchen went out the back door and outside and down into the garden. And it went up to the chicken pens. We used to have chickens, and we sold the eggs, and we'd also sell fryers to the markets in town. But the roosters and stuff that would hatch out, we had a rooster pen, and she would say, "I want two of those roosters killed for dinner tomorrow."

Craig: And this was your job?

Rick: Yeah, we'd go kill the roosters.

Craig: And then you got to pluck them.

Rick: Yeah, we always had to boil the water and scald the chickens to pull the pinfeathers, and she'd take them in the house, and she'd cut them up and get them ready for the next day. That was on a Saturday, cause on Sunday is when we'd have fried chicken dinner. Another thing we did was we hunted rabbit. And you'd go out like on a Saturday night. Me and my cousins would be up there. I hunted all the time when I was up there.

Rick Hudson Growing Up

As close as he was to his grandparents, Rick and his dad had a difficult relationship. This was apparent in the circumstance surrounding Rick's first horse. An old cowboy by the name of Lawrence Crockett often came up to the Hudson Ranch, and he and Rick were good friends. Lawrence had come from New Mexico many years before, riding his horse and working on ranches all along the way. Lawrence knew horses and he knew Rick's dad.

Rick: Well, Lawrence was up there at the ranch one time, and he was sitting in his old jeep. And my grandfather and I was out there. I didn't have a horse of my own for a lot of years. I walked and did everything that had to be done on foot. Anyway, Lawrence Crockett told my grandfather, he said, "You need to get this boy a horse so he can have a horse of his own," and my grandfather said, "He's not my son. It's not my place to get him a horse." Grandpa said it was up to my dad to get me a horse, that's what he said. Lawrence looked at me, and he looked at my granddad and said, "Well, you know, if that boy's dad ever gives him a horse, it won't be much. It'll just be a one-eyed mule or a knock-kneed mare."

So a while later, a couple years later probably, my grandmother got tired of me not having a horse. I walked everywhere I went and did work, you know, on foot. So she gave my dad some money, and she said, "You go get Rick a horse." Well, he got a mare that had been foundered, had a knock-knee. I told Lawrence, "Lawrence, you're right."

Craig: So what . . . did that become your horse?

Rick: It did for a while, but the horse was so poorly that you couldn't even keep a saddle on it. So my grandma said, "That horse's not going to work." And they got me another horse, and it was a big white Morgan, a beautiful horse, a nice horse.

Craig: Were you roping, or were you just moving cattle around?

Rick: I moved and roped, whatever you had to do. I haven't done that for years. I wish I'd never left that kind of work, but I did.

Rick spoke about visiting Alice Reyes at her gas station, and his dad entered the conversation again.

I even rode a bicycle down there [to Reyes Station] cause Bill Jordan, who worked with my dad, came to the ranch one time, and I didn't have a horse. I didn't have anything. Old Bill made bicycles and gave them to, gave them away to poor kids that didn't have any. So he told my dad, he says, "I'm going to bring that boy a bicycle." Boy, my dad lit up. He didn't want me to have any bicycle. Well Bill backed my dad down, told him, said, "Punch," he called him Punch, he said, "Your boy is going to have a bicycle. I don't give a damn if you like it or not." So Bill come up, and he brings this bicycle. Well, I rode that bicycle all over that ranch. It was a good mode of transportation, and I used to take that bicycle down to Reyes Station.

Rick did well in high school and in his sophomore year started taking college prep classes. One day Rick's dad Leo came up to the ranch, and when someone mentioned that his son wanted to go to college, he was furious and gave Rick a cussing that would match anything ever heard in the US Navy. According to Leo, college was the worst idea possible, and Rick was stupid to even think of it. Rick's grandfather waded into the argument and told his son, Rick's dad, to just shut up. Indeed, Rick did go to college and received a teaching degree. Unfortunately when he finished college, jobs for teachers were almost impossible to find, and ultimately he spent the greater part of his life working in the oil fields near Taft.

When I asked Rick if there had been serious accidents on the ranch, his reply was characteristic and also revealing. He denied that anything major ever happened; there were only a few very minor incidents. I kept asking and soon there was a list of incidents that came to his mind. When Percy (Grandpa) was young, he had been in the freighting business, and on one of his trips, the wagon hit a bad bump. Percy fell off, and his neck was broken. On another occasion, Percy was working cattle by the barn when a bull hit him and broke six ribs. He got up and declared, "Hell, I'm all right. I'll be all right." The damage was discovered only because his family took him to the doctor over his protests. Rick also recalled that a visiting neighbor had once been thrown from his horse and then kicked in the head. These were not serious accidents in the minds of either Rick or the people involved at the time.

"Conveniences" on the Hudson Ranch

Jackie and I frequently asked about conveniences that were, or were not, available to the families. When a generator was installed at the ranch in later years, the Hudsons finally had electricity. But for much of the time that Rick lived there, light was provided by kerosene lanterns. These had a wick dipped into kerosene, and brightness was adjusted by changing the length of wick. In fact these never produced much light, but in winter months this was how homework was done. As we talked, Rick pointed at a lantern in his living room. His grandmother had given it to him because it was the one he had used in his bedroom.

More advanced lighting, if it can be called that, came later when Percy bought a "carbide system." Calcium carbide is a solid which produces acetylene gas when mixed with water. Outside the ranch house was a small metal cylinder with a supply of the carbide and a system for dripping water onto it. Gas collected at the top of the bell, and from there it was piped throughout the house where it could be burned in small lamps. Even more curious was a device which Rick called a "carbide clothes iron."

When dress clothes needed to be ironed, the customary instrument was a metal iron that was heated on the wood stove and which remained hot long enough to be of at least some use. A more "advanced" iron had an opening where embers from the fire could be placed and these maintained the heat for a longer time. But the carbide iron was the ultimate convenience for the modern housewife.

> Rick: She had this iron. She had a closet there in her kitchen, and a pipe came into the closet with a valve on it for that gas. There was a hose that went to her iron, and when she'd iron clothes, she'd go to the cupboard and pull her ironing board out and that carbide iron. She would set it there, and then she would get a match, and she would strike that match, and she'd stick it in that iron, and she'd turn that valve open on that iron.
>
> Craig: And it burned inside the iron somehow?
>
> Rick: She'd get this thing going, and she'd light that thing, and it would go whoooo. And you'd sit there, and it would just roar.
>
> Craig: Like a jet engine as it's burning.
>
> Rick: Yeah. All the time she'd be using it.

It could only have been a mercy when the family installed a generator and had electricity for lights, radio, TV, and of course an electric iron.

Rick Moves On

Leaving the ranch and its life was difficult for Rick. As his grandparents became older, it became impossible for them to manage it. Rick had hoped that he could continue there, and indeed his grandparents had once promised him the ranch upon their death. With many siblings, ownership was a complicated matter. A falling out in the family was nearly inevitable, and there was some resentment of Rick's favored position. He never knew the reasons, but in fact the ranch was sold, and the family moved off. Rick's final words on the subject were:

> Yeah, that's what's bad about it. See, I didn't . . . I loved that ranch. It was like a brother to me. I grew up there. When I grew up there, it was me and my grandparents, the three of us. And outside of . . . my grandfather and I worked side-by-side every day, you know, and that ranch was kind of like a spiritual brother. It was like cutting my hand off when they sold it.

A Mystery Solved: Widow Woman Spring

Conversation returned to a lighter note when I asked if Rick knew anything about the "Widow Woman Pasture." This is a quarter section of land at the very south end of the present Carrizo Plain National Monument. It is along Highway 166 near the Stubblefield adobe where Lourena had grown up. With a name like Widow Woman, there had to be a story, but in spite of my efforts I had been unable to find the origin of the name. Richard Rudnick had suggested that the pasture was named for the Widow Woman Spring nearby. Of course this only increased the intrigue without answering the question. Rick related a story told to him by his grandmother, Lourena Stubblefield Hudson.

A Mrs. Southard lived in a shack across the road from the Stubblefield adobe in the 1890s. Lourena's father was sometimes home, sometimes away, and Lourena had dropped out of school to help her mother. Mrs. Southard was apparently a widow, and when Lou's father was home, he sometimes "visited across the road." Lourena told Rick that one day her much older brother Bill came riding up to the little window of their house on a horse. He leaned over, pointed a finger at their mother, and said, "Mom, you get rid of that . . ." Reading the transcript of the interview with Rick, I am not sure if it was Mrs. Southard that was to be banished or if it was Lourena's father. Of course this is gossip, but a century afterward it is even more amusing.

An Itinerant Cowboy: Cliff Hudson

One of the truly remarkable cowboys of the early Plains was Clifford Hudson. As I mentioned, quite by accident I met his daughter Kathleen. Although she lived and worked in Taft, her childhood had been spent on several of the ranches at the south end of the Plains. She spoke warmly about those years with her father.

Clifford's parents were John Beattie Hudson and Henrietta Jobe. John Beattie was brother to Percy Hudson. Although born in Sonoma County in 1865, John Beattie had moved with his family to the large Hudson Ranch south of Highway 166. Henrietta Jobe was one of seven children born to Samuel Jobe and Elizabeth Blackburn. Samuel had been a Pony Express rider, and after the Pony Express had been displaced by telegraph and railroads, he established a homestead at the southern end of the Carrisa Plains. This is where Henrietta had grown up. Known as the Jobe Homestead at the time, many years later, it became the MU Ranch.

Cliff Hudson was born in 1908 on the Hudson Ranch. Cattle, ropes, fences, round-ups, and horses were his life. He never inherited the family property on Cerro Noreste Road, and for his entire life, he worked as an itinerant cowboy for other ranchers. As a child, he was a good student and was particularly adept with mathematics. He hoped to go to college to study civil engineering, but these were Depression years, and his family had no money. At a young age, he worked part-time on nearby ranches, and when he married, he was obliged to take a full-time job. Early during World War II, Cliff received a draft notice, but as a result of several injuries he had sustained previously he was classified 4F and did not serve. During these war years, he worked on a ranch near LeBec. His daughter Kathleen related:

> You know the war . . . from the time I was six months old till I was four, we
> lived in LeBec, and Dad worked for Frank Butler who was a movie writer at
> Paramount Studios. Because of the war effort and what they did – in movie
> theaters in those days, they said "Buy War Bonds," and they made war mov-
> ies – we were provided with a lot of things that were rationed. And they'd
> bring things to the ranch. Mom did have rationing stamps for sugar, but I
> guess they couldn't buy tires.

In the mid-twentieth century, a family named Klipstein owned and worked a great deal of land throughout Southern California and in the Carrisa Plains. Following the war, Cliff went to work for them, first on a ranch near Bakersfield and a year later on a ranch south of Highway 166 in what is today Klipstein Canyon. Three years later that land was sold, and with his wife and three daughters, Cliff was obliged to move again. Kathleen was eight years old at the time, and her home in Klip-stein Canyon had become very dear to her. Kathleen spoke about his-tory in the canyon and about finding Indian relics near their home. The prospect of leaving for a new place and a new life was traumatic, and Kathleen cried when she was told about the move. Her father knew how to make it right.

> And he knew how attached I was to the Klipstein, and he bent down to me,
> and he said, "We're going to be moving, but we're going to be moving to
> where your grandmother Henrietta lived." So right away I felt wonderful
> because that was where my grandmother had grown up as a child. So I had
> no regrets. And I came out there to the Jobe [homestead] and lived. I loved
> it there so much.

Cliff Hudson became ranch foreman for all the Klipstein property north of Highway 166. This included land in the Carrisa Plains north to the Travers' property, parts of the Elkhorn Plain, and still other proper-ties close to Fellows, Taft, and Maricopa. Kathleen spoke of once riding the north boundary of this range, getting off her horse, and finding a flint stone from which Indians had chipped arrow points. Several years after the Hudson family arrived at the Jobe homestead, the house caught fire and burned. For six months while a new one was being built, the family lived at the traditional Hudson home on Cerre Noreste Road. Kathleen said these were difficult times because she had come to love the Jobe Ranch and missed it so much. In 1952 the Klipsteins sold their Carrisa properties to the Rudnick family, and the Jobe house became headquarters for the MU Ranch. Although they no longer lived at the Jobe homestead, Cliff continued working for the Klipsteins until around 1958.

For reasons that were not explained, the family moved one year to Newport Beach in Orange County, and Cliff worked for a relative who ran a hardware store. Kathleen's mother was happy enough to be off the ranch, but it was a hardship for Cliff. He worked regular hours indoors, wore khaki pants and regular shoes: no boots, no Levis, no cowboy hat, and no horses. It was more than he could take.

A year later, the family returned to Klipstein Canyon. There Cliff worked briefly for the Sneddon family who had purchased some of the Klipstein property. He was later working for a friend in the Cuyama Valley when he received a call from Claude Arnold at the Chimineas Ranch at the north of the Carrisa Plains. Claude needed a ranch manager who was a cowboy, and he also needed a cook. These were the jobs that Cliff and his wife had been doing all their lives, and the Chimineas became the new family home. After two years he moved again, this time to the Avenales Ranch near Santa Margarita where he stayed for sixteen years till he retired. Cliff knew cattle; he knew horses; he dealt fairly with other hands; and he understood hard work and long hours. Ranch owners knew who he was, and although he never had his own property, he was never without a job.

The Working Life of a Cowboy

Cliff Hudson was skilled in everything that a cowboy needed to do. He braided *riatas* (Spanish lassoes); he made hackamores (a type of bridle) for the young colts; he made bridle reins; he made saddlebags. All of this was done from scratch starting with a cow on the hoof. He had learned all this from older Spanish *vaqueros*. The hide must be taken off the cow correctly, and then it was stretched out, staked down, and salted. Stretching the hide required a great deal of strength, and it was only in his later years when arthritis handicapped him that Cliff no longer did this work. After a period of time, the stretched hide would be dry and stiff, and then it could be stored with the hair still on it. Later, if a *riata* was to be made, he cut the hide into strings about a quarter inch wide. Kathleen again:

> After he had made it into strings, then he soaked it so it would be more pli-able to work with. He always did this in the winter. His hands were always busy . . . He'd braid the strings. He had a certain way to braid the rope, and then he'd pound it tight with this hammer, you know. Then he made it the length he wanted. And then he took it out and stretched it. He had a set-up for that. He used his pickup truck, and he attached a rope, and he . . . and you have to be careful because you don't want to break it.

In fact when Cliff was a young hand and before he was married, a rope did break as he was stretching it. As it snapped back, it blinded him in one eye. From that time on, Cliff Hudson was a one-eyed cowboy.

On another occasion when he was a young man, a horse fell on him and broke his leg. Surgery for broken bones did not exist in 1930, and the treatment was to pack the leg in sandbags until the bone healed. Cliff had a friend in Los Angeles who was a doctor, and so he was taken there and was flat on his back for three months. The bone did not grow back straight, and for the rest of his life, Cliff Hudson had one leg shorter than the other. Although these injuries kept him out of the military dur-ing World War II, they never prevented him from working as a cowboy. An elevated shoe for the broken leg may have helped, but still . . . There was no disability insurance in those times.

When Cliff was married and the family was living at the Jobe Ranch, he broke a leg again. His wife and two daughters were away on a week's vacation with Cliff's sister at a beach home. When they returned to the ranch, Cliff came out of the barn on crutches carrying a milk pail. Another horse had fallen on him, but mercifully it was the other leg. They asked him, "Dad, why didn't you tell us that you broke your leg?' He said, "I didn't want to spoil your vacation."

It was a miracle that Cliff was never bitten by a rattlesnake until he was into his eighties. By then he had left the Avenales Ranch and was living again on Cerro Noreste Road. He had gone to gather eggs, and in summertime, it was usual to take a stick to check the nest before reaching into it. It was dark when the snake hit him, and he couldn't even tell if it was a rattlesnake. He said, "Oh, just put some turpentine on. It'll be all right." Nothing more would have been done if Kathleen had not taken him to the hospital in Taft where he was given antivenin as a precaution. If it was a rattlesnake bite, they never knew whether he had been envenomated. For an old cowboy, this was just another day.

As a young man, Cliff worked breaking horses. Bruises and broken bones were certainties for this occupation, but the accidents that have already been described were not his only adventures. Kathleen related a gentler story about one of these horses.

For himself, and he broke them for others. He sold them too, and he has an interesting story he told me about a horse he had to sell. One day I was cooking for my dad, and he said, "Cucaracha, Cucaracha." I said, "Who is Cucaracha?" He said, "A horse I once had. I broke him. I sold him to the military because you could get more money from the military." And he said, "I was going to Nevada to pick up some cattle."

In summer days, they took cattle to Nevada to feed. They took them by train, and so he'd go on the cattle train. He was working for Klipstein, and he went with the cattle train, with the cattle. This man in Nevada got to talking with Dad about a horse that he had. Turned out it was Cucaracha. And so one day it came back with the cattle, this horse, Cucaracha. And Dad gave the horse to the Klipsteins, and he said it lived out the rest of his days on the Klipstein's ranch.

Kathleen Works with Her Father

Cattle could not stay all year in the same pastures. When grass was gone at lower elevations, then it was time to move cattle to higher pastures where better feed was available. Today this is done with trucks, but in the 30s and for many years the moves required cattle drives with cowboys on horseback. These were not the month-long drives across Texas that are shown in movies but instead were several days up into the San Emigdio Mountains to the south of the Carrisa Plains. Cattle were also moved shorter distances on the ranches to nearby pastures for better feed or water or to bring them closer to corrals for branding or for shipping. Kathleen spoke about helping with this daily work as a child. She told about her first job trailing cattle:

> The very, very first time my sister and I, on our gentle old horses . . . Dad was going to train us, teach us how to drive cattle, so we always had to take up the tail end. But our horses decided to stay in the shade of a scrub oak. And they stayed there, and no matter how we reined them or how we kicked them, they stayed put. So Dad had always told us, "If you get lost, don't worry about it, the horse will find its way home." Well we waited under that tree for what to a child seems like eternity. Finally, my mom's brother comes to find us. He gets the horses turned around, and we head back home.

A later cattle drive had its troubles as well.

Kathleen: The plan was to help take the cattle from the Klipstein Canyon part of the ranch over across Highway 166 to the Jobe Ranch. It's hilly, you know, out of sight, you can't see. That was our very first time we ever did this. I was probably five years old.

Jackie: Did the cows get where they were supposed to?

Kathleen: Oh yeah, they did. With all those good cowboys. But the next time when I did it by myself and with Dad, I was probably eight. And he's in a field, it's on this side, it's on the south of the Jobe Ranch. We're going into a field west of Soda Lake Road, and he says, "I want you to bring, see that, see that cow there." He'd point. He'd say, "Bring me that cow, that cow, and that cow." Well, if he'd just said, "Bring me all the cows you see in that field," it would have been fine. But no, I wanted to take just the ones he pointed to because my dad was really strict. You had to do just what he said. So here I am, all the cows ahead of me that he had told me to get, and I had the others behind me. They're following behind me like cats and dogs.

And I thought, oh no. I'd say, "Go back, cows, go back. You're going to get me in trouble." And so finally I had to take them to the east side of Soda Lake Road into another field, and Dad went ahead to open gates, cause he figured it would take me forever to open them. So Dad didn't come, and here I am with all these cows, probably thirty, and pretty soon I hear him singing "Red River Valley." I said, "Oh Dad's going to be mad at me," but he was just laughing and having a good time. He probably laughed about that . . .

Jackie: He may have known that the other cows were going to follow.
Kathleen: I said, "Dad, I tried to get just the cows you told me to get, but these came to follow."
Jackie: That's what you actually count on when you go to gather cattle. If you get a couple, a whole bunch more will come with them.

Kathleen and her sister had their own horses to ride while they lived on the Jobe Ranch. She spoke about these:

That was another interesting thing about the horse I rode as a child. The horse I started out with got old, and he had to be taken away, and Dad, that was another time Dad had to bend down and tell me the horse had to go because it was getting old, but here I'd get to have Uncle Sam Jobe's horse, and that was nice. I felt good about that, but I felt so bad for my own horse. This was a new experience. This new horse was completely different. He was a big black horse, very spirited. And I rode that horse, and my sister by that time, she had a little horse that would buck with others but not with her. Oh, she had a good little horse. Its name was Peanut. And then of course my youngest sister had Maude, the mule. And I can't remember Dad's horse, what horse he rode then. He would break horses too. He had different horses he rode.

On Saturdays when Kathleen was out of school, she would go with her father to check fence lines and water troughs. They were on horseback riding the rough country up the steep ridges. Again and again she spoke of how her dad looked out for her on these days in the field. These were the happy days that she remembered from years ago in her childhood, and even as she spoke of them, Kathleen was teary-eyed. When asked about her best memories, she spoke about the quiet out on the Plain, "You can dream. You can . . . there's nothing interfering, no distractions. It's dark at night, and that's a thing too that you can find something in. The sounds you hear at night, the stars above."

Remembering Cliff Hudson

There is one last story about Cliff Hudson that Kathleen told. "My dad said once . . . he was at a funeral, and they talked about a prayer. They said, or they read something from the Bible, something about many mansions. My house has many mansions . . . And my dad said, 'I don't need a mansion. Just give me a saddle and a saddle blanket to rest my head on.'"

Rick Hudson remembered clearly when his Uncle Cliff died. He had been ill for two years, and the end was anticipated. Several of the family gathered at the bedside, and Rick had asked, "Cliff, what advice do you have to pass on to us in the younger generation?" The reply should have been no surprise: "Take life as it comes to you."

Family Ties

These stories show another side of life on the Plains: the close ties between several generations. I only knew one of my grandparents, and although I feel a great respect for my parents, my chief memories of childhood are of schoolyard games, the paper route I carried, and camping with my Boy Scout troop. When the persons of this chapter spoke, it was their families that appeared again and again. Perhaps with fewer community ties than in the north, families were necessarily more important. The elder Wells couple, Percy and Lourena Hudson, and Clifford Hudson were strong and caring people.

With no fixed home and with no certain job, Kathleen's father had nevertheless provided reliably and cared for his family. Cliff knew and accepted who he was, and by all accounts accepted others in the same spirit. Without a doubt, Hiram Wells was an eccentric, but one of his strong qualities was his attention to the grandchildren. He instructed them, he expected them to work hard, and it was also his pleasure to humor them. Rick Hudson was brought up entirely by his grandparents when his own father drifted away, and when family disagreements arose, it was his grandfather who took his side. Forty years after leaving the ranch, Rick still speaks warmly about the garden, the house, and his life on the ranch. In every case, the attention given to the children seemed natural; this was simply the way that families were supposed to be. I'm not sure if I could have held my own talking crops and cattle with these pioneers, but I wish I had been able to meet them in person. These were the types of strong people that I had expected to find when I first arrived on the Plains.

CHAPTER THIRTEEN

Jinx & Barbara Van Matre

Memories of children and grandchildren

Van Matre children. Back row: Duane, Ivy, Bud. Front row: Jennings Jr, Ernest

Chance may have been the biggest player of all in searching for Carrisa Plains history. I had not lost interest in contacting the Van Matre family, but I had given up any expectation of success. Their abandoned home at the very center of the southern Plains had given a hint of their lives, and the possibility that it might be listed in the National Register of Historic Places only increased my frustration. Chuck Kuhnle had suggested that the family was somewhat eccentric, and Doug Wreden had added to this impression with his account of the oldest daughter, Jeanette, and her marriage to Andy McCornack. It almost seemed that the family had deliberately hidden their traces, and I was reminded of an adage that I had once heard: "When people live at the end of a road, they have a reason for living at the end of the road." Some months after reading Dianna Thompson's final tribute to her grandfather, everything was turned upside down. I could not have been more wrong in my impressions.

One Clue Leads to Another

On a whim, I looked again at the posting about Jennings Jr.'s passing on the genealogical website. I had not previously noticed that although the eulogy was written by Dianna, another person had posted it for her. With a bit of searching, this new email address appeared, and with nothing to lose, I sent a note explaining my purpose and asking if I might be put in contact with Dianna Thompson. My message was relayed, and although Dianna was understandably wary concerning my purpose, her reply was polite. She relayed my interest in Carrisa Plains history to her mother, Jeanette, and also suggested that I contact her Aunt Cynthia who was the family historian. It was Cynthia who had worked at the Shandon post office and then moved away with no forwarding address. Dianna suggested that I locate Cynthia through Facebook, and although Cynthia acknowledged me as a "friend," she did not reply directly to my message. A search on telephone White Pages found her in Oregon, and I finally resolved to make a phone call. The result was astonishing and led to a wonderful series of interviews and a wonderful history of the Van Matre family.

Because my son lived in Oregon, I made arrangements to visit him and then to continue on to meet Cynthia at her home somewhat east of Eugene. The lady who met me was friendly and genuinely glad that the history of the Carrisa Plains was being collected. Cynthia had originally moved to Oregon to be nearer to her aging father, Jennings Jr., who had lived in the very north of California. Indeed, it was she and her sister, Charlotte, who had made the trip back to the Plains to spread his ashes.

The interview with Cynthia was a beginning, and with her help, I

was able to contact three others of her family. I had previously sent a letter and request to Charlotte, but had received no reply. Now, at this later
point, the two sisters had already spoken together about the oral history
project, and Cynthia gave me a phone number and implicit permission
to call her sister. I was also given contact information for her Uncle
Ernest, Junior's twin brother. Through Ernest I eventually was able to
contact Ivy, his older sister. Although elderly, Ernest and Ivy were both
vigorous, and like their niece Cynthia, they had also moved away from
Southern California.

Meeting the Second Generation

Ivy, the first child of Jinx and Barbara Van Matre, married while still living on the Plains. Her husband, Sidney, lived and worked with the Van
Matres for a few years, and then he and Ivy moved to Colorado. On their
return to California, they had taken a residence in the Sierra foothills
largely as a matter of convenience, and this was where I met and spoke
with Ivy. Sidney had died and a daughter, Myrna, had come to live with
her mother. The home was an older ranch-style house several hundred
yards off a small, unpaved road in a delightful stand of oak trees. Ivy was
over ninety years in age and insisted that her time on the Plains was so
far in the past that she could only remember bits. Whatever that past
once meant to her, it was clear that she was comfortable with her memories. She was a gentle lady with a nice sense of humor.

Ernest had entered the US Navy in the final year of World War
II, and he served as a heavy equipment operator with the Seabees (the
Navy's construction battalions). Indeed, a number of farmers from the
Carrisa had served similarly in Korea and Vietnam; heavy equipment
had been much of their lives on the Plains. After the war, Ernest returned and worked several years with his family before re-entering the
Navy to make it his career. When I met Ernest at the door of his home
south of Sacramento, he handed me a written record with his memories from the Carrisa Plains – seventy handwritten pages listing family
members, and describing land purchases, homesteading, wheat farming,

cattle ranching, and problems with feral animals. These collected papers are now archived in the library collection at Cal Poly State University in San Luis Obispo.

Although in his eighties, Ernest was articulate and spoke in great detail about his family's history on the Plains. Where his memories differed from those of others of the family, I am inclined to accept his version as most reliable. Some of what I had found earlier was confirmed, but there were also some surprises. Here, then, is the Van Matre family.

Van Matres Acquire Land in the Carrisa Plains

In 1884 Abraham Jennings Van Matre purchased 960 acres at the north of the Carrisa Plains close to Bitterwater Road. At about the same time, he also purchased 284 acres near Creston where he eventually lived with his son Isaac Sobispo Van Matre. Isaac had one daughter and four sons: Henry, Joseph, Leslie, and Jennings (later known to neighbors as Jinx). When Abraham became too old to work, he divided the Bitterwater properties among these four grandsons. When three of the brothers moved away, Jinx elected to stay on the Plains and bought some of their land. In total, he held 480 acres along Bitterwater Road, and these became the "Home Ranch" for his family.

Jinx was born in 1876, and in 1917 he married Barbara Glenn. He was forty-one years old; she was sixteen. Ivy spoke of her parents, Jinx and Barbara:

> My father [Jinx] met my mother Barbara when she came from Arroyo Grande to take care of my Uncle Joseph's wife, Aunt Sadie, on the Estrella ranch where they settled after leaving the Carrisa Plains. Sadie was due to deliver the first of their two children. It was 1915. Barbara was only sixteen years old when she married my father on Valentine's Day 1917. They came back to the Home Ranch, where they lived happily until his death in 1969. Mother was little more than a child. She was not versed in the ways of my grandmother Permelia [wife of Isaac Sobispo Van Matre], who was very religious and a stickler for an immaculate home. It must have been difficult

for her, but my father adored his "child bride" and always did whatever he could to make her happy. They were loving parents to me and my brothers Vernon, Duane, Jennings Jr., and Ernest. In turn, my mother adored Jennings [Jinx] and much preferred to be outdoors working with him and the livestock than to be inside cleaning house.

Barbara and Jinx had five children. Ivy was oldest and was born in 1919. Vernon, known also as Bud, was the second. Maynard Duane, the third child, was born in 1923 and died young in 1953. Jennings Jr. and Ernest were twins, born in 1926. Jennings Jr. had four daughters who have already been introduced: Jeanette, Charlotte, Cynthia, and Roberta.

Jinx was passionate about acquiring land. Shortly after their marriage, he and Barbara filed papers on a homestead about five miles west from the Home Ranch. In order to satisfy the homestead requirements, they built a house, barn, and corrals, and began farming there. When the three-year residence requirement had been met, the family moved back to their main house along Bitterwater Road. At about this time, Jinx bought 127 acres from his cousin, Vincent Van Matre, and he leased a section of land from William Van Husen, son-in-law of Heinrich Wreden. A last purchase was a homestead that belonged to a family friend, Jerry Hagerty. Jerry was a gold miner who had hoped to make a strike, and when this failed, he sold the land to Jinx and left to look for better fortunes. This came to a total of 1567 acres, which the family worked north of Highway 58.

Jinx scanned the San Luis Obispo newspapers regularly looking for county tax sales, lands that were being sold to pay delinquent taxes. There were few of these available near their Home Ranch, but in the south part of the Carrisa Plains it was possible to buy large tracts at minimal prices. Some sources suggest that Jinx farmed 4,000 acres in the south while Ernest gave a figure of 10,000 acres. Whatever the actual number, it was clear that Jinx with his sons worked very extensive holdings. One of the smaller parcels which Jinx acquired in the south was a second homestead that Jerry Hagerty had patented in 1930. This was exactly the site where I had first found the three harvesters, the old house, and several other outbuildings.

Three Separate Properties

Cynthia, daughter of Jennings Jr., was the first of the Van Matre family with whom I spoke, and I asked at some length about the family lands in the south of the Plains. She answered my questions . . . but I had asked the wrong ones. I had assumed all along that the homestead site with the three harvesters was the family's principal ranch in the south. When I later reviewed the interview, I began to suspect my error. The later interviews with Charlotte and Ernest gave a very, very different picture.

This southern homestead site was, as Alden Loucks had suggested, only used seasonally. To be sure, it was the center of their largest wheat farming ranch, but it was not home. The family called it the "Camp." Their true southern home, and the center of their cattle operations, was north of the Camp and south of the Washburn Ranch. It was on the very east side of the Plains next to the Temblor Mountains. Although no one could explain why, the family had chosen to name it after the Hindu god "Vishnu." When Chuck Kuhnle had spoken of the southern Van Matre Ranch as the "Bayou," he had simply not heard the name correctly. Both the Vishnu and the Camp were acquired sometime during World War II, but it was not until the four sons of Jinx and Barbara returned from the war that they began putting up houses, barns, sheds, and corrals.

Ernest was certain that the main house at the Camp had been moved to the site as a two-room unit. It had previously been the family house on the first homestead that Jinx and Barbara had established to the north. The two additions to this house had been built later from scrap material taken from the oil fields near Taft. Ivy had a different memory of this house. She recalled that it was originally a single room and believed further that it had been built by Jerry Hagerty and sold to her family along with the land. This is consistent with the fact that to claim ownership of the land, Jerry would certainly be obliged to build some structure there.

Because this site may be a candidate for the National Record of Historic Places, I was particularly interested in resolving the discrepancy. The most likely resolution of these two accounts would seem to be that Jerry Hagerty had once built a house on the Camp property, but it had been removed at some time before the present structure had been moved from the north. This suggestion is supported by the SWCA report, which estimated a date for the house in the 20s. This was before Jerry Hagerty took claim to the homestead, but it would be consistent with the dates when Barbara and Jinx built on their northern property. This suggestion is also consistent with a vague recollection that Ivy had of moving the northern house "somewhere." Perhaps Ernest had simply forgotten the existence of a single room structure which the family then removed, or perhaps Ivy was mistaken about its existence in the first place. It is unlikely that this question will ever be resolved.

When I asked Ernest about the windmill, corral, water tank, and trough half a mile north of the Camp, he insisted that this never belonged to his family. "No, that was the Kern County Land and Cattle Company's tank. There was a well and a tank there. We didn't use it. We swam in it. That's all, all we ever used it for."

There was much more certainty about buildings at the Vishnu. They had come from the Kern County oil fields but by an indirect route. Jinx and his sons hunted regularly for quail and deer. The bankers in Taft with whom Jinx did business were also hunters, and Jinx often invited them to hunt on his property near the Home Ranch. These same bankers owned a great deal of the land where oil wells were located. When wells went dry and the oil companies walked away, the banks needed to somehow dispose of the derricks and buildings that had been abandoned. They offered the timbers to Jinx at a minimal cost if he would haul them off. Corrals for cattle were the first construction project at the Vishnu. Posts were timbers eight inches by eight inches by nine feet long. These were planted in holes three feet deep, dug out by shovel. The horizontal rails of the corrals were two inches by twelve inches by sixteen feet long. It is difficult to even imagine what such a piece of wood might cost today, but it was only scrap when Jinx acquired it.

The Van Matres needed a house at the Vishnu, and Duane, who had returned from military service, was recently married and needed his own house near the Home Ranch. The same bankers informed Jinx that the military barracks at Gardner Field in Taft were being decommissioned and sold. Was he interested in a purchase? He was, and the family bought an entire two-story structure for a minimal cost. The first floor was largely concrete and of little use, but the second story was of a suitable wooden form. The entire family participated in dismantling the house and moving it. The second story was cut exactly in half, and then the two parts were supported on large horizontal beams, placed on trailers, and hauled to their new locations, one at the Home Ranch and one at the Vishnu. In one sentence, this seems easy enough, but the written description that Ernest gave in his report is very impressive.

Today the Vishnu property is located on a large, private parcel of land within the boundaries of the Monument. This land is fenced, and gates are chained shut with locks. When the Van Matre lands were sold in 1970, they went to the Oppenheimer Company. Cynthia said that in 1980 she and a sister had been south to the Carrisa Plains and had been taken to the Vishnu by one of the Oppenheimer foremen. Their old house had been modified from what they recalled, and it had been surrounded by a chain link fence. The Home Ranch is decaying along Bitterwater Road and is now on property owned by Chuck Kuhnle. The Camp has already been described and stands in the center part of the Plains where the National Monument has stabilized the buildings and intends to install some interpretive signs. Although it was the smallest and most basic of the Van Matre homes, the Camp may be the one that ultimately survives.

Working at the Home Ranch

Fences and root cellars are part of every ranch. The physical work and imagination required to construct them are impressive. Although Ernest was in elementary school when the work was done on his family ranch, he nevertheless provided a detailed description.

> On the homestead, where we lived temporarily to meet the requirements to own the land, my father and my uncle dug a basement cooler about forty feet from the house, twelve feet by eighteen feet and six feet deep. They made steps leading down into it with a closable door. They also made a regular lumber roof over it with rolled roofing. There were shelves for

canned fruit, vegetables, and meat hooks to hang quarters of beef. Also there were two coolers that my father [Jinx] made. These were made with a wooden framework with four shelves. This was covered with heavy burlap. The actual cooling came through a large tin pan four inches deep that was on the top of the cooler. It was cut from a sheet of tin and soldered together. Around the full length of the pan, tiny nail holes were made to let the water in the pan run down and saturate the burlap [where it evaporated and cooled the structure]. It is amazing how well evaporation cooling works. All our milk, butter, and all perishable foods were kept . . . [here]. When the requirements to own the homestead were met, we moved five miles back down to the Home Ranch.

Of course fences are needed to manage cattle, and every rancher will tell you that he spent a good portion of his time, the tedious portion, building fences. Ernest saw the situation as follows:

One of the basic problems a rancher has when owning any number of cattle is: you must always know where each and every one is on your property. Cows do not have a natural stay-home instinct. Instead I believe they all firmly believe in the old adage, "The grass is much nicer on the other side, etc." It was important to make sure you had a good strong fence. Our answer to that problem was our one hundred and sixty acre homestead, one hundred, twenty acres covered with juniper trees and forty acres level enough to raise grain. Post were not expensive but when you need hundreds of them, they were not in the budget.

Theses junipers provided the posts needed on all the Van Matre lands. Juniper trees are better described as very large bushes with up to nine trunks (or large branches) growing from a single root. When it was time to build fences, Ernest and his brothers would head into the hills on the homestead property with a two man bucksaw. A tree was cut, and the poles were trimmed into eight foot lengths and piled up. Then it was on to the next tree. It was impossible to get a truck into these hills, and so some scheme was needed to get the poles out to level ground. For this, Jinx built a sled out of an old truck body and with a hitch borrowed from a harvester. With one of his smaller tractors, he could sled the posts to a waiting vehicle. If the fence under construction was on level ground, then Jennings Jr. would drive the truck, and a hired man would throw the poles off at sixteen-foot intervals. These poles were planted thirty inches deep in holes that were dug by shovel and crowbar. Fences had four strands and each wire was fastened by two staples at each post. There were miles and miles of these fences to build.

Barbara Glenn Van Matre

Barbara was sixteen years old when she married, and her first child was born two years later. Earlier interviews that Jackie and I held with neighbors suggested that she was a truly remarkable woman. Her children confirmed this as fact. Ernest attended the Simmler School about seven miles distant from the Home Ranch where they lived at the time. His mother would drive the children to school. In winter, roads could become horrible bogs, and Ernest recalled one particular occasion:

> One morning on the way to school, we drove into one of these long water holes and somehow the engine stopped. Mother tried the starter, but it would not work, so she had to get out in ten inches of water and crank the engine. It took her some time, but she got the Ford going again and us on the way to the school. There the school teacher informed us kids that we were late, and this would not be tolerated. I thought how fortunate it was that mother had gone straight home and had not gone into the school. It is not wise to make an angry Irish woman more angry.

Knowing something about Barbara made me think of Aunt Lottie, and so I asked if the family knew Lottie. The reply was: "Oh, everybody knew her." Cynthia recalled an occasion when Barbara had somehow fallen and hit her head badly. She was put in bed, and one of her children went to a neighbor and put in a call to Lottie. The family never had a phone or television, and it was only in later years that they even had reliable electricity. Lottie made a house call as she almost always did, and the conclusion was that Barbara had to be taken to town for a real doctor. As the situation turned out, the injury was not serious.

Ernest spoke also spoke of Aunt Lottie:

> Yeah, she took care of my brother, Duane. He thought it would be fun to grab a fence post and vault over the fence, and he did that one day, and the fence post broke, and he ended up on the barbed wire and laid the back of his legs open. We took him over to the King's place, and Lottie sewed up the back of his leg. That's one time when she helped us a lot. There were a lot of times when she helped us out. Whenever anybody got sick in the family, really sick, we'd go see Lottie King.

Minor medical problems in the Van Matre family were treated by Barbara. Cynthia spoke of Corn Huskers Lotion, Bag Balm, and Lava soap. These are not medical treatments, but most people who have memories from the 40s and 50s, no matter where they grew up, will recall some of these. Normally Barbara had no use for doctors. Cynthia reported, "She always raged to us on how doctors are just out to take your money and kill you." Barbara's son, Duane, died of a gangrene infection from a war wound, and she blamed the doctors for that. Cynthia spoke about Jennings Jr.: "My father was the same way. Right before he passed away, he hadn't been to a doctor in twenty years. I mean, he had to go to a doctor when he broke his arm, but other than that he wouldn't go to doctors." Jinx had skin cancer, and ultimately it was necessary to have part of an ear removed. When the cancer returned, he decided that there was no point in seeing a doctor about it a second time. The result of this decision I don't know, but it is also a fact that he lived to age ninety-three.

The subject of dentistry came up, and it is easy to guess that nothing less than an emergency would bring the family to town. Cynthia told about the one time that her grandmother, Barbara, did go to see a dentist, or didn't as the situation had turned out.

> One time she went to the dentist; my dad's wife took her. They put her in the room. My stepmom went out to go have a cigarette. Grandma almost

beat her to the car. She decided she wasn't going to do it after they drove her all the way from Carrisa Plains into San Luis Obispo for her appointment. She walked out and never went back. But, yeah, she had really bad teeth. She wasn't able to, I don't know how she dealt with them other than . . . She dealt with a lot of pain. They did, they were very strong people as far as pain went. Their tolerance was extreme.

Somehow it is right that Barbara and Lottie were friends. I had heard their stories in widely different contexts. Their acquaintance demonstrated, once again, that the Simmler community was a close one. Another story about connections was told by Ivy when I asked her about dances at Simmler. Her memories were very nice: "Yes, when I was a teenager, about thirteen, my Aunt Jean, my aunt told me I had to dance, and she asked this Ernest Garcia, he was a nice, one of the Garcias, she asked him to dance with me. So I danced with Ernest Garcia, my first partner. He probably won't remember."

Harvesting Grain and Raising Hogs

Cynthia had memories of harvest time when the four sisters often helped out. She recalled an occasion when their Uncle Bud was pulling a harvester with three of the girls riding. A gust of wind blew Jeanette's straw hat off and into the header. Trying to grab it, she hit the leveler bar, part of the mechanism that kept the threshing floor level, and the result was to tip the machine wildly and start it down into a gully. They tried to call ahead for their uncle to stop, but there was no way he could hear them with all the noise of the tractor. It was only luck that made him look back. He stopped the tractor, jumped off, and ran back to right the machine. Bud scolded them for nearly capsizing the harvester and getting killed. Jeanette was crying because her hat had been ruined.

Earlier interviews had suggested that Bud was sometimes eccentric in the projects he undertook. Both nieces spoke about his venture in raising hogs:

Charlotte: He had two hundred and sixty of them, about one hundred and thirty at the home ranch and another hundred and thirty up at the Vishnu. The only problem was in the bad weather when you couldn't get to the Vishnu. If you couldn't get up there to feed them, they would attack each other. They're vicious, and they'd attack you too. I remember having to go up there one time, and the grain truck [with feed for the hogs] was parked outside the corral fence. The troughs and everything were empty. It had been like three days, and we had to go and literally crawl across the corral fence to get to that truck because there's no way you could get on the ground. They'd attack you. I was so scared. I'm thinking, "Oh my gosh," because they were banging against the fence, you know, making it sway. "If I fall, I've had it."

Jackie: Yeah, they will kill anything.

Charlotte: They will, when they're that hungry. So we finally talked Bud into getting rid of them. But I've still got a scar right here on my knee where I literally had to jump a fence to keep from getting attacked by his boar. He had a huge boar. He stood about this tall [indicating three or four feet]. His name was Charlie. Oh he was, oh he was mean. Gosh he was mean.

Craig: It doesn't sound as if Charlie was one of your good friends?

Charlotte: Not my favorite, no he wasn't.

Cynthia recalled that Charlie was forever breaking out of the corral and leading his ladies on walkabouts. Nola Twisselman's garden was a favorite destination, and Bud was in frequent trouble for this. They also found a nearby pond where they could cool off in the hot weather. The hogs were not happy when the sisters were sent to bring them back home. It was an epic battle of wills.

Stories about work on the ranch, about failed or foolish enterprises, about barbecues and neighbors, and about the Farm Bureau went on and on. These conversations with the Van Matres were among the later interviews that I conducted. In some ways the stories were already familiar, but when you hear them again from different persons and from different perspectives they take on greater meaning. These were not isolated events that affected only a few people. These were a way of life and provided a common bond throughout that part of California. I will finish this chapter with two narratives which Ernest related, though not about his family and not about daily life. The particular problems and their solutions were somewhat unique, but even that is a common thread through most everything in the Carrisa Plains.

Ernest Speaks of Dogs and Horses

Dogs were a part of every farm and ranch, and for the most part they were necessary to work the livestock. Coyotes were a constant menace for sheep, and large aggressive dogs were one strategy for keeping coyotes away at night. Unfortunately these animals sometimes lost their civilization, and on one occasion, a group of nine had left their ranches and become a wild pack. They had become even worse than the coyotes, and a number of ranchers at the north of the Plains had lost sheep or cattle. Al Stone was one of these. In Ernest's words:

> He [Al Stone] was starting this small sheep herd. The dogs went up there one morning, and he woke up with yipping and bleating of sheep running around. He went out, and there they were. It was a pack of nine dogs killing his sheep. So like all ranchers do out there, we all have rifles and shotguns and pistols and whatever you wanted, cause there wasn't much law against it then. He went out and shot three of the doggone dogs right on the spot. If it had been coyotes, they would have scattered in all directions, but the dogs went down the main road, started running down the road. So he . . . yeah, he got in his pickup and followed them, and about three miles down the road, there were no more dogs. He shot them all. They did a lot of damage, though. They killed a lot of little calves, small animals.

Dogs were not the only farm animals that went feral. In early years, the north of the Plains was used largely for cattle ranching. When it became apparent that more money could be made raising wheat, a great deal of land was converted to farms. The horses that were once used to manage livestock were no longer needed, and some simply went wild. West from Bitterwater Road toward the San Juan Creek is a high mesa that is brushy, seldom used, and well supplied with water. The feral horses made this home, until they discovered that newly planted wheat was better feed than grass on the mesa. When farmers tried to chase the horses off the fields, the result was usually even more damage to their crops. Ultimately the ranchers persuaded the county to send some of their animal control officers to help. Large stock trucks were brought in, several temporary corrals were built, and county riders and ranchers went out for a round-up. The wild horses were driven in and ultimately shipped off.

A Final Visit

Of course I wondered why the Van Matres had left the Carrisa Plains, and it was Cynthia who spoke most directly about this. Among the children of Isaac Sobispo Van Matre, Jinx was the only one who had elected to remain on the Plains; the others had sold and moved away. Jinx died in 1969, and shortly afterwards, nearly all the Van Matre property at the southern end of the Carrisa was sold to the Oppenheimer Corporation. Jinx's wife Barbara wanted to stay at the Vishnu, but there was no one to run the ranch. In fact, most of the money from the sales went for taxes. Jennings Jr., with his wife and daughters, lived for a while on 284 acres of family property near Creston. The farm there was marginal, and when the house burned down, they were obliged to live in a granary on the property. Cynthia's mother was alcoholic, and when she died, her father, Jennings Jr., became seriously alcoholic for a period of time as well. Cynthia lived briefly with her grandmother and her Uncle Bud in a house which Barbara had bought in California Valley. None of the family chose to remain as farmers, and ultimately the four daughters married and moved away. Barbara died in 1984.

What of these ranches today? The Camp with its falling house and wooden harvesters lies within the Carrizo National Monument and is being restored for visitors to see. The Home Place is hidden in a grove of trees off Bitterwater Road on lands that now belong to the Kuhnle family. As for the Vishnu, it stands on private property falling within the Monument boundaries on the east. With sunlight at just the right angle, it is possible to stand on Soda Lake Road and barely see the Vishnu across the open fields. Few people who see the buildings will even wonder what they are looking at. Several times I attempted to contact the owner of the property to ask if I might visit the old ranch. My calls were never returned, and I decided at last to cross the boundary fence and simply walk over the fields. My search for the Van Matre family had started with the decaying house and harvesters farther to the south. It would end when I had finally seen this, their southern home on the Plains.

It was early morning when I arrived at the Vishnu, the sun was low, and the canyons of the Temblor Range were still in shadows. Beside a large barn was a corral with an old windmill, and I wondered if this was the electric plant that Bud had once put up. The ranch house was behind a chain link fence as Cynthia had seen it some years earlier. Not far off was a shed that had been a machine shop at one time, and in a nearby yard was a magnificently preserved wooden harvester. Almost certainly the harvester had not moved since the Van Matres had worked the land. Lastly, on a low hill and closer to the Temblors, stood two huge grain tanks.

I walked to the hill behind the tanks and looked back toward the west. The entire Vishnu lay in the foreground, and beyond that were the open fields of the Carrisa Plains. In the morning light, I could see the Caliente Range in the distance with the Washburn Ranch barely visible at its feet. The silence was complete, and the dry grass before me was yellow and brown.

Although the Van Matres have scattered across California and the American west, their story remains with the Carrisa Plains. The land and the people had become one.

CHAPTER FOURTEEN

Three Women

Unsung heroes

Pioneer on the Plains, 1939

A last part of the story of the Plains, one which is often overlooked, tells of the women who lived, worked, and raised families far from the more settled parts of the state. For the men there was dust, heat, and stubborn animals. Machinery broke down, and there were hired crews to manage. But nearly all the men who worked ranches had grown up doing these things. It was simply the way things were. The women that we met, both directly and indirectly, told different stories and ones that I had not expected to hear. These may be the unsung heroes, heroines really, of the American West.

Some of them grew up on farms and ranches. You have already met Nancy Traver and Lourena Hudson. Some of the farm wives, however, had come from the cities and had to learn an entirely new way of life. There was dirt everywhere, there were insects and mice, there were children to watch and feed, and for many there were farm chores as well, barnyard animals, cattle, canning, cooking, and even field work in some instances. For those who had not grown up on the Plains, all this had to be learned, and learned quickly. Above all, living on a ranch far from neighbors was sometimes an isolated existence and very different from what they had known before. For some this was too much, and after a few years they left. Others adapted, and a few were truly enchanted and would never leave even if given a choice. The lives of women in rural America and the work of women on the Carissa Plains often go unrecognized. They were also pioneers of the early twentieth century.

Debbie Beck

Steve Beck was the second son of Kenneth and Jean Beck and brother of Greg. It was natural and expected that he would be a farmer and work on the family ranch. His wife Debbie was from the coast, and her story is one of those about learning to adjust to a different life. When I spoke with Steve and Debbie, I was impressed with her adaptability and with her energy and spirit in describing the life there. Debbie moved out to the Plains immediately after their marriage in 1974.

A first question to Debbie was: "What is it like to move out to the Plains from the city?" Without a second of hesitation, she replied, "Shocking, utterly and totally shocking." We laughed. Then she went on to talk about the isolation. "If you can't stand to be alone and be by yourself day after day, then it is not a place for people to be." And she spoke of the work, day and night, all the time. Steve, of course, knew about these things, but Debbie said that she didn't know anything. She laughed and said that she was too young, too blissful, and too innocent. Later in the conversation I asked her what was most important for a new wife who arrived on the Plains for the first time, and Debbie answered, "You have to love your husband."

Debbie never drove a tractor on the ranch. However, in the summer months when wheat was being taken in, Debbie drove one of the bulk trucks that brought grain from the fields to the storage tanks. She spoke of an incident when the truck caught fire, and the story gives a flavor of the unexpected that was a normal part of her life there.

The family was harvesting on what they called the Pimentel along the east side of the Plains just below the Temblors. It was their practice to keep the harvesters running without a stop, and the bulk trucks drove alongside them as the grain was unloaded into the truck. Debbie explained that she would take a load from one harvester, then pull up to the next, and when that had been emptied, she would go on to the next. At that time the family had three harvesters working, and it was a big operation. The truck was unloaded at the tanks with a hydraulic dump mechanism, but then of course the last of the grain had to be shoveled out of the back corners. Debbie was between the field and the farm when she began to smell smoke.

She was driving the truck, an old Dodge, onto Highway 58 when the smoke began. It seemed to be coming from the engine, and it was big. But whatever the cause, there was the danger of setting an entire field on fire. There was no cell phone to call for help, but there was a fire extinguisher. She could only hope that somebody would see the smoke and could help. In Debbie's words:

> Something in the engine was burning, and I'm like loaded with wheat, trying to get the truck over to the other side of the road. It's really heavy. And so I'm trying to get the truck on the other side of the road. I got it off the road. I got the fire extinguisher out. I see the harvester coming across this field from the Pimentel. Steve, oh yeah, he saw the smoke. He's driving the harvester across the, you know, he pulls out from the rows, comes over as fast as he can in the harvester, across the fault on the Pimentel. You know,

he's driving as fast as he can.

By the time Steve arrived, Debbie had the hood open and was using the fire extinguisher. It was the powder that is used for electrical fires. It went everywhere.

> Oh my gosh. The powder covered all over the seat of the truck, all over the engine. I'm sitting on the side of the road going, "I quit. I'm done. Take this job and you know what." And pretty soon Dad [Kenneth] drives up. I think Dad probably drove up about that time. He always had a knack for being where he should be right at the right time. I said . . .

In the early 80s, the Becks leased the Goodwin Ranch. This was where Dewey Werling had raised cattle and wheat until he finally gave up ranching and moved to town. For about seven years, the land had been leased to Ray Cavanagh, and following that the Becks assumed the lease, again for cattle. Greg Beck was away and it was principally Steve and Debbie who managed this operation.

The time came to wean the year's calves from their mothers. With four hundred or more calves, the job took two days at least, and a number of neighbors helped with the round-up. The calves were locked in a corral, and the cows were outside in the next field, mooing and looking for the calves. Steve was sick with a bad flu, and the calves had to be fed. This was Deb's job. From bed, Steve had said, "You've got to go down there. You've got to go down there and feed those calves. Hay. Make sure the water's on, make sure the water's on."

Debbie was not eager to leave the home ranch for more work at the Goodwin and said, "I don't want to go down there. I'm tired. I don't want to go down there, and I don't want to go down there. I don't want to mess with all those cows. They're all crying, and their moms are all there. Their moms are all mad, and I don't want to go down there."

Steve: "I can't get up. I can't get out of bed. There's nobody else to do this. You've got to go down there." This was the life of a farm wife. Deb got in the truck and went to the Goodwin. The gates had come open.

Deb: Somebody left . . . the gates were open. All those calves . . . we'd
worked like two days, three days, to get all those calves separated
from their moms, and they're all out. They're all back out with their
moms. I get down there, and all those calves are out sucking on their
moms again. They're all out there in the field. They're all walking
away with their moms. There are no calves in the pens at all. And I
go, "Holy Mother Mary. They're all gone." I'm like, I'm just sitting
there all alone. I'm all alone at the Goodwin. I've got all this hay in
the back of the truck. I don't know how I'm even going to get it out
there. I'm all alone, and they're . . . the only thing I've got is the hay.
Sure, I'm going to put this hay out, and they're really going to want
to eat this hay after they've got their moms. And they're sucking on
their mom's milk, and they haven't had it for three days. Oh, my
God. And they're walking away with their moms. I mean it's like, it
was a total mess. It's like there's no way I'm ever going to get them
back. It was like "Okay, I quit." So I came back home and said,
"Steve, they're all out. They're all gone."

Steve: I didn't say anything. You walked into the bedroom. You opened the
closet. You took your suitcase down, and you started packing. I had a
temperature of 101, 102. I was sick, and I go, "What are you doing?"

Deb told him: "I'm leaving." Steve asked: "What's the matter?" She
replied: "It's the cattle, all the cattle are out. I can't take it."

There was nothing to do but call the neighbors back and spend another two days separating the cows and calves. In retrospect it may have
been funny, but there was no humor at the time. Deb said:

Well, I'd been feeding people for three days to have them help us work.
I'd been feeding them all for three days. I'd been feeding them, you know,
whatever, beans, steak, whatever. I'd been cooking for three days, plus
working for three days getting all these cows separated so we could wean
these calves, we could sell these calves, get them on a truck. We didn't get
them on a truck. Probably we didn't get them on the truck when we should
have. Now they're all back, so it was all a big, this whole week was a waste.
This is total farming.

She said it was like pushing the wrong button in the "dot com" world and erasing everything that had ever been put on your computer. Eventually it was all sorted out, and Steve recovered from the flu as well.

Deb was a cowboy during those years, and one of the jobs that fell to her was riding into the hills of the Chimineas Ranch to find a bull that was destined for market. This was in the national forest not far from the Goodwin Ranch. The bull was leading a pleasant life in the shade of one of the canyons. He was supposed to be producing calves, but apparently this was no longer of interest to him. Instead he ate and slept in comfort where he couldn't be found. It was time to turn the animal into round steak, and it was clear that Deb was not to come back to the ranch unless the animal was with her. The bull was not cooperative, and there was no possible way to round it up and lead it home. It was hot and dry in the summer, and the only possible way to make it move was *water*. Eventually it would be thirsty enough that it had to come out of the brush to a water trough. Deb explained that the rest of the round-up consisted of yelling and letting the dog harass it until it could be forced into a trailer behind the truck. There was no corral or chute in the forest to make it easy. I never heard the conclusion to the story, but the fact was that Deb did finally get home, and there was never any later comment about this animal. The bull had met its match.

There was another cowboy story that Steve and Deb told about the Beck Ranch. The two of them were moving cows from the Pimentel property in the Plains eastward over the Temblors to some property they had leased from Ricky Twisselman on the San Joaquin side. It was a hot day, and with three dogs to help, the cattle arrived at the next pasture. Ricky offered to drive them back to the Beck Ranch, but Steve said, "Naw, we'll ride. We're tough. We'll ride back." They were on horseback.

It was a wickedly hot day, and as they headed home over the top of the ridge, the dogs quit. They lay down and wouldn't move. These were not lap dogs from the house. These were tough Border Collies, born to do this kind of work. But the day had become too much for them, and besides this they had run out of water, and there was no shade anywhere. Debbie was animated telling the rest of the story.

We had no water. All we had was Steve's hat for shade, so he's like under his hat, trying to get some shade. I said, "I don't feel good, Steve." Steve said, "Just keep riding." I said, "I can't ride anymore. I have to walk." I got off the horse and started walking. "Okay, Steve. I've got to sit down. I've got to sit down under a tree somewhere." Steve was absolutely firm, "You can't sit down. You're not sitting down. You can not sit down. I will not let you sit down." Deb: "I can't walk anymore." We got to our truck, ate something, got hydrated, and then we went back and looked for the dogs, found the dogs up on the top. They hadn't moved. They were just lying there "hchh, hchh," almost dead. We had to pick them up and carry them. Big old dogs. They just lay there. They were just lying there. But the cows were safe. Ooooh, yes. Of course. Never mind the wife.

In retrospect, Steve and Deb laughed about the incident. but Deb also said that the ride got her thinking about looking for another life. The ranch was barely providing a living for the two of them, and not too long after this they moved to San Luis Obispo. Deb spent a year getting a master's degree in counseling, and took a job working with troubled kids at one of the high schools. When the kids tell her how hard they are working and how people expect too much of them, Deb can only chuckle. "They have no idea what the word 'hard' means," she told me. Deb had no regrets about moving back to the city.

Jan Cooper

Jan Cooper is one of the true survivors on the Carrisa Plains. When she arrived at the north of the Plains as a bride from the coast, she could not possibly have been more innocent about what lay ahead. She learned to cook for the harvest crew, took up hunting with another friend, Shirley Livingston, and then later worked harvests together with Shirley and with another woman from a nearby ranch. Jan worked in town briefly, became a cowboy for a neighboring rancher, and has lived alone for several years since her husband's unexpected death. Today she speaks easily of her affection for the land and sky. She intends to stay on the Carrisa Plains.

Jan insists that she was not really a city girl. Her family always had animals when they lived in Atascadero and San Luis Obispo, but on the other hand she admits that she had never worn blue jeans till she came to the Plains. Jan was a high school student in Atascadero when she met Jon Cooper. He graduated two years ahead of her, and one of his friends, Walter King, was seeing Jan's sister. This was the connection. It was not till Jon's third marriage proposal that Jan agreed. The first one was on the spur of the moment and something of a joke. The second time Jan insisted that she was too young. Perhaps she couldn't think of a way to dodge the third proposal, or perhaps she had no intention of refusing, but whatever the details, she became a new bride on the Carrisa. This was 1965 when Jan was twenty-two.

Jon's dad, Alfred, was one of four brothers who came to the Carrisa Plains in the late-30s, and the family had become an institution there. All the Cooper children went to the Simmler School. They had married others from the King family, from the Twisselman family, and from the Kuhnle family. Of course Jon's bride was expected to be a ranch wife. Jon's mother asked him, "How is she going to adapt to the life out here? Is she going to want to cook for the hired men?" Jon replied that his wife would not have to cook for hired men unless she wanted to. It was, and still is, characteristic of Jan that because she didn't have to cook, that was exactly what she was going to do. Jon was too smart to insist that his wife would have to cook.

For Jan, cooking became a new adventure all by itself. Jan told of once going on a family picnic with Jon and bringing chicken and cherry pie. The chicken was raw, and the pie crust could have been a competition Frisbee. Jan claims that her family actually did throw it around. In the early days, her job was to feed the farm crew on the ranch, a few miles west of the Simmler School. When Jon and Jan came home from their honeymoon in Las Vegas, one of Jon's uncles was already sitting at the table waiting for his breakfast. Jan would go to the living room to read cookbooks and would sit there from meal to meal teaching herself. She admits to a lot of crying and hiding when meals didn't turn out right. Today Jan's cooking is legendary, and her friends complain that she is responsible for their weight gain.

It was also characteristic of Jan that she became very efficient at this work. If the crew was working all night, she would have to fix something for them when they came in late. Everything would be ready before she went to bed. Bread was sitting by the toaster, the toaster was plugged in, the eggs and pan were out, and the table was set. When the crew came in, the final preparations took only fifteen minutes, start to finish. Later when her first daughter was born, Jan had some help in the kitchen from a neighbor, but initially she worked alone. There were nine men to feed three times a day.

There were other things for Jan to learn, and she laughs about one of the lessons. Shortly after her arrival on the Plains, she needed to feed one of Jon's uncles . . . but there was nothing in the house, and Jan had to go to the store nearby. She put on a nice dress, stockings, and heels. Jon asked, "Where are you going?" and Jan replied that she was going for groceries. Jon suggested that slippers and a robe were what his mom always wore for these errands. Jan was sure that Jon was not the only one who laughed about her naiveté. She quickly adapted to the local dress code.

Another lesson in Jan's initiation occurred when she drove down to the San Juan Creek not far away and got stuck in the sand. They had a Willys jeep, and Jon had shown her how to drive it. Jan was alone when a herd of bulls came up and surrounded the jeep. As she told the story:

> I was scared to death. I thought they were going to get me, and the coyotes. It was getting late, the coyotes were howling, and Jon wasn't coming. And pretty soon I just started crying, I was like, "What am I going to do? I can't get out. The bulls are there, and blah, blah, blah." He finally shows up, and he's laughing at me because I'm just beside myself. I said, "I was afraid to get out because the bulls were going to get me." He says, "Those aren't bulls. They're cows with horns." I just thought anything with a horn was a bull. That's how stupid I was. I didn't know the difference between a harvester and a tractor or any of that kind of stuff, you know, and later on I'd be driving all those things, the harvesters . . .
>
> I started driving the harvesters probably five years into the marriage or

something like that. I always got the harvester with no air conditioner because you couldn't let the hired men have the ones with no air conditioner or they wouldn't do it. So I was the one all full of chaff and sweat, and sometimes I'd have to get off and just run back home and get in the shower and get all that stuff off of me and start over again. Safflower, wheat, and barley.

Several friends helped Jan adapt to her new life on the Plains. A part of the interview which Jackie and I had with Jan is transcribed below. It not only records her adventures, but it tells something of her spirit.

Jackie: You mentioned the Livingstons. That would be Shirley Livingston, Lottie's daughter and Sandy Rowlett's mother?

Jan: Right. Shirley and I would go hunting down at La Panza Ranch. Jake Martin had it, and we were the only ones that were allowed to hunt it, and we would hunt the whole . . . I'm not sure what gave us the privilege, maybe because we were women. I don't know.

Craig: What were you hunting then?

Jan: Deer. We were hunting deer. And we'd get in the Willys Jeep, and we'd go hunting once a week anyway. Drive all over the whole ranch, and we had more fun. We had more fun. Come back with a big buck or something, you know. Jon and Robert, Shirley's husband, they just couldn't believe it. We had a lot of adventures, a lot of adventures. I'd be driving, I drove the Willys jeep one time when it got on a side hill with oak leaves, and it started slipping. I just bailed out of that thing. I said, "I'm not going down with this," and Shirley just gets in the driver's seat, and she just drives it right up, and I totally panicked and left it. She [Shirley] told everybody about another story when I shot this deer right between the eyes. I was eating lunch and had a peanut butter sandwich in my mouth.

Jackie: Davy Crockett?

Jan: We'd been eating lunch and were stopped. We were just outside there eating lunch, and I had a peanut butter sandwich, and I said, "Oh, a buck," and I stuck it in there [the sandwich in her mouth] and grabbed my gun. We had so much fun. I really missed her, really missed her. We just had a lot of adventures together.

In addition to these adventures with Shirley Livingston, Jan had still others at home. Living with her husband Jon was certainly one of them. He was good-hearted and everyone liked him, but he was also eccentric and famously impulsive. One of his ventures was raising hogs, and for a while this was a serious business that he partnered with his brother Wayne. It was more than just a business, however, and Jan insisted that during those years there was always at least one piglet living in the kitchen. It was a runt that would not have made it out in the pig pen. And besides keeping pigs in the house, Jan would have to go sit out in the hog barns when they were farrowing.

All this began with a first pig named Lulabelle, and Jon just loved this pig. It happened that Lulabelle and Jan were pregnant at the same time, and it was very uncertain who was going to "farrow" first as Jan put it. Jan delivered first, and she is certain that it was a good thing. She joked that if it had been the pig, Jon would have been too busy to notice his wife at all. It was that pig that lured Jon into the pig business. Of course Lulabelle got out of her pen and rooted up Jan's garden regularly. Jan thinks that it was a friend who gave him Lulabelle. With a friend like that who needs . . . Eventually the novelty of it wore off, and Lulabelle became pork chops along with her companions.

An encounter with a rattlesnake was another "home adventure." Jan is an extremely practical and adaptable person, and her telling of the story makes this very clear. It occurred some time in the 1970s. The home where Jan lived had a swimming pool, and she and a friend, Susan Diefenderfer, were sunning there by the water. One of the family cats had been digging up a planter, and Jan was casually trying to repair the damage. The cat had been covering its scat, and Jan intended to cover the surface of the ground with some small stones to discourage it. The stones were under another bush by the pool, and Jan reached under to pick them up when she felt something hit her thumb. She jumped and told Susan that she had been stung by a tarantula hawk (a type of spider wasp that favors tarantula larvae). When Jan looked down again, there was a small snake coiled up under the bush. Jan said it was looking up at her as if to say, "I'm sorry. I thought you were a mouse." The snake was hunting, struck her thumb, and never even rattled.

Jan went into the house and told her husband that she had been hit and had to get to town. The exchange was characteristic of these two:

"Well, I guess you'd better take me in to the doctors. I just got bit by a rattlesnake." And Jon says, "Oh, bull." I says, "No, I did. See the blood right there?" He says, "Oh, you did not." Susan comes in. Her eyes are just . . . "Oh yes, she did."

They got ready for the trip in to San Luis Obispo. Jan was still in her bathing suit, so that was something to deal with. Then they made a call to the hospital to be sure the antivenin would be there and ready when they arrived and that it would the right kind for a Western Rattlesnake. Jan said that they seemed to be traveling a hundred miles an hour around the curves on Highway 58 till she warned her husband that death by rattlesnake would be preferable to death by collision. Although it is no longer recommended today, at that time it was normal that a tourniquet be used. Her thumb became swollen and so painful that Jan removed the tourniquet, and then the swelling proceeded up her hand and arm. By the time they arrived at the hospital, her face was sagging, and the thumb was not only hurting but had swollen so much that the skin was stretched almost to the point of tearing. The anti-venom countered the rattlesnake toxin, but it was still necessary to remove a great deal of the skin from the thumb as it had become necrotic, probably from the use of the tourniquet. Jan's allergic reaction to the anti-venom was even more serious.

Ultimately Jan spent four days in the hospital. The allergic reaction was horrible, and she felt as if she would die from lockjaw. She couldn't eat, and every bone in her body hurt. When the treatment was nearly complete, a priest came in to visit, fully expecting to administer last rites. By then Jan was able to laugh and to tell stories, so the priestly concerns were appreciated but not required. A year later Jan felt a small pain in a knuckle of her thumb. She thought that it was a cactus spine and tried to remove it with tweezers. In fact, a part of one fang had broken off and was still in the joint. The only permanent result of the biting incident is that Jan's thumb is still slightly numb at times.

The ultimate challenge, adventure perhaps, was to make a living at a time when family farms were becoming marginal. Raising hogs was a good business for only a short time, and so next Jon and his brother Wayne leased the American and Saucito Ranches and went into the cattle business. This was in the late 80s and was also temporary. Wayne gave up cattle, and moved to Atascadero where he had a business building truck bodies. Initially this was successful, but eventually the long, long hours that were required motivated Wayne to take a job with Pacific Gas and Electric. Jon Cooper returned to college, studied geology, and eventually made this a second career.

Jan stayed on the ranch and operated it while Jon was away at school until this became too much work for Jan to do alone. After a year they gave up their lease, and then Jan split her time between art classes in San Luis Obispo and working as cowboy for another rancher, Tom Foss. Jan checked the cattle to be sure everything was all right, and then went directly to her classes wearing spurs and jeans and covered with dust. During this period, Tom sent Jan to school in Hanford, California, to learn the techniques of artificial insemination. After Jan bred his cattle, there was a shortage of feed, and Tom was obliged to sell most of these cows that Jan had bred. This was the girl who once went to the Simmler grocery in heels, stockings, and a dress.

Jan enjoyed doing work for other ranchers. She liked being a cowboy, and when working for others, she didn't have the stress of directing operations and managing finances. Still, when she and Jon were running cattle on the American and Saucito Ranches, there had been some good years. It was a stocker operation then, which means they bought yearlings, sometimes from Mexico, kept them most of a season to fatten, and then sold the animals. This way they didn't have to worry about feed year-round, and in a poor year when feed was scarce they simply didn't buy as many cattle in the first place. One year Jan invested in futures on the stock market and made enough money to build an art studio on the ranch – a third, or fourth, or fifth career change.

Jon Cooper died in 2007. It was a heart attack and entirely unexpected. Jan chose to stay in the Plains and on the same property where the two had spent most of their adult lives. At the end of our interview,

Jackie commented to Jan that she had come out as a young bride and had been nearly overwhelmed by the experience. Jan corrected her:

> Not overwhelmed by the country because I always kind of lived in the country. I loved it. But just overwhelmed by the cooking and the things that needed to be done around here. And now I have lots to do. I love it out here. Can you hear the birds singing? There's no cars buzzing by my house. I love it out here. Love nature. I had fun when I was working in town also. It was a whole other experience. I worked a couple of years in there, and that was fun. But I'll stay here on the Plains. I don't want to go anywhere. I don't know how much longer I'll be able to take care of this place by myself. There's just a lot to do, and things are always needing repair, and it's hard to keep up with it. I'm not getting any younger, but it has been an adventure.

Cindy Wreden

There is one more woman that should be remembered here. In the course of searching out Carrisa history, I spoke directly with Deb Beck and with Jan Cooper. Cindy Wreden is someone I met only on the telephone, and I never had the chance to ask directly about her life on the Plains. I regret this lost opportunity. Her story is both impressive and sad. It was through her husband of many years, a personal friend of mine, that I knew her.

Doug and Cindy were married in 1968. They first met in Atascadero when a mutual friend took Doug to her apartment. She invited Doug for dinner a week later, and the meal was wonderful. As Doug learned later, it was Cindy's roommate who had prepared everything and put it in the oven. It was steak and salad and wine. This was a scam, and Doug insists that Cindy couldn't even boil water without help. This first dinner date was also a bit odd in that another fellow, a friend of Cindy's, showed up at the apartment, had dinner with them, and then left. Several weeks later, Doug saw Cindy dancing with yet another fellow at a college night club in town. Doug and Cindy danced that night also, and then they became a regular couple.

Their wedding was in Virginia City, Nevada. Their parents had said, "Wonderful. Do go get married. Go and have a good time," but they, the parents, were not able to attend. Doug brought a younger brother and sister as witnesses, and they all stayed with family friends in Virginia City, Nevada. Doug described the weekend:

> We went to this old hotel in Silver City, and Paula Harvey, it was this woman, she kept women there who had had children out of wedlock, and they worked for her, and she sent them out to gather all these wildflowers, and they made a cake for us and did this beautiful wedding cake. We toasted Champagne out of hundred-year-old Champagne glasses. We went down, she got a friend of hers who owned the Union Brewery, which is still there now in Virginia City, to open it up. It had been closed for years. I mean, there were cobwebs, cats running around on the bar. And so they opened it all up. My cousins happened to be at Incline [a town nearby]. They had a condo up there, and they all came down, and my aunt and my uncle. And so it turned out to be a big family deal after all. We got the Justice of the Peace from Story County to come down and marry us in this old bar. And there's a wedding picture of all of us. You can see us in this old antique mirror behind the bar. And then they gave us a big reception up in Tahoe, and bought us the bridal suite at the Tahoe Inn.

The wedding was a party, but the honeymoon was less auspicious. Their plan was to go camping and then fish along the Walker River nearby, but it was cold, cold, cold. They had an El Camino with a camper on it, borrowed from Cindy's dad, but it was not much help. The next night, they drove over Tioga Pass to somewhere near Sonora and got a real room. Doug's father, Bill, owned the Pinole Ranch on the Plains, and that was where the couple returned a day later. The ranch was not what Cindy had expected.

> Cindy was originally from LA, moved to Atascadero, graduated from Atascadero high school, only lived around here a short time. I think she thought coming out to this ranch was going to be something different than what it was. And everyone, without seeing it, imagines the ranch with rolling white

fences and horses and all that kind of stuff. So she cried a lot. She cried a
lot that first year.

Doug and Cindy had no long-term plans when they returned to the
Pinole. Doug was doing the work of a hired hand there, and although
there was already a woman, Francis, who had been working as cook,
Cindy was to be in charge of the kitchen. Francis was a single mother
with a thirteen-year-old daughter, and she was not about to become
helper to some new girl just out of college. Cindy and Francis shared the
use of a wringer washing machine. When Cindy put laundry in, Francis
would throw it out in the dirt and put her own in. Francis was a tough
lady, and she and Cindy had words. Doug called the ranch manager to
settle this, and it was first, "Francis, down the road," and then next,
"Cindy's going to have to start cooking now." Doug said, "Okay." Cindy
said, "But I don't know how to cook."

George, one of the hired men, known as Lonesome George, was
called in. He was a good cook. "I'll teach you, honey," he told Cindy.
"Right, okay George," she answered. So Cindy spent a week learning to
cook, and George didn't have to drive tractor. This was the beginning of
their life on the ranch. A year later, Cindy was taking care of a new baby
and was running the kitchen on her own. They had moved from the
cookhouse where they had started and into the old ranch house. Several
years later Doug became the ranch manager himself. Cindy and Doug
had become ranchers.

Doug's dad had once been a partner raising cattle on the La Panza
Ranch farther west, and in 1974 Doug considered running cattle for
himself at the Pinole. For whatever reason this never happened, and
then partly by accident he and Cindy began raising sheep. The story
of how Cindy went to Montana for a winter has already been told. For
a few years Doug and Cindy made a living raising sheep for wool and
meat, but eventually the market went down, and they had to find yet
another way to make a living. Doug described the end of the ranch:

> I think for a year we kept operating, and I still fixed a few fences. Then I
> finally said, "I quit. I'm tired of playing this game. I'm tired of going to the

bank and projecting we're going to have this and that, and we know it's not going to happen cause it's not going to rain." And so I just called up [his dad] and quit. And Cindy said, "What did you do?" I said, "I quit." She said, "What are we going to do?" I said, "I don't know."

When his dad, who was owner of the Pinole, asked him to stay on, Doug said, "I don't know. We're probably going to go off to the valley or coast and get a job and just be like everybody else." But Doug still wasn't ready for that, and he owned a lot of equipment that he still had to sell. For a time, he would haul scrap steel to the central valley on weekends after spending the rest of the week working on the ranch. These were dozer blades and other pieces of machinery that no longer worked and had to be cut up for a load in the truck. He could sell a load for seven or eight hundred dollars and then spend one hundred of that to fill the truck with gas and spend more yet to buy acetylene and oxygen for the cutting torch. They could get grocery money this way, but there still wasn't enough for them to leave the ranch. They went to swap meets on weekends to sell off what they had accumulated over a lifetime. Again in Doug's words:

> I mean, we were, we were at times just flat broke, and we would go to the swap meet on Sunday and make two or three hundred dollars and then go to the grocery store. Still had two kids in high school, but it was a good experience in that every time we'd go shopping or go somewhere we'd go, "Ah, swap meet item. Don't need that. Don't need that. Don't need this. We just need food" And we had little baby cribs that I fixed up and painted, and we'd sell. That went on for a whole year, but it was a hell of a good lesson that served us for a long time after that. And then we started . . .

During this period, Doug had started a business building fences for other farms and ranches, and eventually it picked up and orders were coming in. He worked all over San Luis Obispo County, at Cal Poly, on the Vandenberg Air Force Base, and even farther off. He and Cindy were traveling all the time. They were in business together, and money was no longer a problem. When I asked about the work, about how they

drove posts for the fences, Doug said they had a two-man auger, and
Cindy would work on one end and he worked the other. Sometimes they
could use a tractor, but sometimes they had to do this by hand. The tractor would destroy kangaroo rat burrows that the BLM and the Nature
Conservancy were trying to protect. One of their jobs was near the Selby
Pasture not far from Painted Rock. They were putting in three miles of
fence in the middle of summer. The ranger, Ed Ruth, would come by
and ask, "Oh, how are you guys?" And Doug would ask, "Why'd you
take a job like this in the heat?" Ed would reply, "Oh well, it's not too
bad." "It was about 110 degrees, and he was driving a truck, and we were
driving poles." Every hour they would duck under their truck for shade.

There was another fellow, an employee of the BLM, who sometimes
came out to check on the work. As Doug described him:

This guy, Sam, comes out and he says, "I'm just here to be sure you don't
kill any rats. You going to finish this today? I said, "TODAY? Maybe next
week." "Oh, it's going to take all that time?" I said, "Yeah. Grab onto this
thing, Sam." And so he watched us drill a few holes, and I said, "There's a
rat burrow." He said, "I can see you really know what a rat hole looks like."
I said, "Oh yeah, if we drag one out of there we'll just throw it back in."
He didn't think that was too funny. He had just graduated from Humboldt
as a biologist, and he was a little overweight, and he was sweating. It was a
hundred and ten, and he was just sweating, and you could tell that he was
not happy being there. Finally he said, "I think you guys know what you're
doing. I'll just see you later." "Okay."

Every afternoon, we would stop and have some watermelon. We had it
all iced down. We'd sit on the tailgate, and every little drop that went on the
ground grasshoppers would just fly in. They'd just be on it like a magnet,
sucking up that water.

Doug spoke about another job they worked:

When I think about it even today, I think, "What the hell were you thinking about? Ask your wife to do that?" And she would have done anything.
She was just always there. We did a lot of projects all over the place. And

we were doing a project in Santa Margarita off of 58, you know, where the winding corners are? Off on the right up in the decomposed granite. We built three miles up there, in that steep nasty country. We couldn't get these posts and wire up on the fire trails, cause you couldn't take a truck up, like it was straight up and down. We'd made the rancher a map, three posts here, two rolls of wire, and he'd go and pack it up there on his pack horses, drop it off, and we just took it off of the bill. But Cindy got sick up there from the heat, and I'm looking all over. "Leland, you seen Cindy?" "I don't know. I think she went down to the truck." Came down to the truck. She's lying across the seat. She says, "I'm not doing this. I'm never going to go with you again. I'm done. I quit." Leland came down, and he picked her a bunch of wildflowers and made this little bouquet and says, "You still going to quit?" "Yes, I'm quitting. I'm never building fence again." Cause she was packing tools, you know, up slopes and . . . It was a rough job.

They thought about quitting the fence business and moving to Atascadero. Doug could get a job as a mechanic, but his dad still wanted him living on the ranch as caretaker. On the Pinole they paid no rent, but it seemed that they were always on the road living in a travel trailer. They built fences in Tehachapi and in Bakersfield and farther south still. Work was dawn to dark. Ultimately the Pinole was sold, and Doug's share made it possible to buy some land and begin building a house.

This was the end of the story as Doug told it. I met him on the Plains in 2003 where he had a regular job doing maintenance for the National Monument. It was a regular, salaried position, at the Monument, and the commute to work was twenty miles only. Doug and Cindy's children were grown and had moved away, so the hand-to-mouth life with fourteen hour days had become a part of their past. My part in all this was to help Doug remove unwanted fences from the Monument – a nice piece of irony in his case. I arranged groups of volunteers and scheduled workdays with Doug. Sometimes I needed to call him at home to make arrangements, and on these occasions, I might talk briefly with Cindy. Eventually we knew each other's voices over the phone.

Cindy developed cancer, and by the time it was diagnosed it had reached its later stages. Surgery was not possible, and the attempts at chemotherapy were painful. Doug reported that she couldn't eat, and Cindy, the woman who had been lambing sheep and driving fence posts, had become rail thin. Cannabis restored her appetite briefly, but the mental disruption it caused was worse than the chemotherapy itself, and it was discontinued. Doug continued working, but he was tired. When I called the house in the early evenings, he had already gone to bed, and Cindy would take a message for him to return my call in the morning.

One evening I called to ask for Doug, and Cindy simply said that it was not a good time to call. Her voice sounded terrible. I apologized and asked if I might call in the morning. The next morning when Cindy answered, she was brighter and explained that she had been too sick to even go get him. Two weeks later Cindy died. At her request there were no services and no memorial was held. I never met her. I was too late.

Pioneers

All three women came from the city and adapted to a very different way of life. They learned to cook for harvest crews; they managed cattle and sheep; they raised families far from neighbors or towns. Deb has returned to a city on the coast, and Jan has stayed on after the death of her husband. Cindy's story ended before these choices were given to her. The challenges that these women met were formidable, and they are certainly to be counted among the pioneers of the mid-twentieth century. I was fortunate to have heard their stories.

CHAPTER FIFTEEN

The Later Years

California Valley and the National Monument

Monument entrance

On my first visit to the Carrisa Plains, I had arrived from the world of the twenty-first century. It was natural that I should have been struck with the relics from the early pioneer days – rusting fences, abandoned machinery, and collapsing homesteads. I had wondered how the early pioneers had survived in such a place, how they had lived, and why they had left. It was history that I sought, but as stories followed stories, the people themselves became more important. I later began to wonder about the more recent changes that had come to the Plains. The National Monument now occupies land that was once used for wheat and cattle, and California Valley is a sprawling community almost entirely disconnected with any agricultural past. The history of these developments intrigued me, but once again the people became the real story.

California Valley

Many of us dream of a place of our own where we can escape from the everyday, where the sky is clear, and where we can smell the earth. When the community of California Valley was created in 1964, it was the embodiment of this dream for those who came there to live. It was once El Chicote Ranch, covered with saltbrush and crossed by seasonal channels draining south to Soda Lake. Were it not for an ambitious developer in the 60s, it might still be the same open ground. Today this community south of Highway 58 is a scattering of small lots, some occupied, most vacant, and with no apparent center. It is a backwater little known in the rest of California.

In the late 50s and early 60s, plans were made to bring water from Northern California to the agricultural lands in the south of the state. One of these plans routed a canal through the Carrisa Plains and onward toward Los Angeles. If the water came, then agriculture would flourish, homes would grow gardens, land prices would rise, and new communities would appear. This was the vision of the developer who bought El Chicote Ranch. Roads were laid out and marked to serve 1500 two-and-a-half acre lots. With little more than hope, the sales began in the early 60s. A lot sold for ten dollars down with payments of ten dollars a month. These were terms that anyone could afford, and the promise was irresistible.

Extraordinary measures were taken to tell the world about this new city. There were fliers, newspaper ads, and radio commercials all through the state. An imposing array of celebrities told the world how they had themselves found their dream in California Valley. The climax arrived in the spring of 1964: an immense sales event was planned. Movie stars came to advertise the properties. Planeloads of prospective buyers arrived from Los Angeles. Tents were put up to serve as sales offices. Tours were planned, and then to provide the ultimate draw, a free barbecue was held. In the spirit of the Old West and the New Opportunity, this was to be a "Buffalo Barbecue" – beef would simply not do for such an occasion.

A movie taken from the air at the time shows rows of automobiles alongside the sales tents. A DC3 sits on a makeshift landing strip in the background, and crowds of people swarm about. The lots sold, and sold, and sold. One of interviews recorded in 1990 and recovered in the "box of memories" was with Ian McMillan, a rancher living some miles north on Bitterwater Road. He told of coming to the scene and watching the crowds. People arrived from far off with checkbooks in hand. Nothing could discourage their hopes. The rancher told of watching one shabbily dressed older man going into a sales tent with his wife and then sometime later coming out with stars in his eyes. The rancher knew the land well and was sad for the old man. There were over 16,000 persons who came for the barbecue. However, when the fire was lit, there was only one buffalo on the grill. Most of the visitors were fortunate to get even beans. The canal was never built; roads were never paved; no utilities were connected; and the developer soon left for Arizona to pursue his other business ventures there.

Water and isolation are the enemies in California Valley. There is no water utility and so everyone must provide their own. Each lot needs its own well, but it is only on the very western side of the development and close to the hills that water suitable for drinking can be found. Wells on the great majority of lots are able to supply water for washing and for watering lawns but for nothing more. The mineral content is high enough that pipes corrode and scale builds up quickly. Located on the margin of Soda Lake, this ought not to have been a surprise. Drinking water must be purchased and brought in. Many wells on the east side came up entirely dry, and for these persons, even wash water must be delivered. Lots were purchased in a rush, and few people asked or appreciated what difficulties would follow.

The isolation that goes with residence in California Valley is both good and bad. It discourages visits from unwelcome in-laws, but it also requires planning that is not needed in a city. Today there is no gasoline for sale, and there is nowhere to buy groceries. There is certainly no movie theater, restaurant, or video store in the community. These amenities are either fifty miles away on the coast or forty miles away to the east. People soon learn to plan their shopping carefully to cover needs for one or two weeks at a time. They buy a freezer to keep foods, and they plan their driving to conserve gasoline. Entertainment is necessarily of the home-grown variety, not a bad thing in itself, but out of step with the urban culture of Southern California.

View from the Air

While some stories of California Valley relate emergencies, disappointments, or even crimes, there are also idyllic reports of a peaceful valley, of friendships and good will. Every year, a hot air balloon festival is held on the edge of the community, and the spectacle of the brightly colored crafts rising slowly over the fields at early dawn is moving. Two persons who spoke about early days of ballooning in California Valley were Gordon and Manetta Bennett. Here are some thoughts from Gordon:

> I started ballooning in 1975, the last few days of the year. I decided to come out here because it was a wide open space. It would be a good place to attempt to fly. So we came out and flew and found it real nice flying weather. Some of our other ballooning buddies that we met from Bakersfield, they came over and flew with us. And consequently they liked it so much that we formed a group and started having balloon rallies out here. They've been continuous ever since that time, ever since 1977.

When the propane burners are fired to heat the air, the noise is intense. When these are turned off, the silence is complete. The valley itself is quiet, and Gordon and Manetta spoke of drifting silently and watching the landscape moving below them. There would be long shadows in the early morning, and their truck and chase crew would be following somewhere behind. Below them were the grasslands and occasional homes or trailers that are scattered north of the Monument. On one occasion, a woman waved up to them as they passed by her house. On an impulse, Gordon brought the balloon down to talk with the lady, and the result was a friendship that lasted many years. On another occasion, they had been obliged to come down on the Beck family ranch north of Highway 58. Initially Greg had been a bit angry watching their descent; however, Gordon is a charming fellow, and they became good friends. Greg was invited on a number of their rides and also spoke about the morning quiet, about launching under an overcast sky, and about passing upward through the fog into brilliant sunshine.

Gordon and Manetta described more eventful flights as well. If winds became greater than five miles an hour, then landings became difficult, and several times the basket had overturned when they came down. Once the air temperature changed and the wind became fickle as they passed over a slough. The basket dropped and even touched the mud before a gust lifted them again. A landing there would have meant a long and difficult effort, perhaps even an impossible one, to extricate themselves. Once they sailed over a grassy field and realized that two golden eagles were following them. The burners were firing, and the noise frightened rabbits as the balloon traveled over the field below. As the rabbits flushed along their path, the eagles dove for their prey. It was all a strange coincidence, but it is unlikely that the raptors were philosophical about their serendipity. Other acquaintances of the Bennetts followed them to California Valley, and balloon rides became a gathering of friends. Although Gordon and Manetta no longer fly, the festival which they started continues, and the sight of balloons rising in the morning sunlight is a peaceful one.

Public Lands

A second major change in the Carrisa Plains occurred when much of the land was transferred to the federal government for protection of natural habitat. During the 70s, it became more and more difficult for grain farmers to make a living. A number of families, chiefly those toward the south end of the Plains, sold their lands and moved away. A few sold directly to the Bureau of Land Management (BLM), but a greater part of these lands went to Oppenheimer Industries, a publicly traded investment firm. Oppenheimer in turn leased the land back to many of the same ranchers who attempted to continue in this way. During these particular years, tax laws in the United States allowed persons who lost money in farming to write off these losses against other more profitable investments. Oppenheimer sold stock to investors who needed these tax breaks. When tax laws changed again in the later 80s, this financial arrangement was less profitable, and Oppenheimer was ready to sell.

At this same time, several persons with the Bureau of Land Management in Bakersfield and several more in state offices in Sacramento became interested in the possibility of preserving habitat in the Carrisa Plains for native wildlife. The area immediately around Soda Lake had never gone into private hands, and the Bureau of Land Management hoped to expand these protected lands. Financial arrangements for purchases were complicated, and although federal money for purchases of this kind had been previously set aside, still an act of Congress was required to authorize its use. The Nature Conservancy, a private environmental organization, stepped into the process, bought much of the land, and then subsequently sold it to the federal government. The change was profound.

The lands that had been transferred to the federal government were designated as the "Carrizo Plain Natural Area." The words "Natural Area" carry no legal stipulations, and in reality, the designation amounted to nothing more than a boundary line on a map. Although there were some constraints imposed by The Nature Conservancy when the land was transferred, the manner of management was essentially an administrative decision in the hands of the Bakersfield BLM office. Farming was discontinued on the acquired lands, and cattle grazing, which was once an arrangement between cattlemen and private land owners, was now much more strictly controlled. Ranchers who still grazed cattle on their own lands to the north of Highway 58 could no longer depend upon additional leased land within the Natural Area. In spite of promises that the new arrangements would "change nothing," of course there were changes.

With no farming on the newly acquired government lands, there was no longer stubble after harvest, and the sandhill cranes which once visited the Carrisa Plains by thousands no longer stopped to feed. Where grazing ceased, wildlife habitat changed. Grasses grew taller and were sometimes rank. Several endangered species were more rigorously protected, and a number of studies of flora and fauna were initiated. In some sense the Plains had become a grand experiment in habitat management. Some residents acknowledged that the land and animals were better protected under government ownership, but this was certainly not universal. The tight community was split in its judgment about the change.

The National Monument

In January of 2001, a presidential decree created the Carrizo Plain National Monument from the previous Natural Area. It was clearly stated that the purpose was to protect natural features and resources. A number of endangered and threatened species were identified. The alkaline wetlands of Soda Lake were cited. Historic ranching structures and prehistoric Native American artifacts were mentioned along with geological and paleontological features. Perhaps most striking was the stipulation that the native California habitat was to be preserved as a functioning ecological unit. Visitors were permitted on the Monument to the extent that these other primary purposes were not hindered. The Monument had not been created for the purpose of human recreation, but rather for preservation of the natural and human history.

The number and variety of persons visiting the Monument depends upon the season and can be impressive. Bird watchers carrying binoculars or spotting scopes are easily identified. They meet each other under trees at the two campgrounds asking if the horned owls have returned to their nests or whether curlews have arrived yet near Soda Lake. Sunset clouds, sunrise shadows, spring wildflowers, and historic buildings bring photographers. Regular tours are conducted to the Painted Rock pictograph site, and inevitably people ask about ground squirrels, reptiles, animal tracks, and early settlements. Understandably there are few tourists when summer temperatures go above 90 degrees, and with the absence of a wildflower bloom in drought years, there will be few spring-time visitors at those times. Hunting is popular during the permitted seasons: deer, elk, quail, and doves.

In the heat of summer and in the cold damp of winter, the attraction of the Carrizo Monument is of a different sort. It is open, unpopulated, and utterly silent. It is possible to sit on a hill above the Visitor Center midweek in August without seeing another person or vehicle for hours. In February, I have sometimes met a single person staying three days in a campground because they want a place away from people and city noises. The ranches of earlier years are no longer worked in the Monument, and so there are no sounds of domestic animals, of tractors or harvesters, of windmills or electric generators. Within an hour of coastal California and in the twenty-first century, the Monument takes you a hundred years backward in time.

Some people that Jackie and I spoke with have regretted the changes. Although he has been a volunteer for the Monument, Bill Garcia feels the absence of the sandhill cranes in a personal way and places some responsibility on management by the BLM. Although the numbers of elk have increased, deer and pronghorn are not so numerous in the most recent decade as the were previously. I found it gratifying that when the management plan for the Monument was finalized, the signing ceremony was introduced by a Chumash Indian elder. She declared that responsibility for the land and its spirit had belonged to her people for centuries. After the historical difficulties between native and white groups, she was grateful that the federal government had included her people in the planning and had now joined them in preserving the land which they held sacred.

From Past to Present – Two Generations

Ann Cochran spent most of her life on the Carrisa Plains. Her daughter, Johna Cochran Hurl, lives there presently and is now manager of the Carrizo Plain National Monument. Their story is an account of life in

California Valley, of the early years of the Monument, and of an attachment to the land during the declining years of ranching. It is the story of two strong women in rural California. Once again, history is best told by those who lived it. Here are Johna's words:

> First we lived in Cuyama for a little bit, not too long, and then we moved to Maricopa where my mom was the librarian. My mom always loved to explore, and so when we were in school one day she went out exploring, and she found the Carrisa Plains on her expedition. She really enjoyed it and fell in love with it [the Carrisa Plains]. I think I was in second grade when we moved out to the Carrisa Plains. She bought a two-and-a-half acre lot on the north side of California Valley just off Belmont Road, and there we built a house.

The family didn't have money to pay for help, and so they had to literally build their house. This was in 1976.

> Yep. Mom, me, and my three brothers built the house. We went out in the oil fields and collected things to bring home. The old boilers used in the oilfields were lined with brick. They were tossed everywhere. We would drive around and collect the bricks . . . then we'd go out every weekend and start cementing them in by hand to make the floor.
>
> We obviously did not know how to do that, so it wasn't the prettiest floor, but it had some very unique things in it. We had one half of a stone grinding wheel that we used as a door step. We bought some railroad ties for the foundation, two by fours and plywood for the walls, and tin for the roof. This was not your best of houses.
>
> We had been working on it for a year, and then it came time to raise the walls and put on the roof. My brothers were in high school at that time, so one day my mom got all the high school kids together and said, "We're going to go have a barbecue lunch, out in the Carrisa Plains, and you're going to help us finish our house." And so they all loaded into the pickup trucks, and out they came. The house was finished, and we moved in. We had no electricity or running water at the time, but that didn't stop my mom from planting numerous fruit trees that all needed to be watered. We called this

home for about a year; then we purchased a house on the east side of the valley with all the amenities.

Water came from the California Valley Service District. The family had a 53 Chevy that they used with a small trailer and a fifty-five gallon barrel to get water on the weekends. They washed dishes in a five-gallon bucket and used a kerosene lamp on the table for light. It was barely enough to see across the table, but still that was where the kids did homework. School was still in Maricopa, and Ann drove them there and back every day, fifty miles each way. At that time, most high-school-age kids in California Valley attended school in Atascadero and lived in the school dormitory during the week. With three teenage boys in the family, Ann wasn't confident that they would manage without direct supervision. She was willing to make the daily drive to keep them in their previous school. Ann was working as a librarian in Maricopa so she could stay in town during the day, and then drive the family back to California Valley in the evening. Johna remembered that one time she, Johna, forgot to bring her sports uniform with her to school, and her mom had to make the trip back, yes, back home to get it for her. Johna promised that this never, ever happened again.

Johna's three brothers had motorcycles, but when the family moved out of Maricopa, she wanted a horse. The story of how Johna and her mom brought the horse home is crazy and wonderful. It was a forty mile adventure.

Mom finally scraped up enough money to buy me a horse. After many months of searching, we found one. It was a 2-year-old filly that had never been ridden. She paid one hundred and fifty dollars for it. The problem was, we needed to go pick it up; however, we didn't own a horse trailer or a truck. The horse was on Highway 58 and O'Donovan Road, a few miles from Santa Margarita. My mom said that it wasn't that far, and we could walk it home. So we got up in the morning at, o'dark thirty, went there, gave them one hundred, fifty dollars, put a lead rope on it, and started walking it home. I started out walking it on foot, but since it was in the middle of summer, I soon got tired, and my mom said to sit on the hood of the car and lead it. She just drove real slow, and we continued on home. Then some gentlemen driving by stopped and said, "Hey, little darling, can I ride that horse?" We knew they were not from around here. We said, "Sure." And the fellows said, "Let's see what she'll do." So sure enough, they jumped on her with no saddle or bridle. He said "Whoo hooh," She moved quickly to the left and tried to get him off, which she did, "That was fun. Thanks!" And he jumped back in his car and left. We continued on our way. We got about to the Camatti Ranch and were looking at their corrals. We thought, "Those are nice corrals. I wonder if they'd notice if there was a horse there overnight?" Even though it was kind of getting late, we decided to move on.

At that time, the bar was open in California Valley. Everybody passed us on their way to town and then passed us on their way back. Of Course we were the topic of conversation in the bar, "Did you see that crazy lady and them kids walking that horse home?" They're all laughing, and giggling. After a while one of the locals said, "I'll go get her." Of course it was four or five o'clock in the afternoon, and he'd been drinking since noon. He gets his horse trailer and starts down the highway looking for us. At this time we're on the San Juan grade coming up. We were sure glad to see him, but we still had to load her in the trailer. The horse had never been loaded in a trailer. "I'll get her in for you." He got ropes out, put them around the horse, and well, after many tries, she eventually got in. It was definitely an adventure. He got in, drove us home, and we unloaded my new horse!

When the library in Maricopa closed, Ann became the librarian in the Simmler community, although it was open only one day a week. She had teaching credentials and tutored kids in the Simmler area. In summers, both Ann and Johna, who was then in high school, worked the harvest for Jon Cooper. All this was while Ann was raising four kids. Johna said, "Poor mom. She was tough. She had to be." Life in the small house was an adventure. Johna told about one of these adventures.

It was Thanksgiving, and Mom always invited anybody over who she thought might not be having Thanksgiving, so we always had people over. She was rushing around cooking a turkey and getting everything ready while my brother, Joe, was out putting gopher poison in the orchard. This is also where my chickens lived. Well, he accidentally spilled the gopher poison, and he and the chickens were picking it up. He called to my mom, so she rushed out picking the poison grain up ahead of the chickens. Suddenly she thought, "The turkey!" So she runs back in, opens the oven up, checks the turkey, and then she runs back outside. She gets halfway out, and she thought, "Oh, I forgot to close the oven." She goes in, slams the oven door shut, comes back out, and continues to pick up the poison grain with Joe and the chickens. They got all the grain picked up before the chickens did, so things calmed down, and then she goes back in the house and hears this "thunk, thunk" in the oven. She thought, "The turkey was dead when I put it in there?" Well, she opens the door, and there's the turkey sitting right there. She hears the sound again, so she pulls the drawer out from underneath it, and out flops the cat. And it just lies on the floor with all four of its feet straight out. But it was alive. We came in to look, and mom said, "Well that one looks well done". We were all upset. However, once the cat cooled off, it got up, dusted itself off, walked away, and was fine! It was a good Thanksgiving after all.

Life changed for Johna when she went to college. This was not easy. She had grown up on the Plains and spent her time riding and exploring. A city and a school were not home. Johna was the youngest and last of the children, and Ann didn't want to be left behind alone, but they both knew that it had to happen. The agreement was that Johna would try it, and if it didn't work out, then they would figure out something else. Johna said it was a big shock after living "out here in the wild." To begin with, there was the dormitory, and then school, and finally a job away from home.

That dormitory room was twelve feet wide and twenty feet long, and another person lived there. And I'm like, "Aaghh." I didn't mind living in the small space because we had a really small house, but a roommate, and being in the middle of the city, and no animals and no . . . so, you know, it was very different, which was fine. I adapted very well. Sure I can live in town. That's not a problem. Do I prefer to live in town? No. And so when I left for college, I thought, "Well, I'll never be back."

Johna's first job was in Fresno with the US Department of Agriculture doing research on packing materials for fruits and vegetables. It was a good job, but Fresno was a big city and was not where she wanted to live. Johna quit and took a temporary job trapping insects for San Luis Obispo County. When that position ended, she found a position out in the Carrisa Plains trapping kit foxes and coyotes on a research project with the Smithsonian Institute. She was an assistant for another researcher and helped put on radio collars, tracking the animals to study the interactions between the two species. When Johna found a dead kit fox, she would do a necropsy. A local trapper employed by the county taught her how to trap coyotes, and Johna claimed that eventually she became good at it.

Johna became assistant manager of the Monument, and then in 2007 became the Monument Manager. This was the girl who had studied by kerosene lamp in the "House that Ann and her kids built" and then had ridden her horse, Juniper, all through the hills. You have to admire someone like Johna.

What about Ann, Johna's mother, during these later years? When Johna left for college, Ann was alone, missed her kids, and then eventually went back to college herself. She studied botany and then came to the Monument to work as a volunteer. With several others, she participated in native plant surveys on the Monument, in the Cuyama Valley, and in still other areas. Next, again as a volunteer, Ann started running the Visitor Center on the Monument. Throughout the time of these and other projects, Ann and Johna belonged to the Volunteer Fire Department. Several years ago Ann died of cancer. There is a plaque near the Visitor Center that speaks of her love and dedication to the Carrisa Plains. Ann had lived through the times of change there. She loved the open land, she lived in California Valley, she volunteered for the Monument . . . and would not leave.

Coming into the Present

The interview with Johna was not the last that Jackie and I conducted, but it was the one which extended most nearly into the present. It had been eight years since I had first arrived on the Plains and had seen the historic relics from the previous century. I had lost my illusions about epic cattle drives and of homesteaders displaced by dust storms of the Great Depression. Instead people talked about their daily lives, about their recreations, and about neighbors. These are the sort of stories I might tell an old friend after a long absence. The people were real, their problems were real, and they accepted their circumstances as a matter of course. The time had come for me to reflect back on what had been found.

CHAPTER SIXTEEN

Honoring the Past

A last visit to the Plains

———————— ✕ — ✕ — ✕ ————————

What had come of my search for a story of the Plains and the people who had left? One of my very last road trips to conduct an interview was to Northern Nevada. Somewhere north of Bishop, California, I had pulled off the highway in the dark to find a camping place. Sitting on a low hilltop along a tiny dirt road the next morning, I drank coffee and warmed my hands. As the sun rose over the White Mountains, I wondered at what I had found in the Carrisa Plains.

No Simple Pattern

The details of lives on the Plains had no simple pattern. For grain farmers, there was a changing cycle of work through the seasons. For cattle ranchers, there were round-ups, brandings, and checking the stock. Hogs and chickens were a staple for some but an extra for others. Everyone made repairs: farmers to their machinery, ranchers to fences and troughs. And everyone put up houses, moved them, added on. The most nearly universal problem was water, but even in this quest, the solutions differed: wells, springs, trucks, a dam, cisterns, cloud seeding. Schools in the north and south of the Plains were managed differently, and the two communities looked in different directions for their social connections and markets. The common theme in the stories lay not in the challenges in their lives, but in the way in which people faced them. Whether life on the Carrisa Plains attracted a certain kind of person or whether it created a type, they were universally self-sufficient and hard-working. There was no alternative. Children found their own amusements. Adolescents worked during school vacations. Their parents rose early, worked late, danced, prayed, drank, argued, endured, or sold out. Whether they left or had chosen to stay, they were marked by the land where they lived.

People Who Stayed/People Who Left

As the sun continued to rise, I reflected on those who remained. Jan Cooper had arrived as a young bride many years ago, and even with the changes in her life, the old ranch house is still home. Sandy Rowlett lives a quarter mile from the old Simmler School, but to stay on the Plains she commutes an hour each way to work in Atascadero. Doug Wreden grew up in Palo Alto, but the Pinole Ranch became his real home. When the economics of farming became impossible, he stayed and took a job with the Monument. Some ranchers living in the north of the Plains have sold a part of their land to companies planning solar energy facilities. With money from these sales, they expect to remain on the ranch that has been in their family for generations.

There are others who left the Carrisa at an early age but returned many years later. After college, Jerry Diefenderfer left the King Ranch to work with Future Farmers of America, to work as a legislative assistant in Sacramento, and then to serve twelve years on the San Luis Obispo County board of supervisors. The family ranch near Highway 58 was never sold, and after many years, he has returned. Colleen Hayes is another of the returnees. She inherited a small part of her family ranch, and after some years away came back to raise horses and tend a garden. Although Greg McMillan has lived for nearly his entire life along Gillis Canyon Road south of Shandon, his employment was in construction along the coast. The commute became a chore, and he returned to raise cattle, grass fed and organic, for a niche market. This is hardly an industry, and in may not even make a living, but it is home.

For some people, life on the Plains had been sufficiently difficult that they were ready to move on. Others were forced to move but eventually accepted that it was for the best. Greg Beck left reluctantly, but later understood that his future on the Plains would have been empty. Joyce Bingeman and Larry Hill relocated to Nevada, literally for greener pastures. They had no regrets about the change. Debbie Beck was glad when she and her husband moved to San Luis Obispo. Work on their family ranch had left them time for almost nothing else, and she genuinely missed the city and its people.

There were a number of persons who moved away but even at a distance still call the Carrisa Plains their home. Gail Edgar lived at the Saucito Ranch from age eight to about twelve. It was a short period, but when you are growing up, those years are your whole life. They stay with you. When Gail showed me pictures of the Saucito as he knew it many years ago, he spoke again and again of his disappointment over the deterioration that he saw in recent visits. My more detached view of the ranch was kinder. I would not have judged that the house was badly neglected, but then I had never lived there, and it was not the home where I grew up.

Karen Linder is a cousin of Alden Loucks and granddaughter of Lew and Nancy Traver. She grew up on the Traver Ranch and attended school in Maricopa. When Karen left for college, her parents remained on the Plains until health forced a move to town. The land was sold to the Bureau of Land Management, and within a few years, the house, her house, had deteriorated so badly that it had to be removed. Today there is a single tree, a large seeding cart, and a water trough where Karen grew up. Even thirty years after leaving, Karen was teary in thinking that the house where her parents invested so much of their lives is now gone.

The Pull of the Land

The most moving testimonial that Jackie and I heard about the pull of the land was given in an early interview that we conducted. After high school, both Marilyn Elliot and her sister Colleen Hayes married and left the Carrisa Plains to live along the coast. Colleen later moved back to the family home, but Marilyn remained in Atascadero. She now returns to visit her sister at regular intervals. Jackie and I sat with them at Colleen's home as they recalled their childhood years:

Marilyn: It was a beautiful lifestyle, and I grew up loving it, I loved the quietness, the solemnness, everything in the country.

Colleen: I get up in the morning and I look out this window.

Marilyn: The sunsets right here are so beautiful. I've never seen any more beautiful, and I remember them from growing up. I've been out here a couple times since my sister returned, and it refreshes my memory.

Colleen: Two of the things I remember as a kid were the jets flying low, they did that then, and the doves cooing in the morning. When I first came back, oh I remember those.

Marilyn: And I love the smell of the Mullein weed when it first rains in the fall and the dirt and the green . . .

More Than History

Two weeks after my trip to Nevada, I attended a wedding in Cayucos, not far from San Luis Obispo. Doug Wreden and Jan Cooper were married on the beach just north of the pier. They had known each other nearly all their lives, and some time after their respective spouses died, they began seeing each other. There were two other weddings on the beach that day, but blue jeans and cowboy boots marked the group from the Plains. Doug wore a white, collared shirt, the first in his lifetime according to Greg McMillan. The bride was given away by her long-time friend Bill Garcia.

The reception could have been a Farm Bureau barbecue. Jan's brother-in-law brought two immense grills for the chicken. Her family brought half a dozen salads. Wine, beer, and soda filled a row of coolers. This was at a city park near the pier, so with swings, slides, and a climbing gym, the younger children were busy and happy. A three-piece country-western combo played music from the past: Waylon Jennings, Merle Haggard, Hank Williams. I thought about gatherings at the Simmler schoolhouse and watched old farmers in cowboy boots and denim shirts dancing with their wives.

Nearly two dozen of the guests were people that Jackie and I had interviewed. I spoke with some about the oral history project and said "thank you." With others, I spent the afternoon talking tractors, harvests, and family. By 6:00 PM, families were starting for home. The reception had lasted five hours already, and most people had a distance to drive. I asked Jan if she and Doug would be staying at the coast for the night, and she only said there that would be a bonfire on the beach in the evening. I thought about how the past and present had met on a single occasion and at one place. These were people I knew well, and in some very real way they had become family.

That evening as I drove back to Los Angeles, I traveled once more through the Plains. It had become a different world from that of my first visit. I drive the roads now, and in my mind a rusting harrow beside a field is still used to cover seed in autumn. The sound of a gunshot at dusk is Joe Garcia hunting deer with his friends. In the north, Dewey Werling starts a cattle drive for the coast, and Greg Beck drives a tractor round and round through the night. Beside the homestead buildings, children are splashing in water troughs, and parents wait and wait, hoping for enough rain to raise a crop. Miss Moore teaches children at the Saucito Ranch, and when I smell smoke in the forest to the west, it comes from a barbecue that Fred is holding once again at the Buckhorn Ranch.

These people were just like us. They were stubborn, and they were adaptable. They were trusting, and they were generous. They made extraordinary efforts to take care of their children, and they were loyal to friends. Some kept to themselves. Some quarreled with neighbors. Some drank, some partied, and some were drifters. Many marriages lasted a lifetime, and others found the work and isolation on the Plains more than their marriage could tolerate. They all worked hard, and many of them truly loved the work they did and the place where they lived. Few of us today would accept the circumstances that were the norm in those earlier years. But even if they had few of the conveniences that we consider essential, still they did not live empty lives. We might learn something of humility from them and draw courage from their examples. It was more than history that I had found.

Five Family Trees

Names in all capitals identify persons who were interviewed.

HUDSON/JOBE FAMILIES

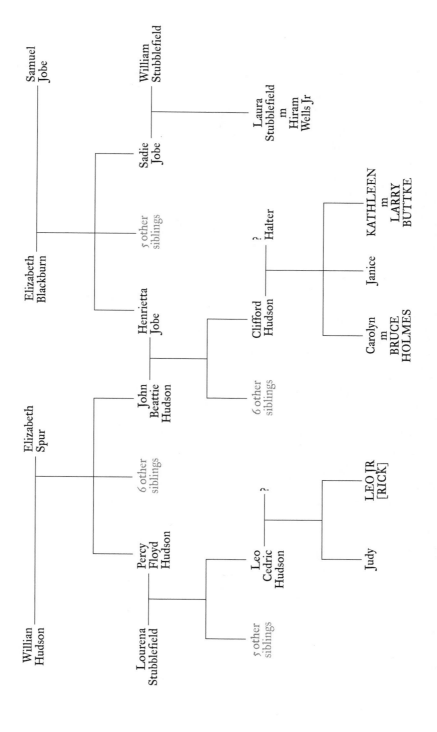

TRAVER FAMILY

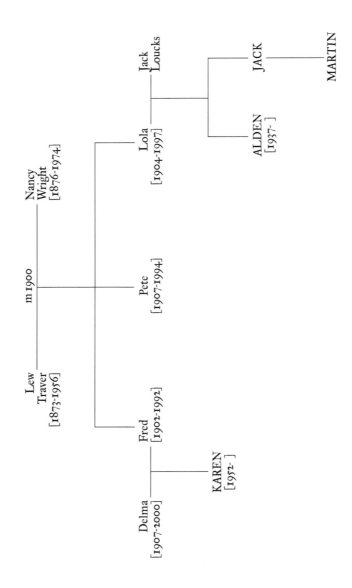

VAN MATRE FAMILY

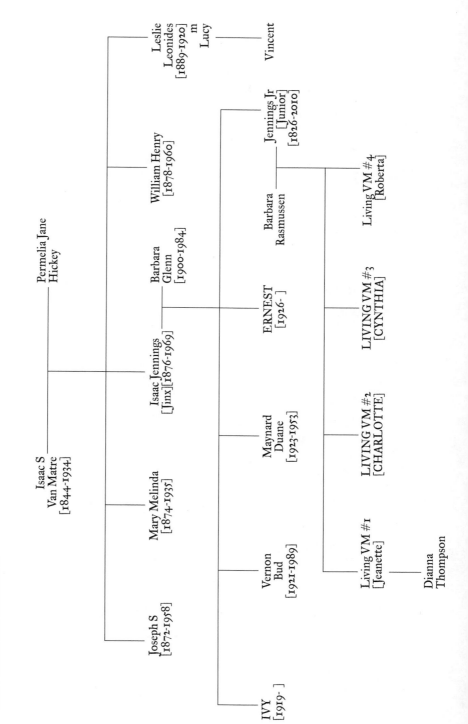

WASHBURN/WILDHARBOR FAMILIES

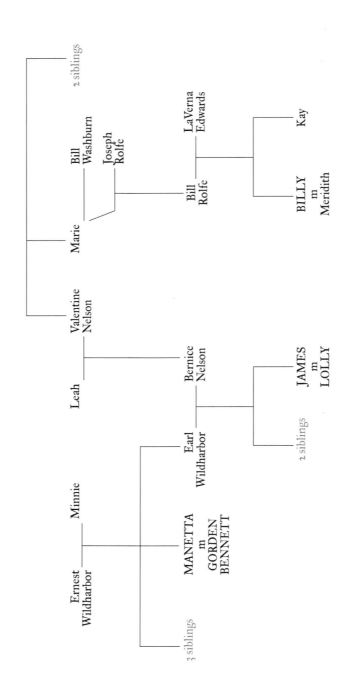

WELLS AND HILL FAMILIES

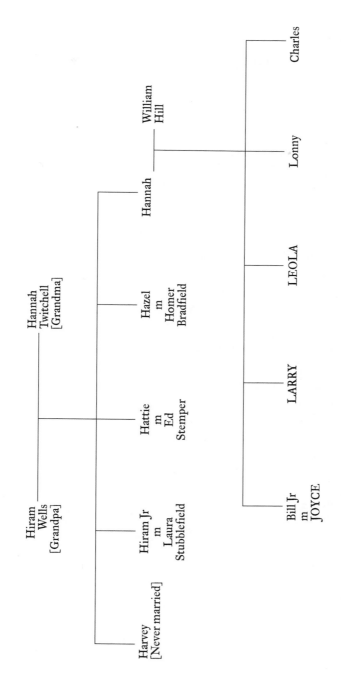

Interview Records

The following persons have been interviewed for the Carrisa Plains Oral History Project. The list is current as of August 22, 2012.

Carol Anderson (worked on Traver Ranch in 80s)
  May 30, 2011, at home of Ken Tack in Taft, CA

Greg Beck (Carrisa Rancher, son of Kenneth Beck)
  August 22, 2009, at home of Jackie Czapla in California Valley

Greg Beck (Carrisa Rancher, brother of Steve Beck)
  October 31, 2009, at home of Jackie Czapla in California Valley

Steve and Debbie Beck (son of Kenneth Beck and third generation Carrisa Rancher)
  July 6, 2010, at home of Steve Beck in San Luis Obispo, CA

Carolyn Bellow/Don Cooper (children of Maurice Cooper)
  August 22, 2012, in San Luis Obispo, CA

Gordon and Manetta Bennett (visitors and balloonists)
  September 29, 2009, at the Monument Visitor Center

Joyce Bingeman (daughter of Ellen Newsome, and owner at Saucito after 1954)
August 2, 2010, at home of Joyce Bingeman in Yerington, NV

Kathleen Buttke (grew up on Jobe Ranch, daughter of Cliff Hudson)
May 4, 2010, at the home of Jackie Czapla in California Valley

Darryl and Anna Candiff (among first residents in California Valley)
July 16, 2009, at Candiff home in California Valley

Howard Cavanagh (son of Fred Cavanagh, nephew of Earl)
August 18, 2011, at his home in Reedsport, OR

Donna Clark (lived on La Panza Ranch, granddaughter of Mae Martin)
June 13, 2011, at her home in Cayucos, CA

Jan Cooper (wife of Jon Cooper and longtime Plains resident)
June 18, 2010, at home of Jan Cooper, Carrisa Plains

Stan Cooper (rancher near McKittrick)
July 26, 2012, at his home near McKittrick, CA

Wayne Cooper (long time Carrisa Rancher, son of Alfred Cooper, brother to Jon Cooper)
March 25, 2009, at home of Jan Cooper, Carrisa Plains

Carissa Cronkright (daughter of Doug and Cindy Wreden)
November 11, 2011, at her home in Atascadero, CA

Ilene Cropper (cook for Lewis Traver family around 1940)
September 7, 2010, at her home in Atascadero, CA

Frank Diaz (worked summers on Chimineas)
July 30, 2012, San Luis Obispo, CA

Eleanor Diefenderfer (daughter of Elmer King)
January 20, 2009, home of Jerry Diefenderfer, Carrisa Plains

Jerry Diefenderfer (King Ranch on Carrisa Plains, and former SLO County supervisor)
April 29, 2009, home of Susan and Jerry Diefenderfer, Carrisa Plains

Susan Diefenderfer (great, great granddaughter of Mary Morris)
March 1, 2009, home of Susan and Jerry Diefenderfer, Carrisa Plains

Gail Edgar (lived on Saucito ranch from 1948 to 1954)
May 2, 2010, at Edgar home in Novato, CA

Mike Ferguson (BLM biologist instrumental in creating Carrizo Plain Natural Area)
August 26, 2010, at BLM office in Bakersfield, CA

Bill Finster (lived on La Panza Ranch, grandson of Mae Martin)
May 31, 2011, at his home in Taft, CA

Don Freeborn (grew up near Simmler community)
March 2 and also June 11, 2011, at his home in Visalia, CA

Bill Garcia (grandson of Jesus Garcia who owned Saucito from 1900 to 1930)
April 22, 2009, at home of Jan Cooper, Carrisa Plains

Bill Garcia (grandson of Jesus Garcia, son of Joe Garcia)
July 17, 2009, at Bill's ranch in Temblor Mountains

Charles Greenall (worked summers on Beck Ranch)
August 22, 2012, San Luis Obispo, CA

Rita Godward (member of Wreden family)
July 2, 2012, at her home in Calistoga, CA

Colleen Hayes and Marilyn Elliot (daughters of Edwin Cooper and Kathleen King)
January 19, 2009, at Colleen's home, Carrisa Plains

Larry Hill (grandson of Hiram and Hannah Wells)
September 26, 2011, at his home north of Winnemucca, NV

Rick Hudson (grandson of Percy Hudson and Lou Stubblefield)
September 3, 2011, at his home in Taft, CA

Cynthia Hurl (daughter of Jennings Van Matre, Junior)
August 19, 2011, at her home in Waltersville, OR

Johna Hurl (grew up in Maricopa and Cal Valley, Manager of CPNM)
July 7, 2010, at home of Jackie Czapla in California Valley

Chuck Kuhnle (long time Carrisa Rancher, son-in-law to Rowland Cooper)
March 18, 2009, at home of Chuck Kuhnle, Carrisa Plains

Chuck Kuhnle (Carrisa Rancher on Bitterwater Road north of highway 58)
February 23, 2010, at home of Chuck Kuhnle, Carrisa Plains

Carol Lauridsen (granddaughter of Fred Cavanagh)
February 16, 2011, at her home in Paso Robles, CA

Alberta Lewis (Lewis family)
March 30, 2010, at her home west of Carrizo Plain

Karen Linder (daughter of Fred Traver, granddaughter of Lewis and Nancy)
March 29, 2010, at her home in Bakersfield, CA

Jim Liston (grandson of William Von Husen, great grandson of Heinrich Wreden)
August 20, at his home in Portland, OR

Alden Loucks (rancher on Carrisa Plains and grandson of Lewis and Nancy Traver)
October 29, 2009, at Monument Visitor Center

Alden Loucks (grandson of Lewis and Nancy Traver)
May 18, 2010, at home of Jackie Czapla in California Valley

Jack Loucks (grandson of Lew and Nancy Traver)
March 20, 2012, at his home in Bakersfield, CA

Harold and Virginia Lowe (summer hand on several Carrisa ranches)
October 1, 2009, at their home in Atascadero, CA

Lisa Marrone (Fire Captain and resident in California Valley)
January 12, 2010, at home of Jackie Czapla in California Valley

Tom McCart (grandson of Peter McCart who homestead Elkhorn in 1896)
April 18, 2009, outdoors at McCart property in the Elkhorn Plain

Steve McCormick (with the Nature Conservancy in 1990)
October 14, 2010, at offices of Moore Foundation in Palo Alto, CA

Bob McDermand (worked for Travers, friend of Hill family)
October 13, 2010, at his home in Lake County, CA

Walter and Harry McDermand (worked for Bill Washburn, friend of Hill family)
September 17, 2010, at home of Harry McDermand in Maricopa, CA

Greg McMillan (Carrisa Rancher, son of Eben McMillan)
February 21, 2010, at his home on Carrisa Plains

Jose and Germain Mendiburu (sheep owners in Cuyama and Carrisa Valleys)
May 25, 2012, at their home in Cuyama, CA

John Miller (friend of Washburn family)
Bill Rolfe (grandson of Marie Washburn)
November 1, 2008, at the Washburn Ranch, Carrisa Plains

Don Messer (longtime friend and cowboy with several of Cavanagh family)
August 20, 2010, at his home in Atascadero, CA

John and Betty Miller (summer hand and long-time friend of Bill Washburn)
November 5, 2009, at their home in Taft, CA

Don Nevins (Wreden family, visitor to family ranch on the Carrisa Plains)
May 3, 2010, on UC Davis campus

Pam Parsons (great, great granddaughter of Chester Rude Brumley)
Dennis Milburn (homesteading family near Pozo, CA)
March 30, 2012, at home of Jackie Czapla in California Valley

Charlotte Penner (granddaughter of Jinks and Barbara Van Matre)
September 9, 2011, at her home in Paso Robles, CA

Joyce Preuitt (lived and worked Wells Ranch with husband Bill Hill)
Leola Wright (daughter of Hanna Hill, granddaughter of Hiram and Hanna Wells)
August 6, 2010, at home of Joyce Preuitt in Maricopa, CA

Chuck and Fran Pritchard (great grandson of Heinrich Wreden)
April 4, 2012, at their home in Paso Robles, CA

Fred and Gladys Rahner (among first residents of California Valley)
September 8, 2009, at their home in California Valley

Carlene Rexroth (daughter of Carrisa Plains rancher)
May 21, 2012, at her home inBakersfield, CA

Joan Rexroth (rancher north of Simmler)
July 31, 2012, at her home in Atascadero, CA

Bill Rolfe (grandson of Marie Washburn, and frequent visitor at Washburn)
June 17, 2010, at home of Jackie Czapla in California Valley

Harold Rowland (summer worker for Dewey Werling on Goodwin Ranch)
June 17, 2010, at his home in Shandon, CA

Sandy Rowlett and John King (granddaughter and son of Walter King)
August 21, 2010, at home of Jackie Czapla in California Valley

John Rudnick (son of Marcus Rudnick, cattle rancher)
April 30, 2012, at the San Juan Ranch in Carrisa Plains

Richard Rudnick (son of Marcus Rudnick and Carrisa cattle rancher)
April 13, 2010, at his home in Bakersfield, CA

John Ruskovich (farmer on Carrisa Plains)
May 6, 2009, at his home in the Carrisa Plains

Harold and Meredith Russell (hired hand eight years for Kenneth Beck)
February 23, 2010, at the home of Chuck Kuhnle, Carrisa Plains

Phil Selby (rancher in Caliente Mountains)
  June 19, 2012, at his home in Pinedale, WY

Judy Selby (daughter of Jack Selby)
  October 1, 2011, at her home in Mancos, CO

Art Steinbeck (rancher and CPNM Lease Holder)
  July 7, 2011, at his home south of Carrisa Plains

Eric Stewart (sheep rancher on the Carrisa Plains and nephew of Frank Galainena)
  September 27, 2010, at his home outside McKittrick, CA

Alberta Stubblefield (rancher in Cuyama Valley)
  August 1, 2012, at her home in Maricopa, CA

Ken Tack (lived on Traver Ranch in 80s)
  October 31, 2010, at his home in Taft, CA

Bill Traver (nephew of Kenneth Beck, worked on Beck Ranch)
  August 22, 2010, at home of Jackie Czapla in California Valley

Gail Traver (wife of Bill Traver and teacher at Carrisa School)
  August 22, 2010, at home of Jackie Czapla in California Valley

Darrell and Nola Twisselman (fourth generation ranching family)
  March 9, 2010, at their home, Carrisa Plains

Ernest Van Matre (son of Jinks and Barbara Van Matre)
  September 10, 2011, at his home in Rio Vista, CA

Maureen Vestal (librarian in California Valley and long time resident)
  June 27, 2010, at home of Jackie Czapla in California Valley

Ivy Wachs (daughter of Jinks and Barbara Van Matre)
September 25, 2011, at her home in Angels Camp, CA

Sharee Washer (General Manager of the California Valley Community Service District)
September 30, 2009, at Community Service District Office, California Valley

Robert and Carol Werling (son of Dewey Werling, lived on Goodwin many years)
August 20, 2009, at their home in Atascadero, CA

James and Lolly Wildharbor (son of Earl Wildharbor and friend of Bill Washburn)
October 17, 2009. at their home in Texas

Jerry Wildman (lived on Saucito Ranch, 1941-1946)
April 22, 2012, at his home in Los Osos, CA

Al Wilkinson (son of Ab Wilkinson, Carrisa *vaquero*)
May 22, 2012, at his home in Santa Maria, CA

Linda Woodard (daughter of Ray Cavanagh, granddaughter of Earl Cavanagh)
March 11, 2011, at her home in Arroyo Grande, CA

Bo Wreden (summers on Pinole Ranch)
October 15, 2010, at his home in Berkeley, CA

Doug Wreden (manager of Pinole Ranch and current BLM staff)
June 26, 2010, at his home, Carrisa Plains

The following interviews were conducted by Nancy Warner in the years 1990-1991. The cassette tapes were in the possession of the Bakersfield BLM office, loaned to Craig Deutsche, digitized, and transcribed in 2009.

Kenneth Beck (son of Nels Beck, father of Greg and Steve, rancher at north end of Plain)
Ernie Garcia (son of Jesus Garcia, uncle of Bill Garcia)
Ian McMillan (Carrisa rancher, brother of Eben McMillan)
Henry Twisselman (third generation rancher on Carriza Plains)
Robert and Catherine Werling (son and wife, respectively, of Dewey Werling)

All the interviews listed above have been transcribed. They are available both as audio recordings and as written transcripts in the following locations:

Special Collections
Robert E. Kennedy Library
California Polytechnic State University
San Luis Obispo, CA 93407
http://lib.calpoly.edu/specialcollections

San Luis Obispo County History Center
696 Monterey Street
San Luis Obispo, CA 93401
http://historycenterslo.org

Taft Junior College Library
29 Emmons Park Dr.
Taft, CA 93268
http://www.taftcollege.edu/library/library.php

PHOTO CREDITS

Where no attribution is given, the photo was taken by the author.

Courtesy of Bill Rolfe: Cover bottom
Courtesy of Linda Woodard: Spine bottom
Courtesy of Bill Garcia: page 44
Courtesy of Doug Wreden: page 71
Courtesy of Greg Beck: page 22, page 122, page 141
Courtesy of Alden Loucks : page 165, page 232, back cover
Courtesy of Yvonne Hawley: page 188
Courtesy of Cynthia Van Matre Hurl: page 216
Courtesy of Lynne Buckner: page 289

Front cover: Bill Washburn on his ranch
Back cover: Alden and Jack Loucks on the Traver Ranch

ABOUT THE AUTHOR

As a volunteer in the Carrizo Plain National Monument, Craig Deutsche became fascinated with the history of the area and together with another colleague undertook an extensive oral history project with former residents. In a former life he was a high school teacher, a distance runner, and a desert conservation advocate. In his present life Craig humors a birdwatching wife and continues to volunteer in the Carrizo Plain National Monument. He insists that the stories of the Plains found him; he did not find them.

Made in the USA
San Bernardino, CA
28 April 2013